Intelligent Democracy

PHILOSOPHY, POLITICS, AND ECONOMICS

Ryan Muldoon, Carmen Pavel,
Geoffrey Sayre-McCord, Eric Schliesser, Itai Sher

Series Editors

Published in the Series

The Open Society and Its Complexities
Gerald Gaus

A Theory of Subjective Wellbeing
Mark Fabian

Intelligent Democracy
Jonathan Benson

Intelligent Democracy

Answering the New Democratic Scepticism

JONATHAN BENSON

OXFORD
UNIVERSITY PRESS

Oxford University Press is a department of the University of Oxford. It furthers the University's objective of excellence in research, scholarship, and education by publishing worldwide. Oxford is a registered trade mark of Oxford University Press in the UK and certain other countries.

Published in the United States of America by Oxford University Press
198 Madison Avenue, New York, NY 10016, United States of America.

© Oxford University Press 2024

All rights reserved. No part of this publication may be reproduced, stored in a retrieval system, or transmitted, in any form or by any means, without the prior permission in writing of Oxford University Press, or as expressly permitted by law, by license, or under terms agreed with the appropriate reproduction rights organization. Inquiries concerning reproduction outside the scope of the above should be sent to the Rights Department, Oxford University Press, at the address above.

You must not circulate this work in any other form
and you must impose this same condition on any acquirer.

CIP data is on file at the Library of Congress

ISBN 978-0-19-776728-3

DOI: 10.1093/oso/9780197767283.001.0001

Printed by Integrated Books International, United States of America

Contents

Acknowledgements	vii
Introduction: The New Democratic Scepticism	1
Defending the Intelligence of Democracy	6
Overview of the Book	12
1. Democracy's Epistemic Problems	18
Do Democracies Need to Make Good Decisions?	20
What Is a Good Political Decision?	24
What Makes an Institution Intelligent?	29
Institutional Diversity and the Priority of Democracy	32
A Note on Method	35
Responding to the New Democratic Scepticism	37
2. The Limits of Elections and Markets	38
The Epistemic Abilities of Elections and Markets	40
The Common Good and Other-Regarding Decisions	44
The Incentive Problem	47
The Information Problem	52
The Invisible Hand of Elections and Markets	59
A Preliminary Case for Collective Politics	63
3. Democracy and the Division of Knowledge	66
Hayek's Division of Knowledge	68
The Division of Knowledge and the Deliberative System	71
A Systemic Division of Epistemic Labour	76
Collective Politics in the Deliberative System	86
Comparing Deliberative Systems	88
Knowledge Gathering in the Deliberative System	94
4. Bias, Misinformation, and the Democratic System	96
Failing to Find the Truth	98
Trust in the Deliberative System	106
A Politics of Bias and Misinformation	111
Not So Biased After All	114
The Benefits of Group Reasoning	117
Error Correction in the Deliberative System	121
Knowledge Evaluation in the Deliberative System	124

vi CONTENTS

5. Polycentricity For and Against Democracy 126
    The Polycentric Critique of Democracy 127
    The Limits of Bottom-Up Selection 133
    The Benefits of Top-Down Selection 140
    Polycentricity within Democracy 143
    Realizing the Polycentric Benefits of Deliberative Systems 146
    Who Should Make Empowered Decisions? 152

6. Diversity and Political Problem-Solving 154
    Can Diversity Trump Ability? 156
    Deliberating with Oracles 159
    How Forceful Is the Force of the Better Argument? 163
    An Alternative Model of Cognitive Diversity 165
    How to Select for Diversity 172
    The Threat of Deliberative Failures 174
    How Far Can Diversity Take Us? 177

7. Elections and Elite Rule 179
    The Conventional Democratic Solution 181
    What Elections Can and Cannot Do 183
    Political Meritocracy and Its Limits 189
    Epistocracy and Its Limits 196
    Is Representative Democracy the Best We Can Do? 202

8. The Sortition Branch 205
    The Potential of Random Sortition 207
    Deliberative Mini-Publics and Their Limits 210
    Randomly Selected Legislators and Their Limits 214
    The Sortition Branch of a Deliberative System 219
    The Sortition Branch as a Democratic Proposal 228
    Intelligent Democracy as a More Participatory Democracy 232

Conclusion: A More Intelligent Democracy 234

References 245
Index 263

Acknowledgements

This project would not have been possible without the help and support of others. I started thinking about many of the issues considered in this book during my doctoral research when I had the good fortune to have Miriam Ronzoni and John O'Neill as supervisors. Miriam's guidance during the early stages of my career has been invaluable and she has never stopped challenging me in my work or offering support in navigating academic life. John's encouragement was an important factor in leading me to an academic career to begin with and he first introduced me to many of the ideas and debates I engage with here. Together they were an excellent team, and I am very grateful to them both. I would also like to thank John Dryzek and Christian Schemmel for examining my resulting PhD thesis and for providing thoughtful and considered comments. John went on to be a great source of advice in publishing this book, and I am grateful for his help.

In the course of completing this project I moved through three institutions where I was incredibly lucky to have kind and generous colleagues. I was fortunate to not only study at the University of Manchester and within the Manchester Centre for Political Theory (MANCEPT), but also to return there on a research fellowship years later. MANCEPT represents a very special group of political theorists who have built an extraordinarily welcoming, friendly, and supportive community. The work in this book owes much to conversations with MANCEPT members current and old. I am very thankful once again to Miriam and Christian, but also to Richard Child, Stephen Hood, Liam Shields, James Patterson, Hillel Steiner, Timothy Kenyon, Stephanie Collins, Giacomo Floris, Vittorio Gerosa, Billy Christmas, Joseph Roberts, and Ruxandra Ivanescu.

At King's College London I got to work with an exceptional group of interdisciplinary scholars from whom I learnt much. Mark Pennington, Samuel DeCanio, and Adam Tebble share my passion for many of the topics covered in this book and I benefited much from having three colleagues who intelligently and kindly disagreed with me. I am also grateful to Paul Sagar, John Meadowcroft, Carmen Pavel, Roberto Fumagalli, Robin Douglass, Adrian Blau, and Rod Dacombe for all of their support. King's provided me with

viii ACKNOWLEDGEMENTS

my first position after my postgraduate studies and it could not have been a better place to further my research and teaching.

I am also indebted to my colleagues at Utrecht University. Having joined Utrecht in the middle of a global pandemic, I am grateful not only for their many intellectual gifts, but also for making me feel very welcome when I moved to the Netherlands and almost immediately into lockdown restrictions. Dorothea Gädeke, Maurits de Jongh, Rutger Claasen, Joel Anderson, Michael Bennett, and others in the Ethics Institute and PPE College were wonderful colleagues in turbulent times.

Throughout the years I have benefited considerably from many conversations and questions at conferences and workshops, from my students, and from the anonymous feedback of reviewers. I am also very thankful to Peter Ohlin of Oxford University Press and all the editors of the PPE book series—Carmen Pavel, Ryan Muldoon, Geoff Sayre-McCord, Eric Schliesser, and Itai Sher—for agreeing to publish and support this project.

Outside of the academy, I am immensely grateful for the support of my friends and family. The contributions of my parents in particular in getting me to the point where I can write this book are immeasurable. Across time and many borders my wife Olatz has been a constant, without whom I would not have been able to finish this project or achieve much else. Moltes gràcies per tot el teu amor i ànims.

Finally, as a dyslexic academic a special thank you must go to my proof-reader Peter Harvey of PWProofreading.

Introduction

The New Democratic Scepticism

Democracy aims to distribute political power equally among the members of a community with little more thought to their ability or competence than that they are of adult age.[1] In many ways, this is a very strange idea. Why should we expect a system of government with such low requirements for participation to make good decisions about the laws and regulations which govern our societies? Political decisions fundamentally affect our prosperity, our liberty, our security, and the health of our planet. When it comes to decisions with such wide-ranging and important consequences, why would we make adulthood the central qualification for participation, instead of intellect, knowledge, experience, virtue, or wisdom? Why would we possibly believe that a political regime that is happy to include any citizen in decision-making will reliably provide or preserve the goods we value?

This critical line of questioning has, of course, a significant history. As long as there have been discussions of democracy there have been those who argue that 'rule by the people' is a recipe for disaster. It was a fear of the incompetence and irrationality of democracy that led Plato to believe that his ideal city of Kallipolis (Καλλίπολις) should be ruled not by the people but by a philosopher king. In fact, for much of history it was simply taken to be self-evident that the average person was ignorant of public affairs and should therefore have little if any influence over them. Whether it be philosopher kings, aristocrats, or monarchs, politics was thought to be an exclusive profession reserved for some small but wise elite, and the public was seen as unable to contribute to politics. Although views such as these may sound outdated or even offensive to our modern ears, they are experiencing a sharp re-emergence in contemporary politics.

---

[1] Some democracies consider competence as grounds for disenfranchising those convicted of a crime and/or those with certain cognitive disabilities. They also often do not give the franchise to resident noncitizens, although this is not normally for reasons of competence.

Intelligent Democracy. Jonathan Benson, Oxford University Press. © Oxford University Press 2024.
DOI: 10.1093/oso/9780197767283.003.0001

2 INTELLIGENT DEMOCRACY

The electoral success of populist politicians with little or no political experience has once again raised the question of whether the general public can be trusted to pick their own political leaders. Whether it is Donald Trump's Republican Party, Boris Johnson and his Vote Leave campaign, or the success of far-right political parties throughout Europe, recent election results are being taken by some as confirmation of the long-held fear that 'rule by the people' is no different to 'rule by the mob'. The polarization of public debate surrounding these elections, and the arrival of fake news and misinformation into mainstream democratic discourse, has further weakened trust in the political competence of average citizens. If public debate consists of little more than a badly informed shouting match, then why allow it any influence over the laws and policies which so fundamentally shape our lives? With today's policy challenges becoming more and more complex, it seems that politics is only moving further outside the competence of the average citizen. As discussions of climate change, global pandemics, artificial intelligence, and internet regulation take centre stage on the political agenda, it is no surprise that the opinions of lay citizens seem less and less relevant, particularly if they continue to select such careless leaders.

While democratic countries are experiencing these problems, success stories are said to be emerging from the nondemocratic world and challenging the monopoly that democracy once had on good governance. Since opening up in the late 1970s, China has managed an average GDP growth of almost 10%, far surpassing the world's developed democracies, while lifting more than 850 million people out of poverty. Those sympathetic to such regimes claim that these results are the product of leaving political decisions to professional bureaucrats and experienced leaders, unburdened by the irrationalities of the national popularity contests which are democratic elections. While many will worry about the human rights records of nondemocratic regimes, the rise of 'illiberal democracies' now questions whether democracy is any better a guarantee of our basic liberties. Whether it is Turkey under Recep Tayyip Erdoğan or Hungary under Viktor Orbán, illiberal democracies are seen by some as evidence that majority rule was never a reliable safeguard of individual rights to begin with.

These democratic anxieties have been making their way into public opinion, even among the citizens of developed democracies. The Centre for the Future of Democracy has found that public satisfaction with democracy has been on the decline worldwide since the 1990s, with 2019 representing 'the highest level of democratic discontent on record'.[2] After a particularly sharp decline following 2005, a majority now say they are 'dissatisfied' with democracy. These declines in public support are often correlated with economic downturns and policy crises, suggesting that it is the bad performance of democracies that is in part driving this discontent. Some of the world's most prominent and populous democracies are also leading this descent into democratic malaise, with the United States seeing dissatisfaction increase by more than a third in just one generation, and Brazil, South Africa, Australia, and the United Kingdom all recording their highest level of dissatisfaction on record. While in the 1990s two-thirds of the citizens of developed democracies felt satisfied with democracy, today more than half say they are dissatisfied.

It is not only the general public which is becoming more pessimistic about democracy, however. It is against this more general backdrop of democratic crisis and dissatisfaction that the academic study of politics has also seen a new growth in democratic scepticism. An increasing number of philosophers, political scientists, and economists are taking critical stances towards democratic politics, with some even claiming that they are now 'against democracy'.[3] Unsympathetic portraits of democracy have, of course, long existed among those who professionally study politics. Joseph Schumpeter, for instance, famously complained about the lack of intelligence possessed by the average voter, arguing that the 'typical citizen drops down to a lower level of mental performance as soon as he enters the political field', and that politics even causes them to become 'primitive'.[4] After the Second World War and then the fall of the Berlin wall, however, anti-democratic sentiments were generally seen as outdated or even vulgar, and it was increasingly claimed that 'we are all democrats now'. It is this democratic self-confidence which is now showing signs of deterioration with the emergence of a 'new democratic scepticism'.

The new democratic scepticism claims that modern social science has confirmed the old fears that the average voter has little in the way of political knowledge, that democratic debate tends to be irrational and polarizing, and that centralized democratic governments are inefficient and ineffective. It also claims such problems cannot be easily solved, as their root cause is

---

[2] Foa, Claystone, Slade, Rand, and Williams (2020, p. 2).
[3] Brennan (2016a).
[4] Schumpeter (1996, p. 262).

4   INTELLIGENT DEMOCRACY

democracy itself. Economics, for instance, is said to demonstrate that the small influence any one voter has in an election makes it only rational for them to remain ignorant and uninformed, while political psychology is reported to show that cognitive and social biases will inevitably lead citizens to be unreasonable about politics. Botched public policies, misinformation, partisan bickering, and the rise of leaders such as Trump, Johnson, and Orbán are not therefore coincidences. They are instead the logical outcome of democratic procedures. As one prominent new sceptic put it, the trouble with democracy is that 'universal suffrage incentivizes most voters to make political decisions in an ignorant and irrational way, and then imposes these ignorant and irrational decisions on innocent people'. We therefore 'get low-quality government because voters have little idea what they're doing' and we 'cannot fix the problem' because it is 'built into democracy'.[5]

The current crisis surrounding democracies is not likely to pass and is instead proof that thinkers such as Plato and Schumpeter were right all along. Rather than trying to hopelessly fix democracy's ills, then, the new democratic sceptics encourage us to look for alternatives. Some, such as the philosopher Jason Brennan, argue that we should remove the most misinformed, morally unreasonable, and irrational citizens from political life.[6] He advocates for a system of 'epistocracy' where political power is conditional on an individual's knowledge and competence. We should therefore make voting rights dependent on one's education or ability to pass a political knowledge test, disenfranchising those who are most responsible for democracy's incompetence. According to Brennan, we should prefer 'rule by the knowers' to 'rule by the people'. Daniel Bell and others look instead to China and Singapore as inspirations for a more competent politics.[7] Their preferred regime is a quasi-Confucian form of 'political meritocracy' where political leaders are determined not by elections, but by their past experience and performance in rigorous examinations. On a Confucian view of politics, Bell argues, 'only those who acquire knowledge and virtue ought to participate in government, and the common people are not presumed to possess the capacities necessary for substantial political participation'.[8]

While new sceptics such as Brennan and Bell wish to restrict politics to the more knowledgeable and enlightened, others believe that we should

---

[5] Brennan (2016b).
[6] Brennan (2016a).
[7] Bell (2016); Bell and Pei (2020); Bai (2019).
[8] Bell (2009, p. 154).

INTRODUCTION 5

reject politics altogether. Perhaps the most influential form of democratic scepticism we see today comes not from supporters of elite rule, but supporters of the free market. Often drawing on the work of figures such as Friedrich von Hayek, these writers claim that problems of democracy originate from the centralized nature of political decisions, and that we should therefore aim to substitute democracy with markets whenever possible.[9] Distant politicians or bureaucrats know nothing of people's local conditions, and we are therefore better off placing our faith in the free market, which gives individuals the greatest freedom to make decisions for themselves. Often inspired by these ideas, other sceptics have argued that we should make politics 'more like the market'. Paul Dragos Aligica, for instance, argues for a polycentric approach to governance which allow private firms, nonprofits, NGOs, and private associations to compete over the provision of goods and services.[10] Citizens will then be able, just like consumers, to 'vote with their feet' as they choose the institutions they believe to be best. The cure for democracy's ills is not therefore to reject the democratic state outright, but rather shrink its size and break its monopoly on governance.

The new democratic scepticism therefore offers a range of alternatives aimed at curing the sickness at the heart of our deteriorating democracies. While not all of these sceptics wish to do away with democracy completely, they all argue that it is fundamentally flawed, and that it needs to be restricted if not removed in favour of some nondemocratic alternative. They are also united in their belief that the flaws of democracy are predominantly epistemic. Whether it is voter ignorance, the failures of political debate, or the limits of democratic centralization, these sceptics are all primarily concerned with issues of knowledge and good decision-making. Democracy is said to lack an ability to acquire, produce, and evaluate information in an effective way, and fail to take decisions in a manner which is informed, rational, and considered. In other words, what these new democratic sceptics are sceptical of is democracy's *intelligence*.

This supposed lack of intelligence points to a core tension in thinking about democracy. On the one hand, many support democratic politics because it treats us all equally and symbolizes our political equality. It is the fairness of giving us all a say in the laws governing our societies which is often thought to justify our supporting democracy both as an ideal and as

---

[9] Hayek (1937, 1945, 2011); Pennington (2003, 2011).
[10] Aligica (2014); Aligica, Boettke, and Tarko (2019).

6   INTELLIGENT DEMOCRACY

a practice. At the same time, we also care greatly about the outcomes of political decisions. We are concerned with whether they produce more or less prosperity, more or less individual freedom, or more or less material equality. Most democrats therefore value the fairness and equality expressed by democratic decisions, while also holding deep commitments to ideals of justice or the common good whose realization is inevitably determined by the effectiveness of political institutions. While many democrats hope for a harmony between these two concerns, the new democratic scepticism aims to pull them apart. By questioning the intelligence of democracy, it challenges the idea that a form of government which treats us all equally can also make decisions which produce good outcomes. It argues that if we want a political system which can promote justice and the common good, then this cannot be a system which respects political equality. Put simply, the new democratic scepticism claims that an intelligent form of politics cannot be a democratic form of politics.

Defending the Intelligence of Democracy

Given the significant challenges democracies are currently facing, and mounting levels of public dissatisfaction with public institutions, it is vital that we can effectively respond to those who claim that our best course of action is to remove or restrict democracy. While we may have simply dismissed the critics during the waves of democratization which followed the end of the Cold War, today we require a more direct response. In a time of democratic crisis and decline, we cannot let claims about democratic incompetence go unaddressed. I therefore aim in this book to defend the intelligence of democracy and in doing so mount a robust reply to the new democratic scepticism. I will show that the sceptics are wrong to reject or restrict democracy on epistemic grounds, and that rather than giving us reasons to question democratic politics, concerns for knowledge and good decision-making give us reasons to embrace it.

The unique intelligence of democracy is that it possesses a range of epistemic abilities which allow it to make good decisions with respect to any reasonable conception of justice or the common good. When considering the best form of government, our task is similar to a handyman selecting a toolbox. The handyman does not know in advance the exact task they will be set. They may have to plug a leak, rehinge a door, fix an electrical socket,

INTRODUCTION 7

or complete many other tasks. The handyman will therefore require a range of tools which can help them achieve any of these various goals. In politics we similarly cannot say in advance what our ends will be. People reasonably disagree over their preferred conceptions of justice and the common good, producing a range of potential goals for our political institutions. We may want them to pursue more material equality, greater individual liberty, or perhaps broader opportunity. Like the handyman's toolbox, then, we will want political institutions to possess a range of epistemic tools which can help them to achieve any of these various goals. Democracy is intelligent, I claim, because it possesses a larger and better set of these epistemic tools than any of the alternatives favoured by the sceptics. Whatever goal we end up preferring, it is democracy which has the best chance of achieving it.

I will therefore argue that we should value democracy not only because it treats us equally, but because it is intelligent. Key to this argument will be a systemic theory of democracy's epistemic value. My view is that no single institution or mechanism can possibly demonstrate the epistemic superiority of democracy over its various alternatives. No election or parliament can on its own acquire all the information needed to address social problems, experiment with all promising alternatives, or motivate all decision-makers towards the common good. To understand democracy's full epistemic value we must see it not as a single institution, but as a broader system made up of a network of different bodies and spaces. A democratic system involves formal institutions empowered to make binding decisions about laws and policies, but also an active public sphere which includes community associations, social movements, unions, and universities. The weaknesses and faults of any one of these institutions can be compensated by others, and a democratic system can therefore achieve epistemic values not found in any one of its parts. Identifying democracy's intelligence therefore requires an analysis of how these different components interact to produce divisions of labour, distributed functions, and emergent properties.

This systemic perspective looks very different from the image of democracy painted by the new democratic sceptics, but also by many democrats. My project builds significantly on what has become known as the 'epistemic turn' in democratic theory.[11] This turn refers to a growing number of democratic theorists who have argued that the value of democracy must rest, at least in

---

[11] For discussion of the epistemic turn see Estlund and Landemore (2018); Goodin and Spiekermann (2018); Landemore (2017); Schwartzberg (2015); Jörke (2010); Urbinati (2014).

8   INTELLIGENT DEMOCRACY

part, on its epistemic quality, and have developed innovative new arguments to explain why democracies can be trusted to make good decisions. While the new democratic sceptics have been increasingly challenging the competence of democracy, it has been these 'epistemic democrats' who have been defending it. Although this book owes much to earlier work on epistemic democracy, this turn has so far been overly narrow in focusing on single democratic institutions, often with the help of formal models. Whether it be applying Condorcet jury theorems to democratic voting, or agent-based models to deliberative assemblies, the focus of epistemic democrats has been on single mechanisms.[12] These approaches can be productive—and I consider formal models of deliberation myself—but we cannot truly understand the epistemic value of democracy without a systemic perspective. The whole burden of effective decision-making within large and complex societies cannot rest on the shoulders of a single institution, and a focus on isolated mechanisms will therefore underappreciate democracy's epistemic abilities. While many such abilities will therefore remain absent on a purely unitary approach, I will show that they can be unlocked through a systemic view. The core and original position defended in this book is that only a systemic perspective can provide a convincing epistemic justification of democracy.

In many ways, my systemic approach has more in common with older epistemic defences of democracy, such as those of John Dewey, which similarly saw democracy as more than the 'political machinery' of government.[13] Dewey conceived of democracy as a 'mode of associated living' and thought that the work of democracy occurred wherever people look to identify and solve problems of public interest, whether this be in families, schools, workplaces, or local communities. Democracy is therefore a 'way of individual life' which requires the 'possession and continual use of certain attitudes', 'personal character', 'desire', and 'purpose'. Democracy is not therefore a single institution for Dewey, but a 'mode of sociality' which should inform 'all areas and ways of living'.[14] Dewey's view falls short of conceiving of democracy as a 'system', however, and it asks different questions to my own approach. Rather than a way of life, the systemic view sees democratic

[12] Landemore (2013b); Goodin and Spiekermann (2018); List and Goodin (2001); Cohen (1986).

[13] Dewey (1923, p. 93; 1927). While many read Dewey as making an epistemic argument for democracy, the interpretation of him as an epistemic democrat is not uncontroversial. Westbrook (2015a), for instance, claims that no epistemic argument for democracy can be found in Dewey's work, while Misak (2013) argues that one can be identified but that it is only partially defended. For further discussion, see Festenstein (2019).

[14] Dewey (1969–1991, LW14:226, LW2:325).

INTRODUCTION 9

values as produced at an aggregate level through the interaction of many institutions within a broader network. Its central question is not how to best cultivate certain democratic attitudes or dispositions in citizens, but how a set of institutions can be best arranged so as to produce collective decisions which express democratic values. The systemic approach is therefore interested in how to best combine democratic institutions (such as parliaments, elections, random sortition, social movements, or community associations) and spheres (such as the public sphere and more formal spheres of government), so as to achieve divisions of labour, emergent properties, and self-regulating tendencies which can improve the democratic quality of the system's decisions. While Dewey is often characterized as elusive when it comes to these questions of institutional configuration, they are central to my approach.[15]

A systemic view therefore involves more than the claim that democracy reaches beyond the 'machinery of government'. It also claims that democratic values come about as the outcome of interactions within a network and that democracy should therefore be judged, wholly or in part, at the systemic level. Elizabeth Anderson's more recent version of Deweyan democracy comes close to this view in focusing on the dynamic nature of democracy.[16] Anderson still gives most of her attention to elections, however, with only limited reference to other mechanisms, such as protest and petition. Her account does not therefore offer a broader understanding of democracy's divisions of epistemic labour, distributed abilities, and self-regulating tendencies. In other words, it does not offer an understanding of how democracy functions as a system, as I will attempt to do here.

While I therefore find much value and inspiration in epistemic democrats new and old, my claim is that we must embrace a systemic perspective if we are to produce a convincing epistemic justification of democracy. Although overlooked by epistemic democrats, the systemic approach is at the cutting edge of much democratic theory. Democratic theory has experienced a 'systemic turn' in recent years and deliberative democrats in particular have increasingly embraced a systemic understanding of democracy.[17]

---

[15] Ryan (1995); Simon (2012); Westbrook (2015b).

[16] Anderson (2006). As Talisse (2011) argues, Anderson's experimental account loses many distinctive features of Deweyan democracy, such as a focus on democracy as a way of life. I critique Anderson's understanding of democratic experimentation in Chapter 2 and offer an alternative view in Chapter 5.

[17] Dryzek (2010, 2017); Mansbridge et al. (2012); Parkinson (2006); and Warren (2017). For a critical overview see Owen and Smith (2015).

10   INTELLIGENT DEMOCRACY

A systemic approach has, for instance, been used to study alternative governance regimes, the value of nondeliberative acts and rhetoric, the appropriate role of experts, the place of deliberative mini-publics, and has been used to inform the design of democratic institutions.[18] While the systemic and epistemic turns represent two of the most significant developments in contemporary democratic theory, they have so far existed in relative isolation. A core contribution of this book is therefore to bridge these turns by developing the first systems based epistemic argument for democracy.[19]

While distinctive in itself, this systemic view also allows for new insights into the epistemic value of democracy and a unique model of its intelligence. Unlike most epistemic democrats, for instance, I question the epistemic reliability of elections. While claiming that they can play an important role as guards against abuses of power, I show how the limited knowledge of voters makes it unlikely that elections will select the best proposals for promoting the common good. Seeing voting as just one part of a larger system, however, allows me to recognize the necessary limits of voter knowledge, while still vindicating the epistemic value of democracy. I argue that while the weaknesses of elections are significant, they can be offset if they are combined with institutions based on sortition and random selection. In their role as voters, citizens lack the information needed for effective political decision-making, but random sortition provides opportunities for more informed citizen participation. I therefore develop a proposal for a *sortition branch* of a democratic system which would grant assemblies of randomly selected citizens significant powers to influence and veto the legislation proposed by elected representatives.

Even a combination of elections and sortition, however, is insufficient for explaining democracy's epistemic value. Instead, I argue that these political institutions must also be connected and supported by an independent public sphere and exhibit forms of decentralization if they are to act intelligently. Without an active and unstructured public sphere democratic institutions could not possibly gather and aggregate the vast amounts of information relevant to social problems, and the public sphere could not possibly filter and utilize all this information without a connection to more formal political

---

[18] Parkinson (2006); Stevenson and Dryzek (2014); Dryzek (2010); Christiano (2012); Curato and Böker (2016); Niemeyer (2014); Dean et al., (2020).

[19] Systemic approaches have been used to analyse epistemic issues, but till now have not been used to create an overall epistemic defence or justification for democracy. For instance, Moore (2017) uses a systems approach to consider the appropriate role of expertise in a democracy, but this is distinct from an argument for epistemic democracy (as Moore himself explains).

institutions. Similarly, without significant decentralization, the amount of self-correction and experimentation which could take place would be greatly limited. While previous views of democratic experimentation focus on single bodies and the feedback from elections, I argue that decentralization allows for processes of emulation and learning between multiple democratic institutions at various levels.

The systemic approach therefore produces a new understanding of democracy's epistemic abilities. Altogether, it will show us that democracies can gather and evaluate information, engage in experimentation and self-regulation, benefit from cognitive diversity, and motivate decision-makers towards justice and the common good. The systemic view then also offers new proposals for how to reform democracy so it can better achieve these abilities and increase its intelligence. As a result, this book does not present a simple defence of the democratic status quo. My aim is instead to engage with democracy's critics in order to mount a positive case for transforming democratic politics. Many chapters will consider and reply to a certain brand of the new democratic scepticism and in doing so highlight the distinctive epistemic abilities of democracy, many of which require some kind of reform to existing institutions. If the lesson of this book for the new democratic sceptics is that epistemic concerns should not lead us to restrict or reject democracy, its lesson for democrats is that if we want to preserve political equality and have political institutions which can promote the common good, then democracy must become participatory, decentralized, and deliberative. If we want a more intelligent democracy then democracy will need to change.

Finally, I also aim to move beyond current debates over epistemic democracy by expanding the range of democratic criticism considered. As we have seen, the new democratic scepticism supports a wide range of alternatives, from free markets, to polycentric governance, to political meritocracy. The literature on epistemic democracy, alternatively, has mostly considered more traditional rivals, such as autocracy and oligarchy. While still important to consider, a sole focus on such conventional alternatives risks not responding to the institutional diversity exhibited by the new democratic scepticism. Accounting for this institutional diversity also requires that one engage with the diversity of philosophical, political, and economic perspectives which inform democracy's contemporary critics. While advocates of epistocracy draw mostly on work from political science and psychology, for instance, free-market sceptics build on Hayekian political economy, and polycentric

12   INTELLIGENT DEMOCRACY

critics on Elinor Ostrom and new institutional economics. This book therefore replies to arguments coming from a broad range of disciplinary traditions, but also uses these different perspectives to inform its own defence of democracy's intelligence. My systemic approach, for instance, is greatly informed by work in deliberative democracy, but also by Hayekian accounts of the distribution of knowledge, political science work on voter knowledge and bias, and Ostrom's insights into the benefits of polycentric networks. The result is a highly interdisciplinary epistemic justification of democracy which can provide a more robust response to the new democratic scepticism.

Overview of the Book

My aim is to defend the intelligence of democracy against the rise of the new democratic scepticism. I will consider the range of alternatives offered up by the new sceptics, examine their limitations, and use this as a basis for developing a systemic theory of democracy's epistemic value. I will therefore argue that we should value democracy not only because it treats us all equally, but because it is intelligent. This argument is developed across the book's different chapters, with each making a particular contribution to the broader systemic model.

The next chapter aims to motivate my defence of democracy's intelligence and spells out the framework I use to develop it. While the sceptics focus on democracy's epistemic problems, many believe democracy's value derives from its intrinsic fairness. It may therefore be claimed that we can simply dismiss the objections of the sceptics as irrelevant to the justification of democracy. I argue to the contrary: that democrats should not retreat to the intrinsic value of democracy, but should rather tackle their critics head on. I argue that conceding the epistemic ground to the critics would not be the best political strategy, but also draw on recent work in democratic theory to claim that we have principled reasons for thinking democracy's value rests, at least in part, on its ability to make good decisions. A central problem for any epistemic conception of democracy, however, is the fact that people reasonably and persistently disagree about what counts as a 'good' decision in politics. I therefore dedicate much of the first chapter to offering a new approach to epistemic democracy which can address this problem, and which will form the framework for the rest of the book. This approach evaluates whether institutions possess epistemic abilities or tools which are important to achieving any of the reasonable conceptions of justice or the common good we may ask them to pursue. I then use this approach to clarify what it means for an institution to be intelligent and the comparative approach I will take throughout the book.

After clarifying some fundamental issues in Chapter 1, Chapter 2 begins the book's comparative analysis by considering the mechanisms of regular elections and free markets. These two institutions have attracted most attention in epistemic debates, with Hayekian political economists focused on the former and epistemic democrats on the latter. I do not, however, make a straightforward defence of elections against the free-market sceptics. Instead, I argue that both institutions possess similar and underappreciated limitations, because both attempt to decentralize decision-making to individuals as either voters or consumers. While both mechanisms possess epistemic abilities when it comes to self-interested decisions, decisions about justice and the common good require individuals to account for the effects of their actions on a large number of distant others. These latter decisions are argued to present significant incentive and information problems for individual decision-makers, and these undermine the epistemic potential of both institutions. The chapter therefore defends the novel position that markets and elections face similar epistemic limitations for the very same reasons. I then use these critiques to set up a preliminary case for the importance of more collective forms of political decision-making, such as the decisions of democratic assemblies and forums, which lay the bases for the subsequent chapters and the development of the system model.

While Chapter 2 points to the epistemic limits of markets, Chapter 3 turns to consider what pro-market critics take to be the central problem with democracy. Hayek and other free-market liberals argue that collective political institutions, such as the democratic state, cannot possibly acquire the information needed to solve social problems, given that this involves local knowledge only known to on-the-spot individuals. After reformulating Hayek's view of the division of knowledge to better account for general scientific knowledge, I start to develop a systemic view of democracy to counter this form of democratic scepticism. I argue that formal democratic bodies are not isolated or cut off from knowledge in society, but are rather connected to an active public sphere involving a range of institutions. This public sphere is shown to possess important divisions of epistemic labour where the task of gathering knowledge is distributed across many autonomous and often

14   INTELLIGENT DEMOCRACY

specialized institutions which locate and acquire information. I also show that it is the open and inclusive nature of a democratic public sphere which allows this division of labour to remain functional. I then finally compare this system model to the workings of markets and defend the provocative claim that democratic institutions are better able to acquire the kinds of knowledge Hayek believed to be so important. Chapter 3 therefore replies to the free-market brand of democratic scepticism, but also demonstrates how democratic systems possess the epistemic ability of knowledge gathering.

After Chapter 3 first introduces the systemic model, Chapter 4 considers some of its most pressing challenges. According to many democratic sceptics, citizens tend to be dominated by partisan bias and motivated reasoning, and democracy is therefore more likely to be a machine for misinformation than a reliable system for gathering political knowledge. I agree with the sceptics that a deliberative system will produce knowledge claims of varying qualities and that it must therefore be able to evaluate the reliability of such claims. I reject their sceptical stance, however, in two steps. In the first, I argue that many prominent approaches to deliberative and epistemic democracy struggle to explain how deliberation can evaluate political information, and that this epistemic ability can only be realized if they expand their conception of deliberation to include appeals to trust and trustworthiness. In the second step, I then consider whether effective trust evaluations can be made in a deliberative system despite claims about hopelessly biased citizens. Surveying empirical research, I question the prevalence of such biases at the individual and group level and argue that there is a division of labour between the spheres of a deliberative system which allows their influence over democratic decisions to be minimized and controlled. This chapter therefore responds to a common range of epistemic objections to democracy, and in doing so shows how a democratic system has the ability to evaluate information.

Chapters 2 to 4 focus on developing a case for collective democratic institutions situated within a wider deliberative system which can gather and evaluate information. There is, however, another form of democratic scepticism which is highly critical of centralized politics. This approach appeals not to Hayek and the free market, but to Elenore and Vincent Ostrom and the idea of polycentricity. These critics argue against a democratic monopoly on the provision of goods and services, and favour limiting democratic institutions in favour of a polycentric approach where private, public, and third-sector institutions compete with each other. Chapter 5 responds to this brand of democratic scepticism by first rejecting its approach to polycentricity. This approach aims to make politics 'more like the market' by emphasizing bottom-up competition and individual exit, but in doing so ends up replicating many of the problems found to affect markets in Chapter 2. I then argue that their polycentric critique of democracy is somewhat misplaced, as on a systemic view democracy is itself highly polycentric. The chapter therefore rejects another form of democratic scepticism, but also develops a polycentric view of a democratic system. It considers how such a system can best realize the polycentric benefits of experimentation and self-regulation and defends greater forms of political decentralization.

At this point of the book, I will have mostly focused on defending democracy against sceptics who favour reducing the scope of politics altogether. The rest of the project turns to those who similarly support collective politics but argue that it should be reserved for the best and brightest. Unlike advocates of markets and polycentricity, elite forms of the new democratic scepticism have received attention from epistemic democrats, and Chapter 6 considers one of the most prominent and sophisticated in the literature. This account is offered by Hélène Landemore, who argues that decisions based on democratic deliberation will be superior to those of even a well-motivated epistocracy, due to its cognitive diversity. I argue that this approach—which is based on the *diversity trumps ability theorem*—underestimates the complexity of political problems and therefore struggles to apply to real world politics. I then offer a simpler and more modest model of democratic deliberation and defend it against deliberative failures often highlighted by the sceptics. This new model—which is based on a *relationship between diversity and diminishing returns*—supports the idea that cognitive diversity is a benefit to democratic deliberation, but rejects the claim that this makes it necessarily superior to elite forms of politics. Chapter 6 therefore establishes that an epistemic defence of democracy against elite rule cannot be based on its cognitive diversity alone.

In the final two chapters I therefore turn to an alternative strategy based on motivations. Although Chapters 2 to 5 established that democracy possesses many epistemic abilities, they did not address how we ensure these abilities are utilized for the common good. Chapter 7 starts by considering the conventional democratic solution to this problem: that regular and competitive elections align the interests of political representatives with the public good.

16   INTELLIGENT DEMOCRACY

I argue that this conventional solution is only half right. While elections can help motivate decision-makers away from the worst political decisions, they are unlikely to motivate them to promote the very best decisions due to the limits of voter knowledge. I therefore argue that the appropriate role for elections in a democratic system is to guard against the worst abuses and misuses of power. The epistocratic and meritocratic alternatives of the new sceptics, alternatively, wish to remove inclusive elections and are therefore left highly vulnerable to abuses, including manipulations of the very procedures which are meant to select more competent leaders or voters. Chapter 7 therefore argues that while representative democracy may have limited motivational value, the alternatives of political meritocracy and epistocracy offer no improvements.

Does this therefore mean that representative democracy is the best we can do? In Chapter 8 I argue that it is not, and defend the use of random sortition for increasing the motivational ability of democracy. By considering two of the most popular sortition proposals—deliberative mini-publics and a randomly selected legislature—I argue that current approaches face significant problems in terms of sortitions influence, its burdensomeness on lay citizens, and its openness to elite capture. I then offer a proposal for a *sortition branch* of a democratic system aimed at overcoming these problems. The sortition branch involves the institutionalization of many short-term randomly selected assemblies with the power to scrutinize and veto legislation, and is argued to involve divisions of labour which guard against the problems of previous accounts. Chapter 8 therefore develops an original and democratic proposal for improving the intelligence of democracy, one which is more promising than the elitist alternatives offered by the new democratic sceptics. I therefore argue that improving the intelligence of democracy requires more citizen participation in political decision-making, not less as the new sceptics claim.

The conclusion brings together the book's epistemic justification of democracy and offers an overview of how it provides a robust response to the new democratic scepticism. It restates how the epistemic abilities of democracy are only produced through the interaction of many different institutions, and how they are therefore dependent on taking a systemic perspective. While any one democratic institution cannot possibly possess epistemic values superior to all of its alternatives, a systemic approach can identify divisions of labour and emergent properties which produce epistemic values at the system level. It also discusses the interdisciplinary nature of this systemic model and the ways it built on the problems and critiques of the sceptics. I then end the book by considering possible ways of improving the intelligence of contemporary democracies and discuss promising new developments.

1
Democracy's Epistemic Problems

Over the course of the twentieth century democracy became one of the most widespread and deeply held political commitments. Few would openly reject democracy or question that it was the best form of government, and even the leaders of regimes with highly questionable democratic credentials started to appeal to the ideal of democracy to legitimize their power. Today, however, this commitment is weakening. Public support and satisfaction with democracy is declining around the world, and there are growing numbers making explicit and direct critiques of democratic politics. In fact, there is now a significant group among scholars of democracy who can accurately be labelled as democratic sceptics. This includes those who would be happy to do away with democracy completely, replacing it with some more elite form of rule, but also those who want to see it limited or restricted. This second group does not reject democracy outright, but is sceptical enough to wish to constrain it in order to make room for something else, such as the market.

It is in reaction to this new democratic scepticism that I aim to defend the intelligence of democracy. I will argue that we should value democracy not only because it treats us fairly or equally, but also because it can make intelligent decisions about justice and the common good. This focus on good decision-making mirrors the central concerns of the sceptics. The new democratic scepticism is in large part an epistemic critique, predominantly occupied with what it sees as the failure of democracy to acquire, communicate, and utilize information to enhance the public interest. Whether it is the ignorance of voters, the biases of citizens, or the failures of public deliberation, the sceptics fear that democratic institutions will make bad decisions about the laws and policies which regulate our societies. Why, however, should we be concerned with such objections? For many democrats it is the intrinsic values of democracy which justify it as a form of rule, not its decision-making ability. If democracy is valued because it embodies ideals of equality, fairness, or freedom, then perhaps we should care little about the epistemic problems highlighted by the sceptics or even see them as 'problems' to begin with.

Intelligent Democracy. Jonathan Benson, Oxford University Press. © Oxford University Press 2024.
DOI: 10.1093/oso/9780197767283.003.0002

DEMOCRACY'S EPISTEMIC PROBLEMS 19

I start this chapter by arguing that the best response to the new democratic scepticism is not to retreat to the intrinsic or procedural values of democracy, but rather to tackle their epistemic concerns head on. I firstly argue that such a retreat is unlikely to be the best political strategy, given that many of our fellow citizens care deeply about the outcomes of political decisions. Secondly, I draw on the recent epistemic turn in democratic theory to argue that we have principled reasons to recognize that good decision-making is an important part of democracy's value, and that there is therefore an important epistemic dimension to democratic politics. One of the most pressing challenges facing any epistemic conception of democracy, however, is the problem of disagreement. If democracy is to be judged in terms of its ability to make good decisions, then how do we deal with the fact that people reasonably and persistently disagree over what counts as a 'good' political decision. While previous approaches struggle with this challenge, I dedicate much of this chapter to offering an alternative.

I argue that if we are to have democratic self-governance, then democratic institutions must be able to lead society down the path towards any of the valued ends we may wish to give it. To do this, however, requires certain epistemic abilities. Just as a handyman needs a range of tools which can complete the many tasks they may be set, democracy needs a range of epistemic tools which will allow it to achieve the many reasonable conceptions of justice and the common good it may be ask to pursue. The reason contemporary democratic scepticism presents a significant challenge to democracy, then, is that it denies that democratic institutions can possess these epistemic abilities. It denies that democracy has the epistemic tools necessary for self-governance. This new approach to epistemic democracy therefore not only helps us deal with the problem of disagreement, but also to understand why we need to mount a reply to democracy's critics. The final sections of the chapter then use this new approach to set out a framework for developing such a reply. I define what it means to say that political procedures are intelligent, explain how the intelligence of democracy can justify it as having an important kind of institutional priority, and discuss the theoretical and empirical tools used in making the book's argument. My aims in this chapter are therefore exploratory and foundational. I will explain the need to defend the intelligence of democracy, the understanding of epistemic democracy endorsed in this book, and the theoretical framework it will use to reply to the new democratic scepticism.

Do Democracies Need to Make Good Decisions?

Perhaps the most frequent complaint among the new democratic sceptics concerns the problem of voter ignorance.[1] Drawing on work from political science and public opinion, they argue that the average voter knows very little about political issues or policy, and that their resulting incompetence at the ballot box is likely to lead to the election of ineffective political leaders. Failures of public deliberation are similarly a key topic in the works of sceptics.[2] They argue that democratic deliberation will likely be ruled by bias and motivated reasoning, and that it is more likely to polarize and turn citizens against each other than it is to improve the quality of public policy. As we will see in later chapters, these are just two of a host of objections which democratic sceptics throw at democracy. They do, however, exemplify the epistemic nature of the new democratic scepticism. This scepticism is not so much concerned with issues of procedural fairness, but with what it sees as a failure of democracy to acquire, communicate, or utilize information in ways that will lead to good political decisions.[3]

What is initially striking about these epistemic concerns, however, is just how much they run counter to the majority of contemporary democratic theory. While the sceptics have claimed that evidence of voter ignorance and irrationality undermine our general conception of democratic politics, these issues are in fact tangential to the central concerns of democratic theorists, who—more often than not—ground the value of democracy wholly or substantially on its intrinsic values. For many democratic theorists it is the fairness, equality, or freedom expressed by democratic procedures which give us reason to value democracy, not its ability to produce good or competent decisions.[4] Perhaps we should not, therefore, find democracy's epistemic problems particularly troubling or perhaps we should not even see them is 'problems'. As long as political decisions are fair and equal, they do not necessarily need to be competent or intelligent.

We should be wary, however, about such a quick dismissal of the recent rise of democratic scepticism. Although a full defence of an epistemic conception of democracy would require a book of its own, we do have some immediate

---

[1] Achen and Bartels (2017); Bell (2016); Brennan (2016a); Caplan (2011); Somin (2016).

[2] Achen and Bartels (2017); Brennan (2016a); Pennington (2010); Somin (2016).

[3] Although greatly concerned with democracy's epistemic failures, Brennan (2014, 2016a) is somewhat of an exception to this rule as he has also dedicated time to criticizing the procedural value of democracy.

[4] Christiano (2008, 2012); Kolodny (2014a, 2014b); May (1952); Fleuß (2021).

reasons for not responding to this scepticism with a retreat to intrinsic values. Firstly, such a retreat is unlikely to be the most effective political strategy. Although many democratic theorists are happy to rest democratic legitimacy solely on its intrinsic value, many citizens of democracies may be less taken with the ideals of procedural fairness. As mentioned in the introduction, satisfaction with democracy is falling around the globe, including in the world's most developed democracies, and the sharpest of these declines are often associated with perceived government failures. Whether it be the global financial crisis or more locally botched policies, satisfaction with democracy tends to dip when governments are seen as failing to take good decisions. Many of our fellow citizens therefore care very deeply for the consequences of political institutions, and they hold democratic institutions responsible when they are seen to take decisions incompetently.

This is also, of course, far from unreasonable. Political decisions affect our ability to put food on the table, educate our children, care for the sick, protect the natural environment, and pursue our life plans. It is therefore only to be expected that many people will wish to have a form of government which can take these decisions in an informed and considered fashion, as well as in a manner which is fair and equal. If we are to convince our fellow citizens to support democracy and reject calls to replace or restrict it, then our best strategy for doing so will not be to concede the epistemic grounds to the sceptics. Instead, we should look to confront their epistemic objections head-on, and persuade others that political equality does not come at the expense of good political decision-making. To appeal only to procedural values in face of the new democratic scepticism may simply be insufficient to reassure many of our fellow citizens that democracy is the best form of rule.

Appeals to the intrinsic value of democracy are also not universally accepted among democratic theorists.[5] Recent years have seen an epistemic turn in democratic theory, with an increasing number of authors arguing that democratic legitimacy depends, at least in part, on democracy's ability to make good decisions.[6] For these epistemic democrats, political decisions can be judged as good not only in terms of whether they were taken fairly, but also by some procedurally independent standard such as a conception of

---

[5] Arneson (2018); Wall (2007).

[6] Epistemic approaches to democracy are not new and date back at least to Aristotle's discussion of the 'wisdom of the multitude'. For discussion, see Waldron (1995) and Landemore (2013b). They have, however, seen a significant revival in contemporary democratic theory. For discussion of the recent epistemic turn, see Estlund and Landemore (2018); Goodin and Spiekermann (2018); Landemore (2017); Schwartzberg (2015); Jörke (2010); Urbinati (2014).

22 INTELLIGENT DEMOCRACY

justice, the public interest, or the common good. Democracy should therefore be seen as analogous to what John Rawls referred to as 'imperfect procedural justice'.[7] While both 'imperfect' and 'perfect procedural justice' assume there are independent criteria which define whether an outcome is correct or better, the former does not take there to be a procedure which can guarantee the right result. Instead, it looks for procedures which tend to produce better results over time. In criminal trials, for instance, the guilt or innocence of the defendant determines the standard of correctness which the jury aims for, but there is no guarantee that such standards will always be met. Instead, we hope that juries tend to convict the guilty and not the innocent with some level of reliability. Epistemic democrats understand politics in a similar way. There are independent standards which define the correctness of political decisions, such as standards of justice or the common good, and while there is no political procedure which can guarantee that the correct decision is always made, we should aim for those political institutions which can most reliably approximate them. We can therefore claim that democracy is valuable to the extent that it tends to produce good decisions over time, or to the extent that it produces good decisions with more reliability than its nondemocratic alternatives.[8]

David Estlund, perhaps more than anyone, has forcefully argued that most defences of democracy either implicitly assume some nonprocedural standards, or remain too weak to justify democratic rule.[9] If only procedural fairness was of value, Estlund argues, we would be just as happy taking political decisions by flipping a coin as we are with majority rule. A random procedure gives equal weight to the preferences of individuals and is blind to these individuals' contingent and morally arbitrary features (e.g. class, ethnicity, and gender). It seems puzzling, however, that we should ground our support for democracy on a single value which would just as likely justify a political regime based on the roll of a dice. To see why democracy is better than a coin flip, we must recognize the importance of standards other than procedural fairness, such as the ability to make decisions about justice or the common good. Democracy must be valued because it can promote justice

---

[7] Rawls (1971).

[8] An epistemic justification of democracy is therefore distinct from a 'correctness theory' where any one decision is legitimate to the extent that it is correct. Rather, democratic decisions are legitimate because democratic procedures will tend to produce correct results over time. See Estlund (2009).

[9] Estlund (1997, 2009). For debate, see Christiano (2009); Gaus (2011); Lippert-Rasmussen (2012); Peter (2007, 2008).

and the common good with more reliability than pure chance. This does not mean that epistemic democrats must deny the intrinsic values of fairness, equality, and freedom. In fact many of them explicitly endorse procedural values alongside epistemic ones.[10] However, epistemic democrats agree with the sceptics in the sense that both take the ability to make good political decisions to be at least one important component in evaluating the value of democracy, as well as its alternatives.

Their claim that there are procedure-independent standards by which we can judge political decisions is a plausible one. In fact, we implicitly accept as much when we engage in political debate and discussion.[11] To reason about a political decision is to presuppose that there are better and worse ways those decisions can be taken. That is, to 'argue in favour of decision A means, briefly, to show that decision A *is the right* decision, or at least, that A is *better in terms of rightness* than other decisions being compared'.[12] The claim of epistemic democrats that there are better and worse political decisions should not therefore feel unfamiliar, as we normally all accept this assumption when we argue over who to vote for or which policy to adopt. The reasons we give for our preferred positions do not attend only to the quality of decision-making procedures, but rather to standards such as justice, the public interest, or the common good. Like lawyers in a court room, we appeal to procedure-independent standards in debating which decision is correct.

An important problem with the analogy between imperfect procedural justice and democracy, however, is the extent to which we share a common understanding of what a good political decision looks like. Unlike a jury trial where guilt and innocence provide the standards by which decisions can be judged, political decisions involve significant disagreement over what defines a good answer or a good outcome. Questions of taxation, redistribution, education, crime, or public health differ from questions about legal guilt, and even more so from questions of science and mathematics. While in law and mathematics there are commonly accepted standards which define what a good or better answer looks like, in politics there is scope for significant and reasonable disagreement. How then can we judge democracy in terms of its ability to make good decisions when we so often disagree about what counts as a good political decision?

---

[10] Estlund (2009); Landemore (2013b).
[11] Ingham (2013); Landemore (2017); Marti (2006).
[12] Marti (2006, p. 29, original emphasis).

24   INTELLIGENT DEMOCRACY

What Is a Good Political Decision?

There are a couple of common strategies for trying to deal with the problem of disagreement. The first is simply to nail one's colours to the mast and specify a preferred standard of correctness. This approach would select a single conception of the common good, such as the maximization of utility or an equal distribution of resources, and then investigate which political regimes best achieve it. The epistemic democrat would therefore be like a maths teacher setting a test. The teacher knows the right answers in advance and then looks to see how reliably her students can find them. This strategy, however, fails to give reason to those who dispute the chosen standards, and can only ever appeal to like-minded citizens. This is a fault that several democratic sceptics fall foul of.[13] They start by assuming some particular account of good outcomes, most commonly a form of utilitarianism, and then reject democracy in favour of an alternative on the grounds that it does not achieve this standard as effectively.[14] Such a strategy, however, does not respect the fact that there is persistent and reasonable disagreement over their chosen account of justice or the common good. Others will reject utilitarianism and the performance of social institutions may look very different on their alternative standards of correctness.

Specifying the nonprocedural standards by which we judge alternative institutions also seems particularly problematic from a democratic point of view. It could quite rightly be objected that one of the most important aspects of democracy is that the question of what counts as a valuable end for society should itself be the subject of democratic deliberation.[15] Taking a position on what defines a good political outcome in advance of a decision would therefore produce the nondemocratic conclusion that such standards should not be set by the democratic process itself. An epistemic argument for democracy which specified the 'correct' or 'true' set of procedure-independent

---

[13] This fault cannot be ascribed to all democratic sceptics. Brennan (2016a), for instance, remains neutral on the preferred standards of correctness in a similar way to epistemic democrats. Brennan does, however, contradict this position somewhat when claiming that a lack of support for certain policies, such as free trade and the removal of price controls, are signals of political ignorance rather than simply disagreements over principles of justice.

[14] Those sceptics who come from an economics perspective, such as Caplan (2011), often fall into this category. It is still an open question, however, whether their epistemic arguments can be applied without specifying a procedure-independent standard. Arguments for the rational ignorance of voters, for instance, are often made in respect to a preference utilitarian framework, but the lack of incentive voters have to acquire knowledge may be problematic on many other conceptions of the common good. See Chapters 2 and 7 for further discussion.

[15] Peter (2008).

DEMOCRACY'S EPISTEMIC PROBLEMS   25

standards seems to be self-defeating, as it would simultaneously undermine a central component of democratic politics, which is for public deliberation to determine our preferred ends.

These problems have led many epistemic democrats to endorse a second strategy. This second approach remains ignorant or agnostic on the standards which define a good answer, and instead looks for those procedures which can discover correct answers, whatever they may be. Epistemic democracy is therefore less like a teacher setting a maths test, and more like the processes of science. We rely on the scientific method to get the right answer to scientific questions not because we know what the truth is in advance, but because its procedures give us confidence that it can find the truth over time. The same could be said of political institutions such as democracy. Just as a 'good justi-fication of a particular scientific research design does not presuppose the hy-pothesis that the research aims to test', an epistemic argument for democratic procedures could focus on 'identifying the properties in virtue of which they tend to produce reasonable decisions, whatever decisions are in fact reason-able'.[16] This second strategy is the one taken by most epistemic democrats.[17] Consider, for instance, arguments for democracy based on the Condorcet jury theorem. According to the theorem, if each voter has a greater than 50% probability of getting the right answer, chooses between two options, and votes independently and nonstrategically, then larger democratic groups will make better decisions than smaller and more exclusive ones.[18] According to this argument, we do not need to know what the right answer is in advance to claim that a democratic vote will be more likely to produce the correct decisions than a nondemocratic vote involving some small elite.[19] On this view, democracy will find the truth 'whatever that is'.[20]

While this second strategy is certainly an improvement over the first, many will doubt that a political procedure will be able to track the truth of political questions in the way it proposes. The reason for this is that it would require these procedures to track the truth of the normative questions which often

---

[16] Ingham (2013, pp. 136, 140).

[17] Estlund (2009); Goodin and Spiekermann (2018); Landemore (2013b).

[18] Supporters of the theorem have aimed to relax these assumptions, extending it to plural voting, cases where voters have lowly correlated votes, or make up their minds autonomously rather than fully independent. See Estlund (1994); Ladha (1992); Landemore (2013b); List and Goodin (2001).

[19] The application of the jury theorem to politics has been repeatedly challenged, including by early supporters, and I consider problems with the approach myself in Chapter 2. For discussion, see Anderson (2006); Dietrich (2008); Estlund, Waldron, Grofman, and Feld (1989); Fuerstein (2008); Gaus (1997a).

[20] Gaus (2011, p. 270).

26 INTELLIGENT DEMOCRACY

underline political ones. Can a political procedure really find the correct answer to questions concerning the balance between freedom and equality, the conflict between aggregate welfare and individual rights, or the permissibility of killing? One reason to be sceptical of this is that it would seem to bring an implausibly swift end to our deeply held and persistent disagreements. The Condorcet jury theorem is a good example in this respect, as it suggests that a large referendum would be almost infallible. A referendum of just 399 people with individual reliabilities of 55%, for instance, would together have a 98% chance of picking the correct answer. The result of such a procedure would therefore provide such strong evidence in favour of one course of action that we would all have to accept it as true. Even if we were deeply committed to an alternative, the procedure with such a high level of reliability would force us to accept that we were wrong, therefore removing all disagreement.

As Sean Ingham points out, even if a procedure could find the answer to such questions with a reliability of only a little over a half, running such a procedure enough times would eventually create sufficient evidence that we would all need to accept its verdict.[21] If democracy can track the truth of questions of justice and the common good, in a similar way to how the scientific method tracks the truth of scientific questions, then our political disagreements would seem to be much more easily resolved than they appear to be. We could simply look to the outcome of a democratic decision, or a series of such decisions, to find convincing evidence of the correct position. This argument does not reject that there are standards of correctness independent of political procedures, but it does question whether any political procedure will likely discover them. Although the scientific approach may therefore recognize the problem of disagreement, unlike the maths teacher approach, it also appears to underestimate its depth and persistence. Both of these approaches to epistemic democracy therefore struggle to deal with the presence of reasonable and sustained disagreement over what counts as a good political decision.

I therefore wish to offer a third alternative, better able to address this problem. This approach, like the second strategy just considered, would not specify any one standard of correctness. Rather than looking for political procedures which can find the true or correct answer to the normative questions of politics, however, it would instead look at whether political institutions possess a range of epistemic abilities which are important to

---

[21] Ingham (2013).

DEMOCRACY'S EPISTEMIC PROBLEMS   27

promoting any reasonable conception of justice or the common good.[22] This approach is therefore based on the idea that there are certain epistemic abilities or capacities which are useful or even necessary for achieving any and all reasonable nonprocedural standards of correctness. Whether we want to maximize utility, satisfy basic needs, or achieve justice as fairness, we will require institutions which can gather and communicate information, as well as use this information to solve social problems in line with these criteria. In other words, there is a range of basic epistemic abilities which we would all want our political institutions to possess, irrespective of the conception of justice and the common good we endorse. While some may want to trade off economic growth for environmental quality, and others the reverse, all will wish to have institutions with the epistemic capacities needed to manage this trade-off. They will wish to have institutions with the knowledge and competence needed to determine, for instance, which options are better for growth and which are better for the environment.

This third approach would therefore judge institutions, be they democratic or otherwise, in terms of whether they possess a range of epistemic abilities which are important to achieving any and all reasonable conceptions of justice and the common good. It looks at whether these institutions have epistemic capacities which are useful in guiding society towards any of the desirable goals we may wish to give it. An epistemic conception of democracy would not therefore be like a teacher setting a maths test, nor would it be like the procedures of science. Instead, it would be more like a handyman selecting the best toolbox. The handyman does not necessarily know what end they will need to achieve. It may be to fix a pipe, put up a shelf, install an electrical socket, or any number of other tasks. They will therefore want a toolbox containing a set of tools which will help them achieve the range of ends they may be set. Similarly, political institutions may be put to many reasonable purposes, such as creating more equality, greater utility, or broader individual freedom. We will therefore want political institutions which possess a range of epistemic tools which will help them to achieve whichever of these ends we may want them to pursue. We will want political institutions to have the epistemic abilities useful or necessary for achieving any reasonable

---

[22] I will work on the assumption that a broad range of conceptions of justice are reasonable (i.e. liberal egalitarian, libertarian, utilitarian, communitarian, etc.) but I will not take a position on exactly what makes any one conception reasonable. The approach I offer below does not require any one account of reasonableness, and will therefore allow the reader to plug in their preferred view. They can do this even if their account of reasonableness is more restrictive than what I implicitly assume in making my argument.

28　INTELLIGENT DEMOCRACY

procedure-independent standard of correctness, and we can judge them in terms of whether or not they do in fact possess them.

This approach to epistemic democracy deals better with the problem of disagreement than either of the previous two. Unlike the maths teacher view, the new approach does not specify any one conception of justice or the common good, but instead considers those epistemic abilities which are needed to achieve any reasonable standard. It can, therefore, offer reasons to all citizens irrespective of their preferred procedure-independent standard. Unlike the scientific view, the new approach also does not claim that democratic procedures can discover the one correct answer to questions of politics. It does not claim that they will discover the one correct goal we should be attempting to achieve, but rather that democracy has the epistemic abilities needed to guide society towards whichever valued end we may wish to give it. The new approach does not therefore need to assume that our reasonable and persistent disagreements can be easily resolved. Instead, epistemic democrats can claim that democracy, like the handyman's toolbox, possesses a range of epistemic tools which can be put to many different uses, or that it possesses more or better tools than its alternatives.

While better dealing with the presence of disagreement, this third strategy also helps to understand the importance of the epistemic objections made by the new democratic scepticism. A key component of the ideal of democratic self-governance is the ability to direct society towards the ends a polity chooses to give it. It involves not only that a polity can select a preferred path, but also that it can 'guide society along' this 'preferred path'.[23] Achieving democratic self-governance therefore requires, at least in part, that political institutions have the epistemic abilities needed to pursue the ends we choose to give them. The common democratic response to political disagreement is egalitarian.[24] We disagree over what our society should look like, but democracy gives us all a say in this debate and weighs our views equally to all others. Being treated equally, however, would seem to be an insufficient response to disagreement if democratic institutions were unable to achieve or approximate the ends we end up selecting. The procedures we use to resolve our political disagreements not only have a bearing on the extent to which we are treated fairly, but also on the extent to which we can achieve these very ends. If I value equality of welfare and you the greatest happiness for the greatest

[23] Gaus (2019, p. 968).
[24] For discussion, see Christiano (2008, 2018); Gaus (1997b); Waldron (1999).

number, then neither of us would wish to settle our disagreement through political institutions which, due to ignorance or irrationality, were incapable of achieving or approximating either standard. Instead, we would both want institutions with the ability to put our preferred standards, or some compromise between them, into practice.

It is here that we can see the force of the new democratic scepticism. If democratic institutions are as ignorant, irrational, and incompetent as the sceptics claim, then they would count our ends equally while taking away the possibility of achieving them. Even if there was consensus over one conception of justice or the common good, or a compromise was struck between two or more conceptions, if democratic institutions lack epistemic abilities they will likely be unable to put it into practice. The epistemic problems highlighted by the new democratic sceptics are therefore 'problems' because democratic self-governance not only requires that we are treated equally, but also that we can guide our society towards the ends we choose to give it. A fair resolution of political disagreement is simply insufficient if we have no reason to believe that our political institutions can achieve or approximate our preferred ends even if they were in the majority or even if they are shared by the whole of society. If democratic institutions are as ignorant and as irrational as is claimed, then we can have little hope that they will be able to achieve any of the conceptions of justice or the common good we value, and we cannot be understood as self-governing in a meaningful sense.

What Makes an Institution Intelligent?

The discussion of the last section did not aim to give a definitive argument for recognizing an epistemic dimension to democratic politics. Such an argument would require a book of its own. However, I did aim to give the reader some reasons, both strategic and principled, to take the epistemic critiques of the new democratic sceptics seriously. I also aimed to provide an epistemic approach to democracy which continued to respect reasonable disagreement, and which I hope will be acceptable to many democrats. Now that we have some idea of why and on what terms we need to reply to the democratic sceptics, I will use the remainder of this chapter to further outline the approach I will take to defending the intelligence of democracy.

Firstly, I need to clarify what I mean when I say that democracy, or any of its alternatives, is intelligent. Following the approach put forward in the

30   INTELLIGENT DEMOCRACY

previous section, an intelligent institution is one which possesses a range of epistemic abilities which are useful to making good decisions with respect to any reasonable conception of justice or the common good. It possesses those epistemic tools which can help guide society towards any of the valuable ends we may wish it to pursue. The more and better tools an institution has, the more intelligent it can be said to be. What, however, are these epistemic abilities or tools? Obvious candidates will include the ability to acquire relevant information, to communicate and evaluate this information, to produce new information, to utilize information for problem-solving and decision-making, and to guard against mistaken decisions or reduce their effects. Whichever conception of justice one prefers, all of these abilities will be important to achieving it. So will certain motivational factors. These concern the incentives institutions create to do such things as acquire and produce information, but also the extent to which decision-makers are motivated to take decisions in respect to the common good. Political decision-makers need to be motivated towards the public interest, and not solely towards their own interests or the interests of some social elite, if they are to make 'good' decisions.

The concept of intelligence used here is therefore a normative one. It matters not only how knowledgeable and rational a procedure is, but also whether it is likely to exercise these abilities towards the right ends. Albert Einstein may be more knowledgeable, logical, and creative than the average physicist, but he would have been a less intelligent physicist if he had spent all his time trying to convince others of falsehoods. Similarly, a philosopher king maybe more knowledgeable, logical, and creative than the average citizen, but still a less intelligent ruler if they spent all their energy maximizing their own wealth and persecuting their enemies. Motivation to take decisions in respect to justice and the common good, as opposed to purely self-interest or the common bad, is therefore an important part of a procedure's intelligence. This epistemic ability does not rule out all self-interested motivations. One's own interests may themselves form part of the common good, and it may also be possible to bring motivations of self-interest in line with the public interest.[25] Adam Smith's famous argument that 'it is not from the benevolence of the butcher, the brewer, or the baker that we expect our dinner, but from their regard to their own self-interest' is a clear example of such a claim.[26] The

---

[25] Habermas (1990); Mansbridge et al. (2010).
[26] Smith (2010, pp. 9–10).

motivational ability of an institution may therefore involve encouraging pure motivations towards the common good, aligning self-interest with the public interest, or some combination of the two.

My claim that democracy is intelligent can therefore be understood as claiming that democracy possesses a range of epistemic abilities useful to achieving any reasonable conception of justice and the common good. It possesses such things as the ability to acquire, evaluate, and produce information, the ability to utilize information for problem-solving and decision-making, and the ability to guard against mistaken decisions or reduce their effects, as well as the ability to motivate decisions towards the common good. Democracy is not, however, the only institution which may possess such abilities. Philosopher kings, epistocrats, or free markets may possess more of the abilities needed to guide society towards valuable ends than democracy. It will be my task then, to argue that democracy has a better range of epistemic abilities than any of the nondemocratic alternatives favoured by the new democratic sceptics.

Before considering these alternatives, however, one brand of democratic scepticism may be thought to directly object to my epistemic framework. While many of the new democratic sceptics similarly wish political institutions to promote the common good, some free-market critics reject the idea that concerns for social justice should guide our political or democratic theories. This view is most associated with Friedrich von Hayek, who famously claimed that social justice was a 'mirage'.[27] Hayek advanced many questionable arguments for this claim. For instance, his belief that justice cannot apply to markets because their outcomes do not result from intentional actions, or that it is an atavistic belief which emerged from the norms of past societies, have been widely discussed and criticized in the literature.[28] One of Hayek's more interesting objections to social justice, however, was explicitly epistemic. He claimed political institutions would fail to achieve social justice as they would fail to possess the kinds of knowledge necessary to apply abstract normative principles to particular contexts. According to Hayek, then, no political institution can be intelligent in the sense I refer to here, as no institution can possess the knowledge needed to make good decisions with respect to some conception of the common good. While I will not spend much time discussing it directly, the argument I develop over

---

[27] Hayek (2013).
[28] Gaus (2021); Johnston (1997); Lister (2013); Lukes (1997); Tebble (2009).

32 INTELLIGENT DEMOCRACY

the following chapters offers a refutation of this claim. Over the course of the book, I aim to show that democracy can come to possess relevant information, including the kinds of local and tacit forms of knowledge Hayek believed to evade political institutions (see Chapters 3 and 4 in particular). While many contemporary Hayekians have abandoned Hayek's mirage claims and have rightly introduced considerations of justice into their work, my argument for the intelligence of democracy aims to dispute the claim that democratic politics lacks the epistemic abilities needed to at least approximate our preferred conceptions of justice.[29]

Institutional Diversity and the Priority of Democracy

An argument for the intelligence of democracy requires a comparison between democratic institutions and the variety of nondemocratic alternatives favoured by their critics. It is this full range of nondemocratic alternatives, however, which has so far been missing from much current work on epistemic democracy. While some confine their analysis to only democratic institutions, those who do consider nondemocratic alternatives have tended to focus on democracy's more traditional rivals. Following a long convention in political philosophy, most epistemic democrats have tended to compare democracy to elite forms of politics, such as aristocracy, oligarchy, and autocracy. These traditional alternatives are important comparisons to democracy, but they do not represent the diversity of nondemocratic institutions supported by the new democratic scepticism.

This narrow scope is perhaps best illustrated by the lack of engagement with democracy's pro-market critics. Hayek's political economy represents perhaps the most influential epistemic approach to social institutions and has become one of the central theoretical justifications for shrinking the state in favour of the market. Despite this, it has been little discussed by epistemic democrats. Hélène Landemore, for instance, states that 'the market is not a political decision procedure' and therefore 'does not offer an alternative' to democracy, while Elizabeth Anderson constrains her analysis to problems of 'public interest' which are said to exclude markets.[30] As a result,

---

[29] For examples of Hayekians who consider concerns for justice, see Pennington (2011); Tebble (2016).

[30] Landemore (2013b, p. 86); Anderson (2006, p. 9). An exception in this regard is the work of Knight and Johnson (2007, 2011), who take seriously the issues of institutional diversity. However, even their discussion of markets does not directly account for the epistemic work of figures such as

the Hayekian objections to democracy have yet to be addressed by epistemic democrats; neither have they produced an epistemic understanding of the relationship between democracy and the market. This omission is symptomatic of a wider neglect of institutional diversity in the epistemic study of democracy.[31] I therefore intend to consider the full range of nondemocratic alternatives offered up by contemporary democratic sceptics, and compare democracy not only to its traditional rivals, but also to markets, polycentric systems, epistocracy, and political meritocracy.

In making these comparisons, I will not claim that democracy is always better at addressing every kind of problem. Given the diversity of social problems confronting modern societies, it seems unlikely that any one institutional form will be best placed to address them all. From the outset of this book, I will accept that there is unlikely to be a 'one size fits all' solution to social problems, and that a society's diverse ills will require an equally diverse range of institutional forms. What I will argue, however, is that democracy should have a particular kind of priority over other institutions. Yes, we will most probably need a range of different institutions to effectively solve society's problems in the name of justice or the common good, but this leaves open the question of how we should select this range of institutions. I will therefore argue that democracy should be granted an institutional priority with the privileged position of determining the scope and role of other institutions.

The idea of institutional priority can be better understood through Jack Knight and James Johnson's useful distinction between first-order and second-order institutions.[32] First-order institutions are those which directly address and resolve social problems. Institutions at this level can include, among others, markets, bureaucracy, expert committees, communities, and social norms. What they have in common, however, is that they are all concerned with directly addressing one or more social problem. A second-order institution, alternatively, does not directly resolve any one problem but rather monitors and adapts the institutions which exist at the first order. As

---

Hayek. Although they begin their chapter on markers by discussing Hayek, they quickly move to an analysis of predominately neoclassical accounts of markets and their failures. For a Hayekian discussion of Knight and Johnson, see Pennington (2017).

[31] A literature has now emerged around the relationship between democracy and epistocracy. See Arlen and Rossi (2018); Bhatia (2020, 2022); Brennan (2014, 2018); Gunn (2019); Jeffrey (2018); Moraro (2018).
[32] Knight and Johnson (2007).

34 INTELLIGENT DEMOCRACY

Knight and Johnson describe it, this task involves coordinating 'the ongoing process of selecting, implementing and maintaining effective institutional arrangements' at the first order, while sustaining an 'experimental environment that can enhance our knowledge' of the conditions under which institutions produce good consequences.[33] A second-order institution therefore has the role of evaluating and adapting society's institutional mix so that a diverse set of social problems can be most effectively addressed.

Institutions which play this second-order role can be similar or dissimilar from the institutions at the first order. If the second-order institution is authoritarian, for instance, then it may decide to address all problems through equally as authoritarian first-order institutions. Alternatively, it may allow markets or expert committees to take care of certain issues, leave others to private associations, and yet others to quasi-democratic bodies. Modern-day China may be one example of the latter, with a one-party state deciding to deal with certain problems itself while allowing markets, corporations, and even local participatory institutions to deal with others.[34] Second-order tasks can also be conducted by more impersonal processes than state institutions. On the free-market views considered in the next chapter, for instance, multiple private firms attempt to solve problems at the first order, while market competition selects between them at the second. Second-order priority is not therefore granted to a fixed institution but to an impersonal competitive process.

What distinguishes a second-order institution, however, is that it has the role of deciding questions of institutional choice as opposed to directly addressing any one social problem. The task of a second-order institution is '(1) to coordinate effective institutional experimentation, (2) to monitor and assess effective institutional performance for the range of institutions available in any society, (3) to monitor and assess its own ongoing performance.'[35] Given the epistemic approach I endorsed above, this monitoring and assessing of first-order institutions will involve the ability to evaluate performance in terms of any reasonable conception of justice and the common good. Given the problem of deep and persistent disagreement, second-order institutions will need epistemic abilities which can allow them to promote any reasonable conception of good outcomes through institutional selection. Importantly, this is not necessarily a requirement for first-order institutions.

[33] Knight and Johnson (2011, pp. 12–19).
[34] He and Warren (2011); Leib and He (2006).
[35] Knight and Johnson (2011, p. 169).

Once it is decided that certain normative criterion should be promoted for any one social problem, then we may wish to select the first-order institution best suited to achieving this specific criterion, even if it lacks the capacity to achieve others. The ability to make good decisions in terms of any reasonable conception of justice and the common good is therefore a requirement for institutions with second-order priority.

My epistemic advocacy of democracy throughout this book should therefore be read as advocating for a priority of democracy at the second order.[36] I will argue that democracy is best placed to monitor, access, and select a society's institutional mix so that a diverse range of problems can be best solved in respect to justice and the common good. The advantage of this priority approach is that it continues to recognize the merits of alternative institutional forms at the first order, and that there will likely not be a 'one size fits all' solution to social problems. This recognition, however, leaves open the question of which second-order institution is best placed to determine when and where different first-order institutions are most appropriate. My answer to this latter question is democracy.

A Note on Method

In defending the intelligence of democracy, this book will engage in a comparative institutional approach. It will introduce prominent alternatives to democracy supported by the new democratic sceptics and compare their respective epistemic properties. This comparative approach is important to drawing any normative conclusions. The epistemic failure of one institution does not give us reason to support another unless this alternative can be shown not to suffer from the same problem. Likewise, the epistemic ability of an institution is not a point in its favour unless others lack this same ability or do not possess it to the same extent. The argument I make in this book is therefore a relative one. It argues that democracy has a better range of epistemic abilities relative to its nondemocratic alternatives. Its argument is also probabilistic. Democracy cannot be expected to always make good or correct

---

[36] It is sometimes unclear whether other epistemic democrats are making an argument for democracy at the first or the second order. Landemore's (2013b, 2014) epistemic argument for democracy, for instance, at first appeared to be at the first order, with examples of democracy directly solving social problems, while in latter work she suggests that her account is best understood as justifying a second-order priority of democracy.

36 INTELLIGENT DEMOCRACY

decisions but it can be argued that it has epistemic tools which make it more likely to make better decisions over time. To say that democracy is epistemically superior (or inferior) to autocracy is therefore to claim that democracy tends (or tends not) to produce better decisions about justice and the common good than autocracy. Such claims about relative superiority do not need to suggest a very high level of absolute epistemic reliability. Given the complexity of social issues we will not be looking for the perfect procedure, but rather the best imperfect procedure. In Churchillian fashion, then, democracy may be the worst form of government, except for all the others.

This kind of comparative analysis is an example of what Elizabeth Anderson calls 'institutional epistemology' or Peter Boettke refers to as 'epistemic institutionalism'. These approaches focus on how alternative institutional designs 'gather and make effective use of the information they need to solve particular problems'.[37] It involves investigating and comparing the rival epistemic abilities of institutions, and in our case whether they can help in the second-order task of institutional selection. Although not always recognized by these names, institutional epistemology and epistemic institutionalism have a long history. Prominent proponents of the approach include Hayek's and Ludwig von Mises's analyses of markets and central planning, Michael Polanyi's account of scientific institutions, and John Dewy's and John Stuart Mill's work on free speech and democratic theory, as well as more contemporary work in informational economics and epistemic democracy.[38] This book is therefore set within, and hopes to contribute to, this rich intellectual heritage.

Consistent with much of this tradition, the analysis conducted here will focus on comparing institutional models. Models are purer or more idealized representations of actual institutions.[39] In reality, we often find imperfect versions of any one institutional type or mixed systems which blur the lines between institutional forms. As a result, it is often difficult to determine whether problems and successes are due to the structure of any one institution, or to that institution not being implemented to its fullest extent. It can be unclear, for instance, whether the benefits and problems of markets are the result of market mechanisms themselves, or the result of their regulation by democratic institutions. Although comparing institutional models

---

[37] Anderson (2006, p. 8); Boettke (2018).
[38] Hayek (1937, 1945); von Mises (2002, 2012); Polanyi (1962); Dewy (1927); Mill (2008, 2011); Stiglitz (1996); Akerlof (1978).
[39] Weisberg (2012).

may reduce the realism of the analysis, it helps to deal with these kinds of problems and makes it easier to identify the epistemic properties of rival mechanisms.

The analysis of these institutional models will be primarily theoretical and will engage with work from a number of fields, such as political theory, social epistemology, political science and economy, as well as economics. It will also consider empirical research where relevant and available in order to inform its more theoretical analysis. Empirical work can help deepen our understanding of how alternative institutions function, and whether the theoretical claims hold in practice. Given the aims of this study, however, I will frequently consider institutional forms which are only roughly approximated by those we find today and can be empirically studied. The empirical evidence will therefore often be incomplete. In such cases, I will attempt to make theoretical claims about the epistemic abilities of alternative institutions which firstly have their own internal plausibility and appeal and are secondly testable and verifiable by future empirical research.

Responding to the New Democratic Scepticism

An important component of any justification of democratic rule will be epistemic. It will be concerned with whether democratic institutions can possess the epistemic abilities needed to make decisions with respect to justice and the common good, and therefore whether they can offer an intelligent form of politics. It is the claim of the new democratic scepticism, however, that democracy lacks the relevant epistemic abilities. Instead, they point to a range of fundamental epistemic problems with democratic institutions, which are likely to undermine their capacity for good decision-making. If we want an intelligent form of politics, then, this cannot be an equal form of politics. The task I set myself in this book is to defend democracy's intelligence and in doing so mount a robust reply to this new democratic scepticism. Through a comparative institutional analysis, I will argue that the unique intelligence of democracy is that it possesses a larger and better range of epistemic tools than its most prominent rivals, and that it is therefore best able to guide us towards any of the reasonable ends we may wish to pursue. Whatever our preferred destination, it is democracy which gives us the best chance of getting there.

2

The Limits of Elections and Markets

When we think of critics of democracy, the picture which most readily comes to mind is of supporters of some kind of elitist politics. We think of advocates for authoritarian political parties, for a privileged aristocratic class, or perhaps for Plato's philosopher kings. Today, however, democratic sceptics are more likely to reject politics altogether than wish for some kind of ruling elite. The most commonly favoured alternatives to democracy are no longer monarchs, autocrats, or oligarchs, but rather markets. Since the late 1970s, many democratic countries have experienced a significant shift towards a greater reliance on market mechanisms, and a reduced role for the state. Markets have spread into many areas of life which had previously been a matter of political control and where they were already established, there has been a move to deregulate them in order that market forces can operate more freely from democratic oversight. Very often, then, solving the ills of democracy has not been seen as requiring a more elite or exclusive form of politics, but rather an expanding role for markets.

As the phrase 'the market *knows* best' suggests, one of the central intellectual defences of this movement is epistemic. The Austrian economist and political theorist Friedrich von Hayek argued that the principal benefit of markets was that they could make use of information inaccessible to any centralized bureaucracy, and a number of contemporary authors have developed his political economy into a more general critique of democratic politics.[1] Rather than having decisions taken by some distant assembly of

---

[1] Writing during the socialist calculations debates, Hayek argued that market economies had important epistemic advantages over centrally planned economies. Today the main alternative for markets is not socialist planning but the institutions of representative democracy, and more recent market theorists have focused on democratic institutions. In many ways the earlier calculations debates are an antecedent to the debates this book contributes to. This has been recognized by DeCanio (2014), who suggests that the more recent work should be seen as a sixth iteration of the calculations debates. For discussion of the previous five stages of the debate, see Roemer (1994). Given the importance of this debate in economic history, and its relevance to the epistemic abilities of political institutions, it is strange that it has generally received little attention from epistemic democrats. To the extent that the next two chapters defend democracy against the Hayekian tradition, they will help to fill this gap.

Intelligent Democracy. Jonathan Benson, Oxford University Press. © Oxford University Press 2024.
DOI: 10.1093/oso/9780197767283.003.0003

THE LIMITS OF ELECTIONS AND MARKETS   39

politicians disconnected from local problems, markets are argued to empower individuals to make the best use of their own knowledge, and to spontaneously coordinate their behaviour through the price system. According to this pro-market brand of the new democratic scepticism, we should, whenever possible, look to replace democratic control with markets. Given its considerable influence on twentieth-century politics, it is somewhat surprising that epistemic democrats have engaged so little with the Hayekian tradition. One likely reason for this oversight is that markets only ever offer a partial alternative to democracy.

Market institutions must rely on an existing set of rules and property rights which will themselves require some other form of governance to create and enforce. There is, therefore, no such thing as a completely 'free' market existing independently of all political institutions, and market advocates do not necessarily reject democracy outright. The new democratic scepticism, however, does not include only those who wish to do away with democracy completely, but also those who wish to significantly restrict it. The Hayekian sceptics fall into the second category. Unlike supporters of elite rule, they do not wish to fully abandon democratic politics, but they do wish to confine its role, as much as possible, to the creation and maintenance of markets which are then granted an institutional priority.[2] As defined in the previous chapter, first-order institutions are tasked with solving particular social problems, while an institution with second-order priority has the job of monitoring and selecting between these lower order institutions. For the pro-market sceptics first-order institutions are private individuals and firms, and the second-order task should be performed by a process of market competition. Democratic governance can still play a role in helping to establish and enforce the rules and rights necessary for the market to function, but beyond that it should simply allow market competition to determine winners and losers. Rather than having democratic bodies directly select first-order institutions, this priority of markets restricts them to the maintenance of market competition.

Over the next two chapters, I aim to address this free-market variant of the new democratic scepticism. While the Hayekian critique of democracy will be the focus of the next chapter, this chapter will compare

---

[2] Many contemporary Hayekians are more radical in this respect than Hayek himself, who actually advocated for a wide range of state interference and regulation, particularly (although not exclusively) in his later works.

40 INTELLIGENT DEMOCRACY

epistemic arguments for markets to those defending democratic elections. In many ways, regular elections and free markets have become the dominant institutions of liberal democratic societies, so it seems only natural to start our analysis with these two giants. My aim, however, is not to provide a straightforward defence of elections against their pro-market critics. Instead, I will make the more distinctive and contrarian claim that markets and elections actually possess very similar and significant epistemic limits. While often presented as competitors, I argue that there is significant overlap in the epistemic abilities commonly attributed to these institutions, and that both face a similar set of problems. When it comes to second-order decisions which must account for justice and the common good, I argue that elections and markets both struggle to realize their epistemic abilities. The reason for this is that both mechanisms aim to decentralize decision-making to a large number of individuals, as either voters or consumers, who will generally lack the knowledge needed to determine how their actions impact the public interest. So while markets and elections have been the focus of Hayekian political economy and epistemic democracy, I argue that they actually share a common set of epistemic problems which limit their intelligence. I then end the chapter by discussing how these limits point to the need for a less individual and more collective form of politics.

The Epistemic Abilities of Elections and Markets

In a simple model of democratic elections, individual voters make decisions about whether to cast their votes for the policy packages of one political party or another, as those parties compete to attract the highest number of votes. Individual voters aim to vote for those policies they consider to be best, and the winning policy package is designed and implemented by a democratic government. In a simple model of markets, individual consumers make decisions about whether to spend their money on the products of one competitive firm or another. Individuals will again aim to choose the product they consider to be best but through purchasing decisions rather than through votes. Products are also provided by multiple private firms in markets rather than by a single democratic government as in elections. Both mechanisms can also involve a certain amount of discussion or deliberation between individuals before making their voting or consumer decisions. More complexity can, of course, be introduced into these two admittedly

THE LIMITS OF ELECTIONS AND MARKETS   41

very simple models. Voters, for instance, may be motivated by a number of factors other than the policy packages of rival parties, and markets can be incomplete and contain significant externalities. I will aim to show how elections and markets confront important epistemic limits even when considering these very idealized models, however, and any introduction of additional imperfections only worsen these problems.[3]

When it comes to the epistemic abilities often attributed to these institutions, there is an interesting amount of overlap between the advocates of elections and those of the free market. Whether it be the pro-democracy traditions of John Dewey (and to a lesser extent John Stuart Mill), or the pro-market tradition of Hayek and his successors, a similar set of epistemic abilities has been used to evaluate these two mechanisms. In this section, I will focus on three of the most common: the ability to incentivize individuals to acquire information, the ability to utilize local knowledge, and the ability to learn through experimentation. Elections and markets do not necessarily possess all of these abilities equally. As we will see, the first is generally considered to be better realized by markets, while the other two are more contested and open to disagreement. It is useful, however, to consider each institution with respect to all three abilities as they will help to identify a common set of problems.

In respect to the first epistemic ability, Mill famously argued that including citizens in politics would encourage them to engage in public discussion and therefore increase their political knowledge.[4] Unlike nondemocratic regimes where citizens are only spectators, democracy includes them in the activity of political decision-making. It therefore makes them responsible for governance and encourages them to learn about the laws and policies which affect their lives. Of course, much contemporary work interested in the motivations of voters is much more pessimistic than Mill. While he may be right that participation provides more of an incentive to acquire information than spectating, the number participating also makes a difference. The possibly millions of votes cast in an election means that the probability of any one vote being decisive is very small, and therefore the expected benefit of an informed vote is much lower than the costs of acquiring information. While

---

[3] One could understand elections not as a mechanism for selecting policy packages, but rather as a mechanism for checking abuses of power. I will consider and endorse a version of this view in Chapter 7.

[4] Mill (2011). Mill was not, of course, a clear-cut supporter of democracy given his endorsement of plural voting based on educations levels. He therefore defends one version of an epistocracy, a regime I consider in more detail in Chapter 7.

42 INTELLIGENT DEMOCRACY

voters confront significant costs in seeking out information about political policies and candidates, they cannot expect that their vote will actually affect the result of an election. Contrary to Mill, then, the costs and benefits of voting are said to make it 'irrational to be politically well-informed'.[5]

Markets, alternatively, are said to avoid this problem of rational ignorance as market transactions have a much higher expected benefit. While voting for the healthcare package of one political party over another is unlikely to be decisive, a consumer's choice between two private healthcare plans has significant consequences for that individual. Markets are therefore thought to provide individuals with a greater incentive to become informed given the decisiveness of consumer decisions. Importantly, these arguments do not necessarily require the strong rationality assumptions found in conventional rational choice theory. Even on a bounded view of rationality where individuals have limited epistemic and cognitive abilities, and are therefore unlikely to calculate the optimal level of information, they can still recognize that markets give them greater reason to acquire knowledge than elections. Both approaches therefore end up in a similar place, although the latter offers a more plausible account of consumer and voter behaviour. Accurately calculating the expected value of any new piece of information, as conventional rational choice assumes, would require knowledge of the content of that information. Such an approach therefore demands that individuals know what they currently do not know.[6] Individuals are therefore more likely to respond to incentives in nonoptimal ways, as suggested by bounded rationality views. Whichever approach one prefers, however, it is the relative decisiveness of consumer choices which is said to provide a greater incentive to acquire information.

The problems that elections face in terms of the first ability may, however, be mitigated by the second, which is the ability to utilize local knowledge. Local knowledge, or 'situated knowledge' in Elizabeth Anderson's terms, is knowledge of specific circumstances which individuals have due to their 'experiences of problems and policies of public interest'.[7] It is knowledge known to those directly affected by political decisions, and therefore often not possessed by policymakers or politicians. As Dewey put it, 'the man who

---

[5] Downs (1957a, p. 259). Also see Downs (1957b), Caplan (2011), and Somin (2016).
[6] Evans and Friedman (2011); Mackie (2012).
[7] Anderson (2006, p. 14). I will use the term 'local knowledge' throughout the book to refer to this kind of knowledge, while I give an alternative definition to the terms 'situated knowledge' in Chapter 4.

wears the shoe knows best that it pinches'.[8] So while a voter may have little incentive to acquire additional information to vote on healthcare policies or welfare programmes, she already possesses a body of local knowledge, due to her day-to-day interaction with government services. The benefit of inclusive democratic elections, then, is that it provides for all an opportunity to utilize their local knowledge, and allows for its inclusion in political decision-making. A similar ability can also be seen in markets.[9] Central to Hayek's epistemology was the importance of knowledge of the particular circumstances of time and place, which is only known to on-the-spot individuals. The benefit of the market is that by decentralizing decision-making to individual consumers and firms, it allows decisions to be taken by those with the greatest knowledge of local conditions.[10] By having decisions taken by individuals, as either voters or consumers, both institutions are argued to provide opportunities for the utilization of local knowledge.

Neither voters nor consumers should be seen as fully informed, however. Rather, they have important but limited local information which can then form the basis of a wider process of experimentation. Drawing on Dewey, Anderson offers an experimental model of democracy where democratic governments test out new policies and citizens then experience their results.[11] Citizens receive direct feedback through their experience of whether a new policy offers improvements over the last, or whether it creates additional problems. Elections, alongside mechanisms such as petitions and protests, then give citizens the opportunity to communicate their satisfaction or dissatisfaction to policymakers, who can then adopt or reform the policy accordingly. Elections therefore provide information to decision-makers about the success or failure of policies, allowing them to improve by trial and error. Hayekians identify a similar experimental process in the market, although with some important differences.[12] Alternative goods are provided by multiple private firms, and consumers have the autonomy to search out the best product at any one time. They can experiment with alternatives, experience their differences, and determine the best on offer. Purchasing

---

[8] Dewey (1927, p. 207).

[9] Hayek (1937, 1945, 2011); Pennington (2003, 2011); Tebble (2016).

[10] Part of this pro-market argument appeals to the tacit nature of some local knowledge. Problems of tacit knowledge will be considered in Chapter 4. Also see Benson (2019a). The local knowledge argument is also closely linked to Hayek's views about the information processes and coordinating functions of market prices. These views are considered later in this chapter.

[11] Anderson (2006).

[12] Hayek (2002); Kirzner (1985, 2015); Pennington (2003).

44   INTELLIGENT DEMOCRACY

decisions then communicate the outcomes of these consumer experiments
to firms, who engage in their own process of discovery as they search out
profit opportunities. Entrepreneurs test new products, and through profit
and loss receive information about whether they were successes or failures.
Over time, private firms can improve their products through a process of
trial and error, as can policymakers in a democracy.

The Common Good and Other-Regarding Decisions

In both pro-market and pro-democracy literatures three epistemic abilities
are commonly discussed. As we have seen, the first is often thought to be
better realized by markets, while the remaining two are commonly attributed
to both mechanisms. Of course, there is still room for debate over which
institution is more epistemically valuable, all things considered. The profit
and loss signals in markets, for instance, have been argued to provide clearer
and more frequent information to firms than can possibly be provided to
policymakers through periodic elections where voters consider large policy
packages.[13] The epistemic value of markets, however, has also been argued to
be limited due to common markets failure, such as externalities and public
goods, as well as by larger inequalities which leave some with little ability
to utilize their knowledge.[14] My aim in this chapter is not to pursue these
debates further, but rather to argue that both markets and elections face a
common set of epistemic problems.

As we saw in the previous chapter, we cannot evaluate institutions epistemically by predetermining the ends they should be pursuing, at least when
it comes to second-order decisions about institutional selection. We cannot,
for instance, assume that elections and markets should aim to maximize aggregate utility, as this would fail to convince those who reasonably dispute
utilitarianism. Instead, an intelligent institution must possess epistemic
abilities or epistemic tools which are useful for making decisions about any
reasonable conception of justice and the common good. My claim, however,
is that the epistemic abilities commonly attributed to elections and markets
are not very useful with respect to decisions of this sort. The reason for this
is that values of justice and the common good are concerned with the whole

[13] Pennington (2011).
[14] Benson (2018, 2019a); Greenwood (2007).

of society or the whole of a community. They are not concerned only with the position of any one individual or group, but rather with such things as the welfare or interests of the general population; with relationships of inequality, domination, or independence between individuals and groups; or with the position of things of moral value which are not persons (e.g. the intrinsic value of nature). In other words, conceptions of justice and the common good involve other-regarding values and taking decisions in respect of them therefore requires that one can account for the effects of their actions on a large number of distant others.[15]

This requirement is as true for voters and consumers as it is for kings or autocrats, because their actions also have consequences for others in society. If they are given the choice between supplies of energy provided by different political parties or private firms, for instance, then the decisions they take will have an impact on more than their own interests. Whether it is through the labour conditions under which they were produced, or the environmental impacts associated with their consumption, the choice between energy policies or private energy companies has significant effects for others. Voters and consumers cannot therefore simply concern themselves only with their own self-interested preferences for warmth and lighting, if they are to take decisions which promote justice or the common good. Instead, they must also attend to other-regarding values concerning the welfare of others, the fairness of the relationship between employer and employee, or the intrinsic value of nature. It is not therefore enough for elections and markets to allow individuals to best satisfy only their own interests. Even if they allow for this, the outcomes of such procedures may still have negative consequences important to many conceptions of justice and the common good. They may have consequences for the state of the environment, human and economic rights, labour standards, wealth and income distributions, discrimination practices, and cultural practices.

This is not to say that every reasonable conception of justice or the common good must involve this full list of concerns (to do so would be to take a position on the procedure-independent standards we use to evaluate decisions). Rather, it is to point out that all such conceptions will involve some set or combination of these or similar other-regarding values, and that promoting

---

[15] Although the ability of markets and democracy to deal with other-regarding or ethical values has been a concern of political theory, this chapter focuses on the specifically epistemic problems such values produce for these social institutions. For more general discussions of the ethics of markets, see Anderson (1995); Brennan and Jaworski (2015); Satz (2010).

46   INTELLIGENT DEMOCRACY

these standards therefore requires making other-regarding decisions. They require voters and consumers to account for the effects of their choices on a large number of distant others. An important distinction, then, is between decisions based on purely *self-regarding preferences*—which are concerned only with self-interested reasons for valuing one option relative to another—and decisions based on *other-regarding values*—which include wider values of ethics, justice, and the common good. While we may often want a first-order institution to only cater to self-regarding preferences, a second-order institution must account for justice and the common good, and must therefore make decisions which account for other-regarding values.

This distinction between two different forms of decision-making, and two forms of values, is often recognized. Mark Sagoff, for instance, draws a similar distinction between decisions which concern only people's 'consumer preferences', which refer to self-regarding wants and desires related to the satisfaction of private interest, and decisions which concern 'citizen preferences', which refer to their beliefs about what is good for the community.[16] Importantly, the distinction is also recognized by epistemic supporters of markets despite often being associated with assumptions of self-interest and egoism. Hayek, for instance, made his epistemic case for markets based on the assumption that market actors may be 'wholly egotistical or highly altruistic'.[17] He claimed that markets allow individuals to make the best decisions using their local knowledge, irrespective of whether the reasons for their decision were purely self-regarding or other-regarding.[18] Contemporary market theorists have followed Hayek in this respect. Mark Pennington, for instance, has argued, in direct reference to Sagoff, that markets allow individuals to make effective decisions in respect of citizen preferences and not just consumer preferences.[19] He claims that individuals can select one product over another for other-regarding reasons, and this will be reflected in the market price for those goods just like any other consumer choice. It is not the case, then, as often supposed, that market advocates see markets merely as a mechanism for self-interested desires.

If elections and markets are to be intelligent in the sense defined in the previous chapter, their epistemic abilities must apply not only to decisions

---

[16] Sagoff (2007).

[17] Hayek (2013, p. 270).

[18] The same is true of standard theories of rational ignorance which assume individuals to act strategically but not wholly out of self-interest. See Downs (1957a); Somin (2010).

[19] Pennington (2005, pp. 49–51).

concerning self-regarding preferences, but also other-regarding values. They must, in other words, apply to decisions which need to account for their effects on a large number of distant others. In the following sections, I will argue that the epistemic abilities commonly attributed to elections and markets fail to do this. The next section will focus on the first epistemic ability, while the subsequent section will consider the remaining two. These sections point to two connected problems facing both elections and markets when it comes to other-regarding values: the *incentive problem* and the *information problem*. Taken together, these problems suggest that voters and consumers will face significant informational burdens when it comes to decisions about justice and the common good, and that they will have little incentive to overcome these burdens.

The Incentive Problem

The first epistemic ability concerns the incentive for individuals to acquire knowledge and is generally thought to be better realized by market mechanisms, as informed purchasing decisions have a higher expected benefit than voting decisions. This difference between the two mechanisms, however, only holds for self-regarding decisions concerned with self-regarding preferences. In the case of other-regarding decisions and other-regarding values, neither elections nor markets provide a strong incentive for individuals to take on the costs of getting informed. Consider, for instance, the example of an individual choosing between different energy suppliers as discussed in the previous section. In the market, an individual will choose between the energy supplied by rival firms and then purchase the one they prefer, while in an election they will choose between the alternative energy policies of rival political parties, and vote for the one they prefer.[20] If individuals need only to be concerned with their own self-interest, then the individual consumer will have an incentive to become informed as their purchasing decision will have a significant effect, while the individual voter has no such incentive, given the small probability that their vote will be decisive.

[20] The latter case could involve choosing between policy proposals for a national energy company. The example of energy is chosen simply because it is a good which has been often supplied by both private firms and democratic government.

48   INTELLIGENT DEMOCRACY

When other-regarding values are involved, alternatively, neither mechanism will produce a strong incentive to get informed. This is because the single purchasing decision of one individual is, like a voting decision, unlikely to have significant costs and benefits in terms of values such as justice and the common good. What is at stake in the case of self-regarding preferences is the welfare and interests of the individual themselves, such as their interest in a warm and well-lit home, and the purchasing decision of that individual is likely to have a significant effect on such interests. Purchasing decisions are likely to be decisive in terms of one's self-interest in ways that voting in elections will not. On the other hand, what is at stake in the case of other-regarding values is the welfare, interests, and relationships of others affected by the production of the different suppliers of energy, such as through their labour conditions or environmental impacts. The labour conditions under which energy is produced or its effect on the environment, however, are not determined by any one consumer choice. Rather, they result from a much larger aggregate demand of which any one individual consumer only makes up a very small part. The loss or gain of one single customer will therefore likely do little or nothing to change how the product is produced, and therefore its effects on things such as labour standards and the environment. An individual purchasing decision is therefore just one vote, so to speak, among a great many purchasing votes which together affect the things being valued.[21]

The individual consumer is, therefore, in much the same situation as the individual voter when it comes to other-regarding values such as justice and the common good. In both cases their individual decisions are unlikely to be decisive. Just as the benefit of voting informed is outweighed by the costs of acquiring information, the possible benefit of making informed consumer choices about other-regarding values is very small in comparison to the costs involved in gaining information about the alternative products on offer. Both voters and consumers will, therefore, tend to be rationally ignorant when making other-regarding decisions, since they have no incentive to take on the costs of becoming informed. Of course, individuals may also have self-regarding preferences for a good, and consumers will have reasons to acquire information in this respect. However, the point is that they will remain rationally ignorant *to the extent* that their decisions need to account

---

[21] As with the original problem of rational ignorance, the size of the group makes a difference. Elections and markets with just a handful of voters or customers, for instance, may not face a motivational problem. This argument, therefore, applies to large societies.

for the effects on others. Consumers may therefore learn about the effect of alternatives on their own interests, and yet remain ignorant about how they affect the public more broadly. When it comes to decisions concerning justice and the common good, then, both markets and elections will lack the epistemic ability of incentivizing individuals to acquire information.

The lack of knowledge on the part of the average voter is well supported empirically, something which is often pointed out by the new democratic sceptics.[22] With much research conducted, it has been consistently found that voters do not have significant knowledge of the policies offered by competing political parties, let alone the likely consequences of these policies for the public interest. This is not to say that all of the claims of the new sceptics are correct. Some of the evidence of voter ignorance they point to is rather weak and involves serious methodological concerns.[23] For instance, some studies only test for what could be reasonably seen as 'political trivia' which does not appear to be vital to casting an effective vote (e.g. naming past representatives or the number of representatives in the legislator). Others employ elitist standards to judge voter knowledge, such as using the opinions of economists as a proxy for the truth and then claiming that any deviation from these opinions is a sign of ignorance (e.g. if a citizen supports price controls they must be ignorant).[24] These elitist standards therefore disregard the fact that people may reasonably and intelligently disagree with economists, due to differences in theory, fact, or value. While we do not therefore need to accept all of these findings or all of the claims of the sceptics, the evidence still suggests that voters do not possess a large amount of information about the policies on offer at election time. Without such knowledge, however, voters will struggle to account for the effect of their decisions on others, and therefore cast their votes in line with other-regarding values.

While they are fond of discussing evidence for low levels of voter knowledge, what the pro-market critics of democracy pay little attention to is the evidence concerning consumer knowledge. Research into how much information consumers possess about the wider social or ethical implications of the different products they buy is no more promising than the research conducted on voters. Work on ethical consumerism, for instance, has found

---

[22] Bartels (1996); Campbell, Converse, Miller, and Stokes (1980); Friedman (1998); Zaller (1992).

[23] Landemore (2013b); Lupia (2006).

[24] For examples of democratic sceptics using these forms of evidence for voter ignorance, see Brennan (2016a) and Caplan (2011). For a broader critique of the role of neoclassical economics in the arguments of some democratic sceptics, see Gunn (2019).

50   INTELLIGENT DEMOCRACY

that consumers generally struggle to identify or rank firms in terms of their ethical conduct or their social responsibility.[25] Although they are sometimes aware of some specific cases of corporate misconduct which have received significant media attention, consumers are generally not knowledgeable about the ethical or unethical conduct of rival firms, and therefore the consequences of alternative purchasing decisions for others. Just as the average voter is therefore unlikely to have much knowledge of how alternative policies are impacting the common good, the average consumer similarly lacks significant knowledge of the wider consequences of supporting particular products or private firms.

While both elections and markets therefore face rational ignorance problems when it comes to other-regarding decisions, consumers may have even less of an incentive to act on concerns for justice and the common good than voters. This is because markets produce uneven trade-offs between self-regarding and other-regarding values. Trade-offs are common given that the products produced under better labour conditions or with less environmental impact, may well be of lower quality or come at a higher cost. These trade-offs are uneven, however, because of the different likelihoods of a purchasing decision being decisive. Given that purchasing decisions are likely to have a significant impact on satisfying a consumer's self-regarding preference, but little impact on their other-regarding values, consumers will face a clear incentive not only to remain ignorant about the latter, but not to act on them at all. This is not the result of individuals placing less importance in their other-regarding values but rather the result of the costs and benefits presented to them by the structure of market transactions and the incentives they produce. If the individual placed equal importance on their self-regarding and other-regarding values, for instance, then the costs and benefits of market transactions would still produce an incentive to act on the former over the latter. This uneven trade-off means that markets not only provide a weak incentive to acquire information about other-regarding decisions, but also a strong incentive to favour their self-interest over other-regarding concerns. In other words, markets give individuals little reason to consider the common good.

This uneven trade-off may, in part, help to explain low levels of ethical consumerism. In what is often referred to as the 'ethical purchase gap' or the 'attitude-behaviour gap', it has been found that there is a significant difference

---

[25] Boulstridge and Carrigan (2000); Carrigan and Attalla (2001).

THE LIMITS OF ELECTIONS AND MARKETS   51

between the number of consumers who express a concern for ethical consumption and the number who actually engage in such behaviour.[26] While 30% of consumers state that they would purchase ethically, for instance, only 3% were found to do so in practice.[27] If the market produces an uneven trade-off between self-regarding and other-regarding values, however, then it makes sense that even ethically concerned consumers may not act on their other-regarding values in the marketplace, let alone do so in an informed manner. A recognition that market transactions are unlikely to make much difference in terms of other-regarding values has also been found to undermine the motivation to act on such values in the marketplace.[28]

Although the incentive may be somewhat worse in markets, it is still the case that both mechanisms face difficulties when it comes to incentivizing the acquisition of information. Voters may not face an uneven trade-off between self-regarding and other-regarding values—their vote has the same effect for both kinds of preferences—but the low probability of their vote being decisive still leaves them with a very weak incentive to get informed. Both mechanisms therefore face an *incentive problem* when it comes to making decisions about justice and the common good which require them to consider their impact on others.[29] There may be exceptions to this general epistemic problem, however, which need to be considered. The kinds of other-regarding values which face the incentive problem are those which are concerned in some way with the outcome of the individual's decision. In our simple example of energy suppliers, for instance, the individual consumer or voter wishes to decrease the prevalence of bad labour conditions and environmental damage. The individual aims at a certain kind of outcome through their actions. Not all other-regarding values, however, are concerned with outcomes. Someone may not want to buy energy produced in bad conditions not because they think it will change this fact, but because they do not want to be involved in this morally problematic phenomenon. In other words,

---

[26] Carrigan and Attalla (2001); Carrington, Neville, and Whitwell (2010); De Pelsmacker, Driesen, and Rayp (2005); De Pelsmacker and Janssens (2007).

[27] Futerra (2005).

[28] Scott, Kallis, and Zografos (2019).

[29] This problem not only reduces the amount of information individuals are likely to acquire but also the amount of consideration they give to this information and to other-regarding values themselves. When it comes to values of justice or the common good it is often thought to be important that decision-makers take time to reflect and possibly challenge their beliefs before taking decisions. Taking time to consider one's other-regarding values can lead to a revision in these values, particularly when done in relation to new information about the subject. Given the costs and benefits facing the average voter or consumer, however, they will have little incentive to engage in such reflection.

52   INTELLIGENT DEMOCRACY

they want to 'keep their hands clean' even if this does not reduce the ethically problematic action. If this is the motivation, however, then the individual may wish to purchase or vote for a good irrespective of their influence within the procedure, and the number of decision-makers will not affect their incentive to get informed.

This second kind of other-regarding value may, in part, help to explain why a minority of voters and consumers are much better informed than their peers.[30] If this minority has other-regarding values which have little concern for the outcome of their actions, then they will retain an incentive to acquire knowledge in order to make informed purchasing and voting decisions.[31] The problem facing these two mechanisms, however, is that promoting many conceptions of justice and the common good will require one to be concerned with the outcomes of decisions. They are concerned with producing particular states of the world, whether they be resource distributions, welfare improvements, cultural practices, or human relationships. For an institution to have institutional priority at the second order, then, it needs to be able to make effective decisions in relation to other-regarding values, and this includes those other-regarding values which are concerned with the outcomes of decisions. Individuals in elections and markets, however, have little incentive to acquire and consider information when it comes to such values.

The Information Problem

Both elections and markets face an incentive problem when it comes to decisions about justice and the common good. At this point, it may appear that these decisions only produce a distinctive problem for markets, since elections also suffer from rational ignorance when it comes to self-regarding decisions and self-regarding preferences. What makes other-regarding values a distinctive problem, for elections as well as the market, is that they also create problems in terms of the other two epistemic abilities. As we saw earlier, these abilities can help mitigate the problem of rational ignorance

---

[30] Achen and Bartels (2017); Boulstridge and Carrigan (2000); De Pelsmacker and Janssens (2007).

[31] Another reason an individual may purchase or vote ethically is to increase their social status and appear virtuous to others. Notice, however, that these are not other-regarding values as the reason for the action is self-regarding. There can also be a large gap between appearing virtuous and acting virtuously.

THE LIMITS OF ELECTIONS AND MARKETS 53

faced by elections. Although elections do not incentivize individuals to acquire more information, voters can rely on their existing local knowledge and continue to learn through experience. The problem, however, is that other-regarding decisions also create significant problems in terms of these two epistemic abilities.

I should start by noting that there is weight to the claim that elections and markets can utilize valuable local knowledge, at least when it comes to self-regarding preferences and decisions.[32] Knowledge of an individual's own circumstances of time and place will likely be relevant to decisions about their interests. As Dewey rightly puts it, 'the man who wears the shoe knows best that it pinches.'[33] The issue, however, is that decisions about justice and the common good are not concerned only with a voter's or consumer's own welfare but rather with their impact on a possibly large number of distant others. Concerns for justice and the common good reach beyond the position of any one individual and attend to the position of the wider society or community. The relevance of information about one's own circumstances is therefore greatly reduced, if not removed, when it comes to decisions about other-regarding values. While I may know best whether my shoe pinches, I do not necessarily know how the production of my shoe, and its possibly very long supply chains, affect others in society who are likely very distant from myself. Similarly, if an individual is choosing between different suppliers of energy, then knowledge of their own local conditions will be relevant to their self-interest, but will not inform them of the consequences for the distant others involved in the supply and production of these goods.

In the case of other-regarding values, then, there is a separation or distance between the individual taking the decision and the effects they need to consider. Individual voters and consumers need to tend to the consequences of these actions for a large number of distant others. Knowledge of their own specific circumstances will therefore be unlikely to inform their decision in the way it informs decisions about their own interests. The ability to learn though experimentation is then weakened for the very same reason. Although the experimental process in elections and markets differ, both require that voters and consumers can learn through experience which policy or product best reflects their values. They require that individuals receive feedback about the effects of products and policies so they can learn if they

---

[32] I consider exceptions to this rule in Chapter 5.
[33] Dewey (1927, p. 207).

54 INTELLIGENT DEMOCRACY

represent improvements, and so they can provide accurate information to governments and firms through their votes and purchases. This feedback is likely to be present in the case of self-regarding preferences as individuals will normally be able to tell if a new product or policy improves or reduces their welfare. It will not, however, be present in the case of other-regarding values as individuals will not have direct experience of how new products or policies are affecting possibly very distant others.

The consequences of a new supply of energy for the environment or for those involved in its supply chains, for instance, are not directly experienced by the individual consumer or voter. They do not receive direct feedback about whether this new supply is an improvement in terms of environmental quality or labour standards. When it comes to other-regarding values, the separation between the individual and things they value removes the clear feedback they require to learn through experience.[34] This does not stop governments and firms trying out new policies and products, of course, but it does stop them from learning about the success or failure of these experiments. If consumers and voters cannot tell if a new product or policy is better than the last in terms of the public good, then their purchasing and voting decisions will not communicate effective information, and they will not help firms and governments to make improvements over time. The epistemic ability to utilize local knowledge and the ability to learn through experimentation is therefore weakened if not removed for both markets and elections when it comes to decisions about justice and the common good.

The result of this is that elections and markets will face an *information problem* when it comes to these other-regarding decisions. An individual's local knowledge will not inform their decisions and they will not be able to learn through experience. To make effective decisions they will therefore require a significant amount of additional information about how rival products and policies affect a large number of distant others. An individual looking to purchase or vote for a particular supply of energy, for instance, would need to discover information about the labour conditions involved in the production of different supplies, including their possibly very lengthy

---

[34] In previous work I therefore referred to the problem of 'low feedback goods'. These goods are disconnected from the individuals who value them, in terms of either time or space, and therefore do not provide the kind of feedback information necessary for individuals to determine the effects of their actions. When goods are valued for other-regarding reasons, they will often possess this property. See Benson (2019b). Lisa Herzog (2020) has similarly pointed to the lack of information individuals are provided by makers when it comes to ethical decision-making, and how this can undermine their moral agency.

supply chains, and their varied environmental impacts. Other-regarding decisions therefore come with a sizeable burden for information which is not necessarily required to act on one's self-regarding preferences. As was the case with the incentive problem, the information problem exists to the extent that one needs to consider others. For instance, if I suffer from bad working conditions then I may have some local knowledge of how to improve them. However, supporting better labour standards for a large number of distant others also requires knowledge of their working conditions, which may differ in important ways to my own, as well as the wider societal effects of any proposed changes. In some circumstances, for instance, better labour conditions could increase the costs on employers, disincentivize hiring, and increase unemployment. To the extent that decisions are other-regarding, then, they come with a need for additional information about how alternative options affect others in society. This burden will often be large and difficult to overcome even for the well-motivated.

This information problem is more often recognized in the case of elections than it is for markets. Determining which political party offers the best environmental policy for the community, for instance, is often thought to require a certain level of knowledge about the impact of environmental problems, their causes, and their potential solutions. Similar epistemic problems, however, also confront ethically minded consumers in the marketplace. Is it more environmentally friendly to buy local food, possibly grown with the use of pesticides and artificial heating, or food which needs to be transported from further afield but without such production methods? Is it better to buy energy produced by nuclear power given its reduced greenhouse emissions, or avoid it because of the risks produced by its generation and waste? Is it enough to reduce the number of flights one takes and purchase carbon offsets, or does one need to stop flying altogether? Is it better to buy genetically modified crops because of their increased yields or not because of their possibly negative health and environmental effects? Like voting decisions, answering these questions requires a significant amount of often technical knowledge about environmental problems and the best methods for dealing with them.

Similar questions face alternative other-regarding values, such as economic and social rights, wealth and income distributions, cultural practices, and discrimination practices. For instance, is it better, in terms of labour rights and income distribution, to purchase a product made in a more affluent and regulated country, or one made in a less affluent but less well-regulated labour market? Which supply chains are likely to involve more, or

56 INTELLIGENT DEMOCRACY

worse forms of, discrimination towards minority groups? Is it best to purchase products from cooperative firms because they give workers greater economic autonomy, or do such firms create two-tiered labour markets where noncooperative members receive worse terms? Answering such questions requires a large amount of information about how different options affect often very distant others, and this can be difficult to acquire even for well-motivated consumers. Again, this is not to claim that all reasonable conceptions of justice and the common good must include such concerns. Rather, it is to point out that all such conceptions will involve some set of these or similar concerns, and that addressing them requires individual consumers to possess a significant amount of information. We have already seen that consumers, as well as voters, are empirically found to have little knowledge in relation to their ethical preferences. However, they also consider themselves to be insufficiently knowledgeable when it comes to purchasing in an ethical manner, and that they lack enough information to take effective decisions.[35] This suggests that consumers find other-regarding decisions to be more complex than self-regarding decisions, as the information problem claims, and that they lack the knowledge required to take such decisions effectively.

While both markets and elections therefore face the informational problem, the problem is likely to differ somewhat between the two institutions. Elections, for instance, often involve choosing between different bundles of policies, while a single market transaction normally involves choosing just one kind of product. The information required to cast a vote will therefore be larger than that required to make a purchase. Consumers, however, engage in many more decisions in markets than voters do in periodic elections. So, although any one purchasing decision is less information-intensive, a consumer's informational burden increases over time, since they engage in many more decisions than voters. Interestingly, the regularity of market transactions turns from an advantage of markets to a cost. While in the case of self-regarding preference it was a benefit because it allowed more opportunities to utilize local knowledge and experiment with alternatives, in the case of other-regarding values it increases the epistemic burden placed on individuals as they must acquire more information more often.

There are a couple of immediate replies which could be given to this information problem. The first is to claim that although voters and consumers

---

[35] Bray, Johns, and Kilburn (2011); De Pelsmacker and Janssens (2007); Gribben and Gitsham (2007).

THE LIMITS OF ELECTIONS AND MARKETS   57

require additional information, they are typically provided with it in the normal course of political campaigns and market advertising. Political parties and firms have a clear incentive to provide information on the benefits of their respective policies and products, and therefore help voters and consumers overcome the information problem. The trouble with this solution, however, is that these groups also have a strong incentive to provide misleading or false information, and trust in both branding/labelling and political campaigning is empirically low as a result.[36] The lies and misdirections of elected politicians are, of course, a staple complaint among democratic sceptics. However, as Naomi Oreskes and Erik Conway have documented, private companies also work to conceal damaging knowledge from their consumers, and actively spread doubt and misinformation about the harmful consequences of their products.[37] Branding and advertising also often offer only low-quality forms of communication compared to the complexities of social problems, compressing information into slogans and soundbites. This low quality is often inevitable given that parties and firms need to communicate to large numbers of individuals who have little incentive to consider it (a point I will return to in more detail in the next chapter). The empirical evidence on voter and consumer knowledge supports this, suggesting that these strategies have not led to a significantly well-informed electorate or consumer base.

The second reply is that voters and consumers do not need to acquire such information because they can rely on shortcuts or heuristics, such as the endorsements of relatively more informed proxies.[38] Individuals can, for instance, follow the recommendation of a trusted campaign group, charity, or journalist when voting or purchasing, overcoming their own lack of knowledge. I recognize that these heuristics often play an important role in both elections and markets, allowing individuals to cope with complex environments where they cannot acquire all information or think through every issue for themselves. The first thing to note about the move to heuristics and shortcuts, however, is that it already accepts that the epistemic abilities normally attributed to elections and markets cannot be realized. If voters and consumers are having to rely on the recommendations of proxies, then elections and markets will neither be utilizing the local knowledge of

---

[36] Citrin and Stoker (2018); De Pelsmacker and Janssens (2007); Nicholls and Lee (2006).
[37] Oreskes and Conway (2011).
[38] Conover and Feldman (1989); Erikson, MacKuen, and Stimson (2002); Lupia (1992).

58   INTELLIGENT DEMOCRACY

individuals nor providing feedback about their experiences with new policies and products. Instead, it will be these informational proxies which possess the needed knowledge, and we would not necessarily require mechanisms of markets or elections to access this information. Secondly, such shortcuts are, of course, imperfect substitutes for directly acquiring knowledge as they are dependent on individuals correctly determining which proxies are reliable, and overcoming the informational asymmetries which will exist between them.[39] Voters and consumers will still face the significant burden of determining the reliability of proxies across different areas of concern (the environment, labour rights, discrimination practices, etc.), and determining what to do when these proxies inevitably disagree with each other over which option is best in terms of any one criterion.

Importantly, the information problem is not affected by whether an other-regarding value is concerned with outcomes. Whether an individual wishes to increase or decrease the presence of some ethical phenomenon, or simply to 'keep their hands clean', their local knowledge will still not adequately inform their decisions, nor will they learn effectively through experience. So, although non–outcome focused preferences may not suffer from the incentive problem, they still suffer from the information problem. A set of other-regarding values which may not be affected by the information problem, however, are those which are very narrow in scope, such as those which involve a concern only for close friends and family. If an individual values the welfare of their direct family, for instance, then their own local knowledge may well be informative, and they may be able to receive feedback about the effect of their actions on these individuals. Markets and elections may not, therefore, face an increased information burden when it comes to these and similarly narrow other-regarding values. The problem for these two mechanisms, however, is that conceptions of justice and the common good involve other-regarding values with much broader scope. Such concerns spread outside of one's immediate companions and apply across large numbers of distant others. In complex and interconnected societies, purchasing and voting decisions have wide-ranging impacts which need to be considered in order to promote the common good. When it comes to these concerns, however, voters and consumers will not be informed by their local knowledge, will struggle to learn through experimentation and experience, and will instead face a significant burden for information gathering. The ability

[39] Thompson (2004).

THE LIMITS OF ELECTIONS AND MARKETS 59

to utilize local knowledge and learn through experimentation is therefore weakened, if not removed, when it comes to decisions about justice and the common good.

The Invisible Hand of Elections and Markets

The last few sections considered the two institutions which have attracted the most attention from those interested in epistemic questions. While Hayek and his successors focused on the epistemic benefits of markets, many epistemic democrats have independently concerned themselves with elections and voting. Both these institutions, however, were found to have significant limitations when it came to decisions about justice or the common good. Such decisions involve other-regarding values which require decision-makers to consider their effects on a large number of possibly very distant others. In such cases, elections and markets are unlikely to motivate decision-makers to acquire information (the incentive problem), and individuals will face significant burdens for information as they will not benefit from their local knowledge or learn through experimentation (the information problem). Combining the incentive and information problem, both mechanisms will face a large epistemic burden when it comes to other-regarding values, and they will produce little motivation to overcome it. The intelligence of these two mechanisms as second-order institutions is therefore greatly limited.

A possible line of defence, however, is to appeal to an 'invisible hand' style argument. This kind of argument would accept that individual voters and consumers may be limited in their ability to make decisions about justice or the common good, but claim that the aggregation of votes through elections or the coordination of consumers through markets allows for a more indirect promotion of the common good. If this is possible, then it would not matter if individuals lack necessary information, as long as they are led by an invisible hand to collective outcomes superior to those they could achieve alone. Both Hayekian market advocates and many epistemic democrats appeal to some kind of invisible hand style argument, so it is important to see why they cannot be used to overcome the problems of the previous sections.

The Hayekian version of the invisible hand places particular weight on the coordinating role of market prices.[40] While any one firm or consumer

---

[40] Hayek (1945).

60 INTELLIGENT DEMOCRACY

has limited information, through acts of buying and selling they can influence the formation of market prices which then allows their actions to be coordinated with others. If the actions of many individuals change the demand or supply of tin, for instance, then this will be reflected in its price, and other individuals will know whether to consume more or less of this good as a result. Hayek therefore argued that the price system had a communicative function which allowed market actors to adjust their behaviour to one another. Market prices do not give marching orders, nor do they communicate the reasons behind any changes. Instead, prices act as 'knowledge surrogates' which allow individuals to adjust their actions 'as if' they possessed the relevant information.[41] A consumer of tin, for instance, does not need to know if an increase in price is due to a new source of demand or a restriction in supply. The change in price is sufficient to inform them that they need to start consuming less tin and more of its substitutes. While any one market actor is therefore ignorant of most of the information needed to coordinate the supply of goods in an economy, they can still make decisions about their own preferences, and these decisions are then coordinated spontaneously through a system of market prices.

Notice, however, that the logic of this argument requires that individuals do possess a certain amount of information. Although they can lack knowledge of much economic activity, they still require information to make appropriate decisions about their own preferences, and these more informed decisions can then be reflected in price signals and coordinated with others. While there may be some truth to this claim when individuals act on their self-regarding preferences, the previous sections have shown that this is not true for other-regarding values. When it comes to acting on other-regarding values, individuals will have little incentive to get informed, nor will they be able to rely on their local knowledge or learn through experience. They will therefore lack sufficient information to act on such values in the marketplace, and these values will not be accurately reflected in the price system.[42] If individuals do not know which goods are best for the environment, for instance, then demand for environmental values will not be accurately reflected in the price of goods, and these values will not be coordinated by the market's invisible hand. Even if the price mechanism works as effectively as

---

[41] Horwitz (2004).
[42] Market prices also cannot possibly provide individuals with such information, given that they act as knowledge surrogates which do not allow individuals to come to know the circumstances of others.

THE LIMITS OF ELECTIONS AND MARKETS   61

Hayek believed (e.g. even leaving aside issues of market failure), then this co-ordination will only account for self-regarding preferences where individuals often possess the knowledge needed to make appropriate decisions. It will not effectively coordinate other-regarding values as individuals lack the necessary knowledge.[43]

The invisible hand of the market will not, therefore, reflect concerns for justice or the common good as a result of the incentive and informational problems. Of course, market advocates could fall back on self-regarding preferences and argue that their coordination is sufficient to promote the common good. They could claim that as long as these preferences are registered in price signals, the market will coordinate economic activity in a manner which best promotes the public interest. The problem with this argument, however, is that it relies on a controversial conception of justice. It relies on the idea that the common good is reducible to a greater satisfaction of self-interested preferences (a kind of preference utilitarianism), but this will be rejected by those who endorse other reasonable conceptions. Even if markets could perfectly coordinate self-regarding preferences, this could not provide a convincing epistemic argument for giving markets second-order priority. This version of the invisible hand argument therefore simply violates the epistemic standards defended in the previous chapter.

Epistemic democrats have also appealed to an invisible hand logic in defending elections. While I have so far focused on Deweyan style arguments, others appeal to the benefits of aggregation.[44] Two of the best-known arguments rely on the Condorcet jury theorem and the miracle of aggregation. According to the jury theorem the probability that a group will vote for the correct answer tends towards 1 as the group gets larger, as long as (1) individuals vote independently; (2) they vote sincerely rather than strategically; and (3) they have a greater than 0.5 probability of selecting the right answer. The miracle of aggregation, alternatively, argues that voting will tend to select the best option because uninformed voters are simply cancelled out through aggregation. If uninformed voters vote randomly then their votes will be evenly distributed across the options, and therefore the outcome will end up being decided by the informed voters. In both cases, then, not all

---

[43] Notice that the problem here is not that consumers do not have perfect information, something Hayekians do not claim, but that they lack sufficient information to act on other-regarding values.
[44] Landemore (2013b).

62 INTELLIGENT DEMOCRACY

voters need to be perfectly informed, as the invisible hand of aggregation can still lead to the selection of the best option.

There are a number of problems with these arguments. Neither, for instance, provides an account of how the best option comes to be on the agenda in the first place. What is relevant for the discussion here, however, are their informational assumptions. The jury theorem, for instance, requires that voters have an above 0.5 probability of selecting the right option. The miracle of aggregation, alternatively, requires that the proportion of informed votes is greater than any uneven distribution of uninformed votes. While the argument assumes that uninformed voters vote randomly, lacking certain forms of information can often create systemic errors. For example, if on the surface policy A appears superior to policy B, but unbeknownst to lots of voters policy A will actually cost ten times as much and risks a budgetary crisis, then this will lead many voters to systematically vote for the wrong policy. The number of informed voters therefore needs to be great enough to outweigh these systematic errors among the uninformed. The problem is that neither of these informational assumptions is likely when it comes to decisions about justice and the common good.

Given that voters in general face a significant epistemic burden when making decisions about other-regarding values, and little incentive to overcome this burden, we have little reason to think that they will reliably select the best options more often than not. In fact, their reliability may drop below 0.5, with the result that a democratic vote will almost certainly select the incorrect option, assuming the other conditions of the jury theorem hold (which is fortunately also unlikely). Similarly, such problems provide us with little confidence that there will be enough informed voters in the electorate to outweigh the significant systematic errors of the uninformed. The information and incentive problems of the previous sections therefore question the informational assumptions of these invisible hand arguments for elections, at least when it comes to decisions about justice and the common good. Of course, defenders of elections could fall back on self-regarding preferences and argue that the common good is achieved through their aggregation. This version of the invisible hand argument would rely on a controversial conception of justice, however, and cannot therefore ground a claim about second-order priority. Epistemic democrats cannot therefore defend elections against the information and incentive problems through appeals to invisible hand style arguments, just as Hayekians cannot overcome them by pointing to the invisible hand of the market.

A Preliminary Case for Collective Politics

When it comes to second-order decisions concerning justice and the common good, both elections and markets will face significant incentive and information problems. They will face a large epistemic burden when it comes to such decisions, and they will produce little incentive to overcome it. Why is it, however, that elections and markets share this similar set of epistemic problems? The answer is that both mechanisms possess a common structural feature, in that they both decentralize decision-making to a large number of individuals. Whether it is as voters in elections or as consumers in markets, both mechanisms place individuals at the heart of decision-making. This structural feature creates many advantages when it comes to self-interested decisions, allowing individuals to make the most of their own local knowledge, and provide feedback signals which can aid trial and error learning. When it comes to second-order decisions which must account for justice and the common good, however, this feature limits the epistemic value of elections and markets.

Having one vote among millions of voters, or one purchasing decision among a much larger aggregate demand, means that individuals can expect little benefit from becoming informed about the common good. Decentralizing decisions about the common good to a large number of individuals therefore creates the incentive problem. Similarly, while any institution will require large amounts of information to promote justice, in elections and markets this significant epistemic burden falls on the shoulders of lone individuals who will likely struggle to acquire all the information relevant to understanding the public interest. The decentralization of decisions to individuals does not therefore create the information problem—any institution would require the relevant knowledge—but it does place this problem at the feet of individual consumers and voters who are unlikely to overcome it (an issue discussed further in the next chapter). So while the kinds of individual decision-making found in elections and markets have advantages in terms of self-interested decisions, they introduce important epistemic problems when it comes to decisions about justice and the common good.

Importantly, these epistemic problems do not stop these mechanisms from playing a role at the first order. While second-order decisions must account for justice and the common good, this is not necessarily a requirement of first-order institutions. If it is decided, for instance, that the main goal when it comes to providing a certain good is to satisfy the public's self-interested

64 INTELLIGENT DEMOCRACY

preferences, or that justice-based concerns can be met through appropriate regulation, then markets may be an effective first-order institution (subject to the likelihood of market failure and the prior distribution of resources). The decision to simply satisfy self-interested preferences in a given domain, however, is a second-order decision. It is the task of the institution with second-order priority to determine the settings in which it is acceptable to simply maximize this criterion or to pursue some other principle of justice. The incentive and information problems facing voters and consumers limits the role they can play in these second-order tasks, as it limits their ability to consider the impact of alternatives on the common good.[45]

If it is correct that the problems of elections and markets result from their decentralization of decision-making to individuals, then this suggests a preliminary case for focusing on more collective forms of politics. Collective political institutions, such as the institutions of the democratic state, involve small groups of individuals empowered to make decisions on behalf of others. Whether it be the decisions of parliaments, assemblies, bureaucracies, or town halls, collective political bodies involve groups of citizens coming together to take decisions for the community. Given that they involve far fewer decision-makers, these institutions do not necessarily exhibit the problem of rational ignorance, and they often have far greater resources to gather large amounts of information. Collective forms of politics do not necessarily have to involve significant centralization to provide these benefits, only that they are more centralized than the decisions of millions of individual voters or consumers. In fact, we will see in later chapters that there are epistemic advantages to not carrying out all political decision-making centrally.[46] Whether at the national, local, or community level, more collective forms of political decision-making may offer more promise when it comes to decisions about justice and the common good than focusing on the individual decisions of voters and consumers.

This is, of course, only a very preliminary case for collective political institutions. How, for instance, are these institutions supposed to acquire the information they need, and how do we ensure that they will be motivated to

---

[45] Of course, these institutions may have other advantages not considered in this chapter which could contribute to second-order tasks. In Chapter 7, for instance, I will argue that democratic elections have a role in motivating political leaders away from some of the worst uses and abuses of political power, and that this is important to the intelligence of democracy as a second-order institution. Elections on their own, however, do not create an intelligent democracy, and must instead be combined in a system with other institutions, as I will argue in Chapter 8.

[46] See Chapter 2 and predominantly Chapter 5.

take decisions which enhance the common good? Additionally, can elections still play some role in the selection of these collective institutions despite their epistemic limits, or should we instead prefer oligarchic, epistocratic, or meritocratic mechanisms? My aim at this stage, however, is only to suggest collective political institutions as a more promising point of focus. The limits of elections and markets at least point us in this direction, and therefore plot a course for the following chapters. In the next chapter, for instance, I will turn to the objections which Hayekian critics level at democracy, objections which directly challenge the possibility of a competent form of collective politics. So far, however, I have argued that the intelligence of elections and markets is likely to be limited and that we should therefore look to more collective forms of political decision-making as an alternative point of departure.

3
Democracy and the Division of Knowledge

One of the most common and influential variants of the new democratic scepticism comes not from supporters of elitist forms of politics, but from defenders of the free market. It comes from those who believe that markets possess a unique ability to gather, discover, and utilize information, and that it should therefore be given priority among our social institutions. This brand of democratic scepticism, however, is as strongly tied to beliefs about the ignorance of political institutions as it is to the merits of the market. The central epistemic problem facing society, according to Friedrich von Hayek, was how to make use of 'knowledge which is not given to anyone in its totality'.[1] He argued that the knowledge necessary for social decisions does not exist in any centralized or coherent whole, ready to be utilized by some political authority, but is rather fragmented and dispersed in the minds of on-the-spot individuals. Collective political bodies will therefore likely remain ignorant of much of the knowledge needed to make good decisions, and as Hayek's successors have pointed out, this includes the political institutions of democracy. Mark Pennington, for instance, argues that the division of knowledge which Hayek identified entails that no democratic parliament, assembly, or forum can possibly obtain the many pieces of information which are so vital to solving our social problems.[2]

Hayekian democratic sceptics will therefore have many doubts about the preliminary case for collective decision-making put forward at the end of the previous chapter. That chapter explored the epistemic limits of markets which resulted from attempting to decentralize decision-making to individual consumers. If collective forms of politics are to offer a more intelligent alternative, however, they cannot lack the ability to acquire relevant knowledge as Hayek believed. We must therefore address the Hayekian critique of democracy and particularly the problems it sees as resulting from the division of knowledge in society. This is the task I set myself in this chapter. After

---

[1] Hayek (1945, pp. 519–520).
[2] Pennington (2003).

Intelligent Democracy. Jonathan Benson, Oxford University Press. © Oxford University Press 2024.
DOI: 10.1093/oso/9780197767283.003.0004

DEMOCRACY AND THE DIVISION OF KNOWLEDGE   67

revising the Hayekian view of this division to better account for the importance of general scientific knowledge, I will argue that the key to overcoming this division is to take a systemic perspective. Once we understand it in systemic terms, democracy can be seen to possess not only an ability to gather relevant knowledge, but an ability even greater than that of the market.

For Hayek and his successors, democratic institutions appear as isolated islands of decision-making cut off from the sea of information spread throughout society. My claim, however, is that democratic bodies are not detached or secluded, but rather fastened to an active public sphere within a broader deliberative system. This public sphere involves important divisions of epistemic labour where a broad range of institutions locate and gather information relevant to problems of public concern, and this division is itself dependent on the public sphere's democratic character.[3] While the Hayekian knowledge problem may appear insurmountable if we think of collective democratic decisions as taking place in a single isolated institution, a systemic perspective allows us to see how it can be overcome. It also helps us to see that collective democratic institutions play a central role in solving this problem. In returning to Hayek's wish to leave decisions to the market, this chapter argues that more centralized political institutions possess important advantages over markets, and better allow a system to acquire both local and scientific knowledge.

I therefore defend not only the view that democratic institutions are better able to address the division of knowledge than Hayek and his successors believed, but also that they can address this problem better than even the market. At least when it comes to second-order decisions concerning justice and the common good, it is democracy which is best placed to acquire relevant knowledge spread throughout society. While Hayek's claims about the information aggregating advantages of markets are widely accepted, even by those not sympathetic to his free-market prescriptions, I argue that it is a more collective democratic politics which can make best use of fragmented and dispersed information. The division of knowledge Hayek identified does not therefore undermine the intelligence of democracy, but instead gives us reasons to support it.

---

[3] I introduced an early version of this model in a paper in *Political Studies*. See Benson (2019b).

68 INTELLIGENT DEMOCRACY

Hayek's Division of Knowledge

At the heart of Hayekian economic and political theory is a concern for the kinds of knowledge relevant to social decisions and those groups most likely to possess it. The mistake of those who favour an interventionist state, Hayek argued, was that they placed too much faith in the general knowledge of the natural and social sciences. Concerned with abstract laws and statistical patterns, this general knowledge was thought to be possessed by experts and policymakers, rather than lay citizens, and could be utilized by these groups to understand and regulate society. In terms of who had access to this general knowledge, Hayek was in agreement, claiming that 'a body of suitably chosen experts may be in the best position to command all the best knowledge available'.[4] What Hayek disputed, however, was that this general scientific knowledge was the only or most important kind of knowledge relevant to social problems. He instead pointed to the existence of a significant body of local knowledge whose subject is not general laws or principles, but rather the particular circumstances of time and place.

This second kind of knowledge does not produce grand theories or predictions but includes knowledge of such things as the conditions of resources, the nature of individual preferences, the options open to individuals, and the uses and effects of different goods. What is important about such knowledge, according to Hayek, is that its particular and contingent nature means that it is only known to those 'people who are familiar with the circumstances'.[5] It does not therefore exist in any centralized or coherent whole, as the best scientific knowledge may be seen as centralized in the academy, but is rather fragmented and dispersed in the minds of on-the-spot individuals spread throughout society. It is this distribution of local knowledge which for Hayek represented the fundamental division of knowledge in a society, and it was this division which frustrated the political regulation of that society. While collective and centralized political institutions may be able to access general knowledge which is known to a relatively small number of experts, it cannot come to possess information which is only known to a very large number of dispersed on-the-spot individuals.

As Mark Pennington has pressed, many democratic forms of decision-making are among those undermined by this understanding of the division

---

[4] Hayek (1945, p. 521).
[5] Hayek (1945, p. 524).

of knowledge.[6] Democratic parliaments, assemblies, or forums all involve centralized and collective forms of decision-making, where decisions are taken on behalf of others in the population. Such institutions must therefore somehow gather, aggregate, and then centralize the vast amount of local knowledge which is only known to on-the-spot individuals with direct experience of local conditions. The collective nature of these democratic institutions is therefore in conflict with the dispersed nature of relevant knowledge. This problem is also not eradicated by decentralizing democracy. Even at the local level, democratic bodies are still more centralized *relative* to local knowledge which is only known at the individual level. Decentralizing democratic decision-making may therefore help to reduce the challenge of the division of knowledge by bringing assemblies and forums closer to individuals; but it does not remove it. Knowledge which is only known to on-the-spot individuals must still somehow be communicated to a relatively more centralized collective democratic body so that it can be utilized for decision-making.[7]

The division of knowledge can instead only be solved, according to Hayek, through a market mechanism which leaves decisions to individual consumers and firms who have access to local conditions.[8] These individuals can make the best use of their own local knowledge, and then through acts of buying and selling influence the formation of market prices which then allows their actions to be coordinated with others. If the actions of many individuals changes the demand or supply of tin, for instance, then this will be reflected in its price, and other individuals will know whether to consume more or less of this good. While prices do not communicate the reasons behind any changes, they act as 'knowledge surrogates' which allow individuals to act 'as if' they had such information.[9] Markets are therefore able to utilize fragmented and dispersed forms of knowledge, by removing any need to centralize this information to some political authority.

We have already seen the limits of this Hayekian view of the market in the previous chapter. While individual consumers may pursue their self-regarding preferences based on their local knowledge, and have these

---

[6] Pennington (2001, 2003, 2011).

[7] Of course, democratic forms can also include the local knowledge of their members, a fact that is sometimes given in support of more direct forms of democracy which include citizens in decision-making. However, there are necessary limits on the number of people who can be included in face-to-face decision-making, and therefore much knowledge will still be left outside the forum.

[8] Hayek (1937, 1945, 2002); Pennington (2003, 2011).

[9] Horwitz (2004).

70   INTELLIGENT DEMOCRACY

preferences coordinated through the invisible hand of the market, they are at a loss when it comes to other-regarding decisions concerning justice and the common good. As knowledge surrogates, price signals do not allow individuals to come to know the local circumstances of others, and therefore do not provide the information needed to understand how one's decisions impact the common good. Knowing the impact of market decisions on such things as labour standards, wealth and income distributions, discrimination practices, the environment, or human rights, therefore requires information which is not provided in market prices. Even if the price mechanism can therefore coordinate individuals as effectively as Hayek believed, this will only be true in terms of coordinating their self-interested actions, the aggregation of which may not promote many reasonable conceptions of justice. So while markets may allow individuals to use their local knowledge for self-interested purposes (subject to market failures and the distribution of resources), their focus on individual decision-making is limited when it comes to second-order decisions about institutional selection, which must account for standards of justice and the common good.

While the Hayekian solution to the division of knowledge is therefore limited, Hayek's formulation of the division also provides only a partial picture. Although he was right to highlight the importance of local knowledge, this too often led him to underestimate the necessary role of general scientific knowledge in addressing social problems. Although not denying its relevance, he argued that there will always be 'an even greater store of knowledge of special circumstances that ought to be taken into account in decisions'.[10] The division of knowledge therefore becomes a problem of acquiring local and dispersed forms of information, with general knowledge not entering the picture. As John O'Neill has pointed out, however, Hayek's reasons for downplaying general scientific knowledge are far from convincing.[11] Even if local knowledge forms the 'greater store' of information, surely the relevance or significance of information to the problem at hand are more important epistemic criteria than size or volume. When it comes to problems such as the use and abuse of the natural environment, the protection of public health, or the regulation of new technology, scientific knowledge is crucial not only to finding an effective solution, but to even recognizing that there is a problem in the first place. Even if local knowledge is more voluminous, general

[10] Hayek (2011, p. 494).
[11] O'Neill (2012).

DEMOCRACY AND THE DIVISION OF KNOWLEDGE 71

knowledge remains essential in such cases. It is more plausible that the relative importance of local and general knowledge will vary from problem to problem, and that any institution with second-order priority will require an ability to access and make use of both.

The division of knowledge is therefore best seen as a two-pronged problem. An institution with second-order priority will need to access both local knowledge which is dispersed in the minds of on-the-spot individuals, and more centralized general scientific knowledge which is known to particular experts or expert institutions. The division of knowledge described by Hayek therefore only provides a picture of half of this division. The question for the rest of this chapter, however, is whether collective democratic forms of decision-making, such as the decisions of forums and assemblies, can overcome this reformulated version of Hayek's division of knowledge.

The Division of Knowledge and the Deliberative System

On a unitary view of democracy, one which focuses on a single institution in isolation from others, overcoming the division of knowledge appears as a Herculean task. The entire burden of gathering all or sufficient knowledge would fall on just a single forum, whether centralized or decentralized, meaning that it would itself need to collect the very large amounts of information relevant to problems of public concern. The bureaucratic and administrative task befalling this single institution would therefore be colossal. This is not only a problem of how such a body would collect and aggregate knowledge, but also of how it would locate such knowledge in the first place. In order to even start gathering relevant information, this single forum would need to know in advance what forms of information to look for and where to look. The members of a single forum, however, may well be ignorant of when and how a social problem affects certain social groups, or that it has a negative impact on the natural environment, meaning that they would not know to search out such information. The local effects of social problems, and the ways in which scientific knowledge has a bearing on such problems, are not self-evident or likely to be known to any one institution. In fact, a single body may not even know there is a problem for which information needs to be acquired.

This unitary view of democracy is the one found in the work of Hayekian sceptics, who see democratic bodies as isolated islands of decision-making

72   INTELLIGENT DEMOCRACY

set apart from the sea of knowledge which surrounds them. It is also an image which can be found in the works of many democrats. Deliberative democrats, for instance, have often focused on single deliberative bodies, such as parliaments or mini-publics, and consider the exchange of information and reasons between the members of such forums. This singular focus, however, fails to explain how these deliberative bodies can access relevant knowledge which is possessed by those who will inevitably be left outside of any one assembly. As Pennington characterizes their position, these deliberative democrats seem to suggest that the coordination of information 'could be resolved if only all the relevant actors could be assembled into a deliberative social forum (a logistical impossibility in itself)'.[12]

Many epistemic democrats are in a similar position, focused as they often are on formal models of single democratic institutions. Models of face-to-face deliberation, however, do not show us how democracy can acquire and utilize knowledge possessed by those not engaged in small group deliberation, and this is sometimes explicitly stated. Hélène Landemore's influential model of deliberation, for instance, explicitly assumes levels of knowledge as given, therefore taking the question of gathering knowledge off the table.[13] Focusing on elections also provides little additional help. Models of democratic voting, such as the Condorcet jury theorem and miracle of aggregation, claim to show that an aggregation of votes will tend to select the best of two or more options, but they do not explain how democratic institutions acquire the knowledge to come up with suitable solutions in the first place. More generally, while the aggregation of votes does yield some information for collective institutions, elections offer only blunt signals given that they do not provide the reasons behind any one vote—and therefore the content of local or general knowledge—and they are also limited by low levels of voter knowledge.[14]

These mostly unitary approaches, however, do not offer the only possible conception of democratic politics, nor the most realistic. Rather than an isolated island of decision-making cut off from the rest of society, democracy in practice extends far beyond any one body or institution. This has been

[12] Pennington (2003, p. 729).

[13] Landemore (2013b). This is not necessary a criticism of Landemore, who makes this assumption in order to focus on the issue of political problem-solving. However, the assumption does mean that her approach will not speak to how small deliberative groups can access information from the wider society. See Chapter 6 for a more detailed engagement with Landemore's approach.

[14] For broader critique of the use of jury theorems and the miracle of aggregation by epistemic democrats, as well as Anderson's experimental model, see Chapter 2.

the claim of the 'systemic turn' in deliberative democracy research which, unlike previous unitary approaches, sees deliberation as distributed across a broad system.[15] The systemic turn emerged in deliberative democracy scholarship in large part as a reaction to what many perceived as an overly narrow focus on discrete areas of deliberation, such as those found in mini-publics and citizen assemblies, or individual deliberative acts, such as instances of rhetoric. While individual mini-publics were often found to produce high levels of deliberation, they also often went unnoticed by the wider public or were ignored by elected politicians.[16] So while internally they appeared highly democratic, this missed the fact that their lack of impact on other actors and institutions limited their democratic potential. Similarly, while many democrats have often been quick to condemn acts of rhetoric, these condemnations often missed that nondeliberative acts can sometimes give voice to groups or concerns otherwise marginalized in public debate and can therefore help to promote democratic values.

The systemic turn therefore claims that any one institution or act should not be assessed in a purely unitary manner, but rather in relation to a broader network of institutions. They should be evaluated in terms of the role they play in a wider deliberative system and how they contribute to producing democratic values at the system level. No single institution, no matter how internally democratic, can possibly legitimize all the decisions taken in a democracy, and we must therefore consider how democratic goods are provided by a system of different institutions possessing alternative virtues. To be more exact, a deliberative system is 'deliberative' in that it offers a 'talk-based approach to political conflict and problem-solving'. It is also a 'system' in the sense that it consists of 'a set of distinguishable, differentiated, but to some degree interdependent parts, often with distributed functions and a division of labour, connected in such a way as to form a complex whole'.[17] Deliberation on such an approach is therefore spread across a number of 'differentiated yet linked components' which make up a wider democratic system, and which interact to produce democratic goods.[18]

---

[15] Christiano (2012); Dryzek (2010, 2017); Goodin (2005); Mansbridge et al. (2012); Parkinson (2006, 2012). While the systemic approaches were developed against overly unitary conception of deliberative democracy, it is in many ways a return to older theories of deliberative democracy, such as those of Habermas (1975), which thought in systemic terms.

[16] See Chapter 8 for more discussion of mini-publics.

[17] Mansbridge et al. (2012, pp. 4–5).

[18] Stevenson and Dryzek (2014, p. 27).

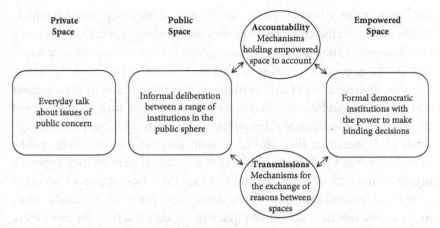

Figure 3.1 A deliberative democratic system

Following John Dryzek, these components can be grouped into three different parts or spaces within a democratic system (see Figure 3.1).[19] The first is *empowered space*, which involves formal political institutions such as representative parliaments, state-established citizen assemblies, government agencies, and bureaucracies. Empowered space is therefore made up of the more recognizable machinery of democratic politics. What is distinctive about this space, however, is that these institutions have the power to make collective democratic decisions which are binding on the population. Unlike other actors in a deliberative system, they can exercise political authority to produce laws and public policies. While they therefore play a very important role, empowered institutions are by no means the only actors in a deliberative system.

The second key area is *public space*, which involves more informal and open sites of deliberation. This space includes a much broader range of institutions, whether they be universities, trade unions, think tanks, social movements, citizens' associations, business groups, newspapers, television and other media, nongovernmental organizations (NGOs), or charities.

---

[19] Dryzek (2009, 2017); Stevenson and Dryzek (2014). Dryzek's approach is useful for my purposes as provides a broader schema for a deliberative system without specifying institutional details. It is therefore not fixed to any predetermined set of institutional arrangements (e.g. the traditional institutions of representative democracy) and allows one to more easily discuss which roles different institutional forms can play in such a system. This will, for instance, become important in Chapter 5 where I advocate for forms of decentralization and in Chapter 8 where I propose adding a sortition branch to the democratic system.

DEMOCRACY AND THE DIVISION OF KNOWLEDGE   75

Deliberation within this public sphere can therefore take place in physical sites, such as in town halls and protests, but can also be more distributed, such as the discussions found in new and old media. Unlike empowered space, no public space institution has the power to make binding and enforceable decisions. However, much deliberation prior to binding decisions occurs in this more unstructured or wild area of civil society. This space can also make nonbinding decisions about things such as what an acceptable topic of debate is, norms of civility, what takes priority in the public agenda, or what should and should not be settled through the state. The third and final part of the system is then *private space*. This space is the least formal in that it involves the discussions of citizens within private settings, such as households and workplaces. In her formulation of a deliberative system, Jane Mansbridge calls these private discussions 'everyday talk'.[20] Everyday talk does not refer to just any conversation, but private discussions which are directed towards political and social issues.

Although empowered, public, and private spaces can be conceptually distinguished, components in each space can 'consider reasons and proposals generated in other parts'.[21] Empowered and public spaces, for instance, are linked through mechanisms of *transmission* and *accountability*. Transmissions refer to different routes through which the deliberations within public space can come to influence the deliberations and decisions of empowered institutions, and vice versa. Through campaigns and lobbying, for instance, the discussions in NGOs or think tanks can impact the decisions of parliaments. Advisory and parliamentary committees, public consultations, citizens' juries, public inquiries, as well as campaigns and protests can also all play a role as mechanisms of transmission. Alongside these transmissions there are also mechanisms for ensuring that empowered space is held accountable to public space. The most common of these mechanisms are elections, but they can also include more informal mechanisms, such as media criticism or protests. Such mechanisms aim at making empowered bodies responsible to the public and can motivate them to consider the discussions of other spaces.[22]

What is important about the systemic approach is not only that democracy is made up of multiple institutions, but that we should judge democratic

[20] Mansbridge (1999a).
[21] Mansbridge et al. (2012, p. 23).
[22] Dryzek (2009, 2017); Stevenson and Dryzek (2014).

76 INTELLIGENT DEMOCRACY

values, at least in part, at the system level. Given that no one institution can provide all democratic goods, or legitimize all decisions, we should not focus only on how democratic any one component is. Rather, we should also consider how these different components connect and combine in order to produce a system which is democratic as a whole. How, for instance, do the different components allow for forms of inclusion, voice, and participation so that these values can be realized at the level of the democratic system? The systemic approach claims that it is by analysing how the different spaces and components work together that we can determine the overall democratic character of the network.

Democracy's epistemic value, or its intelligence as I have put it, can also be judged at the system level. Its epistemic abilities do not need to be found in any one institution, but can rather be distributed across the different actors in the system. In other words, a deliberative system can involve functional divisions of labour, emergent properties, and self-regulating tendencies which work to produce epistemic abilities at the level of the system which none of its components possess in isolation. Similarly, not all institutions need to contribute to producing all of democracy's epistemic abilities, as the system can involve forms of specialization. Any one component may in fact possess epistemic failures or weaknesses, but a systemic perspective allows for the possibility that other components can compensate for these deficiencies so that they do not adversely affect the system as a whole. While epistemic democrats have not significantly engaged with the systemic turn in democratic theory, I will argue over the course of this book that a systemic perspective allows us to better identify the epistemic abilities of democracy and that it is essential to producing a convincing epistemic justification of democratic politics. I will argue that we require a systemic perspective if we are to truly understand democracy's intelligence. The next sections starts this task by applying the deliberative systems approach to the Hayekian critique of democracy and the problem of the division of knowledge.

A Systemic Division of Epistemic Labour

On a systemic approach to democracy the division of knowledge should not be seen as a problem befalling any one democratic body, such as a single parliament or deliberative forum. Instead, the ability to gather local and general forms of knowledge is a task which can be distributed across a number of

DEMOCRACY AND THE DIVISION OF KNOWLEDGE 77

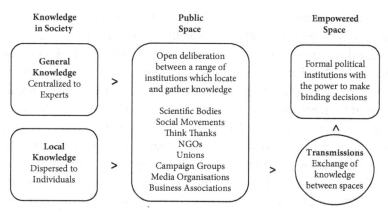

Figure 3.2 Knowledge gathering in a deliberative democratic system

different institutions within a broader democratic system. A systemic perspective allows for an 'economy of reasoning' where the cognitive burden of acquiring information is shared by many actors.[23] Important to overcoming the division of knowledge is how this economy of reasoning allows for a division of epistemic labour within the public space of a deliberative system. Empowered democratic institutions are not isolated islands of decision-making cut off from the sea of knowledge spread throughout society, but are connected to an active public sphere. On the epistemic model of a deliberative system proposed here, this public space involves a range of institutions who play a role as epistemic intermediaries between empowered bodies and the knowledge which is spread throughout society. They play a role in locating forms of knowledge relevant to problems of public concern, gathering and aggregating such information, and then communicating it through transmissions to empowered institutions with the aim of influencing their binding democratic decisions.

This epistemic reading of a deliberative system is represented in Figure 3.2. On the right-hand side of this model are empowered institutions which take binding decisions. We saw in our earlier discussion that decentralization can help reduce the problems associated with gathering local and dispersed information, so we can imagine that empowered space will involve some form of decentralization.[24] On the left-hand side of the diagram, we can

---

[23] Warren and Gastil (2015).
[24] For a further discussion of the epistemic benefits of political decentralization, see Chapter 5.

78   INTELLIGENT DEMOCRACY

see the different forms of knowledge which are relevant to social decision-making. Given my reformulation of the division of knowledge, this includes both local and general scientific information. It includes the knowledge of individuals spread throughout society and the relatively more centralized scientific knowledge of experts. This knowledge is not, however, completely separated from empowered democratic institutions. Instead, at the centre of the system is public space and the range of institutions which make it up. It is these institutions within public space which play a crucial epistemic function in that they work to locate, gather, and aggregate knowledge which is dispersed in society, and through mechanisms of transmission, communicate it so that it can come to influence the binding decisions of empowered institutions.

Some examples can help clarify this epistemic model of a deliberative system and the role of public space institutions within it. Consider, for instance, the connection between the scientific deliberations of the Intergovernmental Panel on Climate Change (IPCC) and international negotiations on carbon emission reductions. As a scientific institution, the IPCC plays the role of locating and gathering the state of the art in academic research on the causes and likely impacts of climate change. It focuses on acquiring the best general scientific knowledge of this problem of public concern, aggregating it into an overall picture, and then communicating this knowledge as best as it can to empowered institutions which have the authority to take decisions to address climate change. The political deliberations of the United Nations Climate Change Conference (COP), as well as the policy decisions of individual states, are then informed by this information. In other words, these empowered deliberations and decisions are influenced by knowledge which is located and aggregated by a public space institution. Other public space institutions, whether it be universities, scientific associations, or research centres, then play a similar role but for other social problems and other fields of scientific knowledge. All of these bodies, however, have an epistemic function in that they gather and communicate general forms of knowledge so that it can be utilized by empowered institutions.

While institutions such as the IPCC may be concerned with general scientific knowledge, public space also involves a range of actors whose role is to locate and acquire more local forms of information. A grassroots social movement, for instance, will generally form around one or a set of social problems which affect their members, whether it be housing, healthcare, environmental quality, and so on. In doing so, however, they are made up of and work with affected individuals who have local knowledge of the on-the-spot consequences and impacts of such issues. In organizing for change, these groups then communicate this information to empowered institutions through alternative mechanisms of transmission, so that it can come to influence democratic decision-making. The Platform for People Affected by Mortgages (PAH), which started in Barcelona and spread internationally, was formed by those whose housing was affected as a result of the 2008 financial crisis. In campaigning for changes to local and national policies associated with evictions and foreclosure, it functioned as an organization which transmitted the local knowledge of these affected parties with the aim of having it influence empowered actors. This is not to say that every social movement necessarily plays this epistemic role or that it is their principal role in a democratic system. Black Lives Matter, for instance, may have many functions in a deliberative system by representing certain discourses or the interests of certain social groups. However, in giving voice to problems of concern which are not being heard by the broader system, it also transmits local knowledge of how issues of systemic racism, discrimination, and police violence affect individuals and communities, and then communicates this information with the aim of influencing empowered spaces.

Social movements are, of course, just one example of the kind of public space institution which work to locate and gather local forms of knowledge. The public sphere contains a variety of alternative institutions, big and small, which play a role in transmitting the on-the-spot effects and impacts of social problems to more empowered actors. Charities, NGOs, labour unions, community associations, local business associations, and a range of other organizations work on particular issues or with particular groups, and in representing their interests help to communicate their local knowledge to others. Charities such as Oxfam or Shelter can access and communicate information about the local conditions of those they aim to help and represent, while labour unions acquire and produce information about how specific policies or problems are affecting their members' interests.

There are a couple of important divisions of labour within this epistemic model of a democratic system. Firstly, while it is the role of empowered institutions to use information for binding democratic decisions, much of the task of acquiring this knowledge is borne by the institutions of the public sphere. Empowered democratic bodies do not therefore carry the full burden of good decision-making, as public space plays a central role in terms of

80   INTELLIGENT DEMOCRACY

identifying and acquiring relevant information.[25] This division is not strict, as empowered bodies may of course acquire some information directly, but it does show that the majority of knowledge acquisition is performed by other parts of the system. Secondly, there is also a division of epistemic labour within public space itself. This space involves a diversity of institutional forms, such as scientific bodies, campaign groups, academic groups, unions, charities, and social movements. No one of those institutions is responsible for gathering all forms of knowledge, as there are instead forms of specialization. Scientific bodies focus on subject-specific expert knowledge, social movements on local knowledge of particular issues they organize around, unions on information relating to the interests of members and trades, and charities on information about their particular issues of concern. The burden of discovering and gathering information is therefore distributed across the different institutions of public space, so information is acquired by a wider network rather than by any individual component. The epistemic burden which is placed on any one part is therefore reduced through this systemic division of labour.

There will, of course, be some significant overlap within this division. There may be more than one scientific organization, charity, or campaign group organized around a single issue or problem, often providing alternative perspectives. Similarly, a social movement may be interested in the scientific research conducted on the issues it organizes around, as well as the local knowledge of people's experiences, and it may therefore draw on the knowledge produced by other components of the system. A climate movement, such as Extinction Rebellion or Greenpeace, for instance, may draw on the general scientific knowledge of the IPCC. The components within public space are therefore interconnected in the sense that they can share and draw on the knowledge-gathering work of other components. Generally, however, it is the different forms of specialization within the division of labour which allows a vast and varied amount of information to be discovered and transmitted in a deliberative system.

There are also different mechanisms of transmission which allow these public space institutions to communicate their knowledge to empowered

---

[25] This division therefore has similarities to Habermas's (2015, pp. 307, 300) two-track model of democracy. On this model formal political institutions play the role of 'justifying the selection of a problem and the choice among competing proposals for solving it'. They are not, however, involved in 'discovering and identifying problems' nor 'new ways of looking at problems'. Instead there is a public sphere which operates as 'a far-flung network of sensors that react to the pressures of society-wide problems and stimulate influential opinions'.

institutions. Some of these mechanisms are more formalized, as is the case with the relationship between the IPCC and COP negotiations, or between government statistical bodies and government departments. Similarly, transmissions can also take the form of advisory and parliamentary committees, public consultations, or public enquiries. There are then less formalized but still relatively direct transmissions, such as the activities of lobbyists, or the relationships political leaders may have with charities, think tanks, or campaign groups. These mechanisms of transmission are less formalized than things such as parliamentary committees, but still play a day-to-day role within empowered spaces and are often accepted by empowered actors. Then there are the least formal forms of transmission which come from the 'outside', such as local campaigns, protests, boycotts, and petitions. These mechanisms are the least formalized but are often important in communicating forms of information which are otherwise excluded from empowered spaces, or which empowered actors do not seek out or even wish to hear.

The different institutions within empowered space may use one or a variety of these different mechanisms. Social movements may have existing relationships with some empowered actors, for instance, allowing for more formal transmissions. For example, some prominent members of the PAH came to hold public offices, such as the former Barcelona Mayor Ada Colau, creating a more formal channel of communication. For other empowered actors, however, this group would not be provided with the same access and may need to engage in less formal mechanisms of transmission. Similarly, while the IPCC has very formalized relationships with intergovernmental organizations, many climate scientists have also spoken out publicly against a lack of action on climate change, therefore utilizing more informal channels. It is through this variety of transmission mechanisms, however, that the information gathered by public space institutions can pass into empowered spaces.

When taking a systemic rather than a unitary perspective then, democratic bodies should not be seen as isolated islands of decision-making greatly separated and disconnected from the knowledge which is dispersed around them. On the contrary, empowered democratic bodies are instead connected to a range of other institutions within public space which act as epistemic intermediaries between those bodies which have the power to make binding decisions and the knowledge which is spread throughout society. What these public space institutions have in common is that they (1) locate forms

82   INTELLIGENT DEMOCRACY

of knowledge relevant to problems of public concern; (2) gather and aggregate such information through their internal procedures; and (3) communicate this aggregated knowledge through transmission so that it can influence empowered decisions. It is by distributing the epistemic ability of gathering knowledge across these many different actors, then, that the deliberative system as a whole can acquire and utilize both the local and general knowledge which exists in society.

Importantly, the effective functioning of the division of labour within public space depends on the democratic structure of the public sphere. For instance, it is important that public space and its processes of knowledge-gathering are generally undirected by empowered space. Empowered democratic bodies may set up general rules and regulations which govern the public sphere, such as the regulation of free speech or a free press, and they may set up knowledge-gathering institutions aimed at acquiring certain kinds of information, such as government statistical or scientific bodies. However, the general division of labour is not directly controlled by any one institution, but is rather an open and spontaneous process. Institutions such as social movements, campaign groups, and unions have autonomy from empowered institutions when it comes to determining their organization and focus, while scientific bodies can determine their own internal procedures for generating and aggregating general knowledge.

This autonomy is crucial to the epistemic function of public space for a couple of reasons. Firstly, if empowered institutions had too much control over the organization of public space institutions, then they could work to silence information which was thought to be damaging to empowered actors. By directing them towards certain issues and away from others, or changing their internal procedures, they could weaken the epistemic function of the public sphere by having it influenced by the interests of those in power. This is a problem which can be easily seen in more authoritarian regimes which directly intervene in the public sphere to stop the spread of certain kinds of information.[26] Chapters 7 and 8 deal more directly with how to resist abuses of power from empowered actors, but we can at this point recognize the threats that such abuses create for the ability of the public sphere to gather relevant knowledge. Secondly, even if those in empowered spaces are benevolent, a directed public space would remain a poor system for knowledge

---

[26] Some democratic sceptics, such as Bell (2016), argue for nondemocratic regimes with legal protections for freedoms of speech. These approaches will be addressed in Chapter 7.

DEMOCRACY AND THE DIVISION OF KNOWLEDGE 83

acquisition. Part of what makes the division of knowledge so challenging is that no single institution can be aware in advance of the different kinds of local and general knowledge relevant to a given social problem. The local effects of social problems on different sections of society, and the ways in which scientific knowledge has a bearing on such problems, are not self-evident. As a result, empowered institutions simply do not always know what information to look for or where to look. Instead, relevant knowledge in society needs to be located or discovered by a more open process. Just such a process can be found in the democratic public sphere whose institutions are granted autonomy from empowered actors.

Social movements, for instance, can form and organize around issues they themselves see as important, and in doing so locate local forms of information which empowered institutions will likely miss. Similarly, unions may be aware of issues affecting their members which others are not, and can then go on to conduct research on these issues if they are given the autonomy to do so. Scientific institutions are no different in this respect, often requiring the freedom to study what they see as most vital and with the methods they determine are most likely to produce results. If the process of knowledge acquisition within public space was fully directed, then, it would fail in its task, as no empowered democratic body can possibly be aware of all the knowledge it needs to acquire. The division of knowledge necessarily implies that not all information is known to any one person or institution in totality, and therefore no one person or institution will be aware of what information will be relevant for any given problem. Even if they can be aware at any one point in time, democratic policy interventions and the emergence of new social problems into the future would disrupt this position, as it would change the facts on the ground. The autonomy of public space from empowered space is therefore important to its epistemic function as it allows institutions to search out and discover forms of information of which any centralized authority would simply remain ignorant.

The epistemic value of a deliberative system is, therefore, in part connected to its democratic character. Unlike nondemocratic systems which often involve the tight control of public space by empowered actors, a democratic system provides greater forms of autonomy. Legal protections for freedom of speech and association, as well as strong norms supporting such freedoms, help to protect the autonomous and open nature of a democratic public sphere, and in doing so also protect its epistemic quality.[27] If public space

---

[27] I am not here endorsing an epistemic argument for free speech in the form often attributed to J. S. Mill. Free speech is important to public space because it allow actors to search out and

84 INTELLIGENT DEMOCRACY

becomes overly directed by more invasive forms of politics, then its division of epistemic labour will begin to break down either because of the pernicious interference of empowered actors, or because these actors simply do not know which kinds of information to search for.

While the open nature of democratic space is therefore important, so is its inclusiveness. Knowledge which is broadly distributed throughout society cannot be uncovered if certain groups or individuals are excluded or silenced within the public sphere. Although general scientific knowledge may only be known to certain institutions or actors with specific expertise, local knowledge can be possessed by any individual citizen. The exclusion of certain social groups can therefore leave the system without access to possibly important forms of knowledge. This is particularly true given that those commonly marginalized from public space often suffer from discrimination or a lack of resources more generally and are therefore likely to be disproportionately impacted by many social problems. The fact that no empowered body can locate all the relevant knowledge in advance therefore requires that public space remains inclusive as critical information may come from anywhere in the system. Empowered actors cannot necessarily predict who will have relevant information about problems of concern moving into the future, and needed information may well come from unexpected places.

Part of what is preserved by the inclusiveness of a democratic public sphere, then, is diversity. Differently situated individuals are likely to be differently impacted by social problems and to see these problems from different points of view. They will therefore be alive to alternative problems and the alternative forms of information relevant to their conceptualization and resolution. Inclusiveness therefore allows the perspectives of a diverse range of individuals to be utilized in a democratic system. It also makes possible a diverse range of institutional actors who will look for problems and information in different places and apply alternative ways of aggregating and interpreting this information. Without some level of diversity the division of epistemic labour within the public sphere would bear little fruit, as the many actors in this space would simply return similar forms of knowledge. The inclusiveness of a democratic public sphere, however, allows for a level

---

communicate the information they see as important, not that 'the marketplace of ideas' will necessarily tend towards truth. In fact, an open public space is likely to produce many false knowledge claims, a problem returned to in the next chapter. This argument also does not necessarily defend an absolutist position on free speech. While I will not address such issues here, this epistemic argument does not rule out prohibitions against such things as hate speech.

of diversity which makes this division of labour productive. This is not to say that the democratic public spheres we see today are fully inclusive or that they do not exclude or marginalize certain groups or voices. Democracies certainly do suffer from such problems. What this discussion does suggest, however, is that we have epistemic reasons to rectify these forms of exclusion, and we can still recognize that democracies today allow for more open and inclusive public spheres than do today's nondemocratic regimes.

The division of epistemic labour that allows a deliberative democratic system to address the division of knowledge is therefore connected to the open and inclusive nature of a democratic public sphere. It is these democratic characteristics which allow public space to locate and gather forms of local and general knowledge about which any one empowered institution would be ignorant. Of course, a public space which is open, undirected, and inclusive may also produce imperfections and flaws into a deliberative system. It would, for instance, allow for the inclusion of epistemically unreliable actors who knowingly or unknowingly propagate false and misleading claims. Indeed, a deliberative system will include the scientific claims of the IPCC, but also climate denial groups. Similarly, an open public sphere will be unstructured, if not 'wild' or 'anarchic' as Habermas called it, making it difficult to determine who to listen to, especially for deliberators who will likely have their own biases and prejudices.[28] Much of the next chapter will be dedicated to dealing with the imperfections of the democratic public sphere, and how a deliberative system can identify which of its varied knowledge claims to accept. At this point, however, I wish to claim that the open and often messy nature of a democratic public space is, in fact, a necessary component of a democratic system's ability to gather knowledge. It is only if the public sphere remains open and inclusive that it can possibly locate and acquire the local and general forms of knowledge relevant to social problems.

Before turning to consider the problems of the public sphere in the next chapter, I want to return now to the role of collective political institutions within its division of epistemic labour. This section has focused on the institutions of public space, and how they allow deliberative systems to locate and acquire forms of relevant knowledge. However, the structure of decision-making within empowered space is also critical to understanding the system's ability to gather information, and here the collective nature of democratic decisions plays an important role. In explaining this role, I will

[28] Habermas (2006b).

86 INTELLIGENT DEMOCRACY

aim to further develop the preliminary case for collective democratic politics with which I ended the previous chapter.

Collective Politics in the Deliberative System

On the Hayekian view, the division of knowledge fundamentally challenges the epistemic reliability of collective political decision-making. Given that knowledge is spread throughout society, Hayek thought that collective democratic institutions would be ignorant of much of the information relevant to social problems, and that leaving decisions to individual market actors was the only option. The systemic model of democracy put forward here has pushed back against this charge, explaining how collective democratic institutions are connected to an active public sphere which allows them to acquire information. The systemic perspective, however, actually allows for a more radical reply to the Hayekian critique of democracy. It is not only that considering the wider deliberative system shows us how collective democratic institutions can deal with the division of knowledge, but that these institutions are themselves important to overcoming this division, and that they possess advantages in this respect over markets. In other words, the systemic perspective shows us that collective forms of democratic politics are, in fact, part of the solution to Hayek's division of knowledge.

To see why collective democratic bodies are important to a democratic systems division of labour, we can compare such a system to one based on the free markets favoured by Hayek and his successors. In the previous chapter we saw that individual consumers face an information problem in making decisions about the common good. It is at least conceivable, however, that they could acquire this needed information from institutions in the public sphere. The simple model of markets considered in the last chapter allowed for the possibility of deliberation between consumers, and Hayekian theorists have similarly noted how markets can utilize linguistic forms of communication alongside price signals. Pennington, for instance, has pointed to advertising, trade magazines, gossip, books, and other such media as forms of explicit communication which contribute to market society.[29] While these market theorists do not go as far as to propose a model of a market-based

---

[29] Pennington (2001). For a further discussion of the markets reliance of other communicative mechanisms, see Herzog (2020).

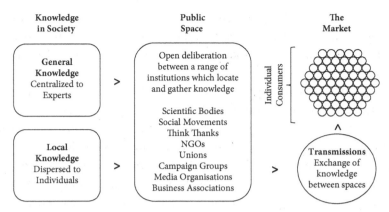

Figure 3.3 A deliberative market system

deliberative system, it is not a large leap to think of these forms of communication in deliberative and systemic terms. We can think of markets as situated within a wider deliberative system, and connected to an active public sphere which gathers and communicates information.

It is well recognized in democratic theory that deliberative systems can take many shapes and sizes, and that the final decisions of such systems can be taken by a variety of political institutions, democratic or otherwise.[30] What is not well recognized is that deliberative systems can also be applied to economic systems, such as markets. While the deliberative system discussed earlier terminated in the decisions of collective democratic institutions within empowered space, we can imagine a deliberative system which instead terminated in the decisions of individual consumers in the free market (see Figure 3.3). Public space institutions, from charities to campaign groups, would therefore aim to communicate their information to individual consumers in order to influence their decisions in the marketplace, rather than empowered political bodies. Environmental groups, for instance, often make information campaigns aimed directly at influencing consumer behaviour, directing them towards more environmentally friendly products and services. Similarly, social movements, charities, medical associations, and private firms all often use advertising and other media to inform consumers about the benefits and costs of alternative products. Just like political institutions, then, markets do not operate in isolation from the

[30] Mansbridge et al. (2012).

88   INTELLIGENT DEMOCRACY

rest of society. Instead, consumers and firms operate in connection with a broader public sphere which aims to influence their behaviour. It is therefore plausible to conceptualize markets as existing within a broader deliberative system.

Just as the systemic approach can show how collective democratic institutions can come to acquire the knowledge they need, perhaps the systemic perspective can do the same thing for markets. Perhaps public space institutions can locate, gather, and communicate to individual consumers the information they require to make their market transactions in respect to justice and the common good. If so, then the market may be able to overcome the information problem highlighted in the previous chapter, drawing on the epistemic role of public space. The reason deliberative systems cannot do for markets what they do for collective democratic bodies, however, is that the collective nature of these bodies is actually important to the ability of the system to gather and communicate knowledge. Having a deliberative system terminate in the decisions of collective political institutions helps it to better address the division of knowledge compared to a system which leaves decisions to the market, as Hayek preferred.

Comparing Deliberative Systems

In comparing a 'deliberative democratic system' based on collective democratic institutions, with a 'deliberative market system' which leaves decisions to individual market actors, I will make one important simplifying assumption. This assumption is that the ability of public space to locate and gather information is equal in both systems. Some have argued that market forces can be corrosive of both civil society and scientific institutions, the result of which would be that they reduce the ability of the system to acquire information. While arguments along these lines have force, I will aim to show that a deliberative democratic system still possesses several important advantages when it comes to the division of knowledge, even if the quality of public space in a deliberative market system is held equal. Having decisions taken by democratic institutions reduces the costs associated with transmissions of information from public space, increases the quality of transmission between these spaces, and it reduces the cognitive and epistemic burden placed on decision-makers.

The first two of these advantages are linked to the number and distribution of decision-makers in both systems. In a deliberative system where decisions are left to markets, relevant knowledge needs to be communicated to a very large number of individual consumers spread throughout the market. It needs to be communicated to possibly millions of market actors spread throughout the economy. In a system which terminates in the decisions of collective democratic bodies, alternatively, relevant knowledge need only be communicated to a relatively small number of empowered institutions. As a consequence, the costs associated with the transmission of information from public space are significantly increased in a market-based system.

Consider first general scientific knowledge, which tends to be relatively centralized to particular experts or expert institutions. In a market system, this scientific knowledge would need to be communicated to possibly millions of individual consumers so that it would be utilized in their economic decisions. A market system will therefore face the opposite epistemic problem when it comes to such knowledge, to that which Hayek identified as facing the communication of local knowledge to a central authority.[31] Rather than centralizing large amounts of dispersed information to a centralized political body, a market system would need to disperse large amounts of centralized scientific knowledge to a very large number of dispersed market actors spread throughout the economy. The transmission of information from public space institutions to so many decision-makers will therefore be highly costly, if possible at all. A democratic deliberative system, on the other hand, reduces the costs associated with transmissions by reducing the number of decision-makers to whom knowledge needs to be communicated. Given that there will be far fewer empowered democratic bodies than consumers in the economy, the communication of scientific knowledge in a deliberative democratic system will therefore be far less challenging and costly than a market system. When it comes to general knowledge, of course, Hayek would not necessarily disagree that political institutions are in a better position to acquire relevant information. What is more striking from the Hayekian perspective, however, is that we can now see that democratic bodies are also in a better position to acquire local knowledge.

---

[31] O'Neill (2012) makes a similar point when considering the role of scientific knowledge in environmental markets. His analysis, however, focuses on the problems of scientific knowledge for markets and takes for granted that market mechanism are better placed to utilize local information. As I will argue, however, markets actually face similar difficulties in respect to local knowledge.

90　INTELLIGENT DEMOCRACY

Recall that when it comes to second-order decisions about justice and the common good, it is not enough for consumers to make use of their own local information, nor will market prices provide them with the local knowledge of others affected by their actions. A market system would therefore need the local knowledge of others to be explicitly communicated throughout the market by the institutions of public space. In doing this, however, such a system will face an even greater challenge than a democratic deliberative system. Rather than requiring that a large amount of dispersed local knowledge be gathered and then communicated to a handful of more centralized democratic bodies, a market system requires that this dispersed information be gathered and then communicated to an equally large number of equally dispersed market actors. In such a system, local knowledge will need to be communicated to possibly millions of consumers spread throughout the economy in order that it can be utilized in market transactions. As was the case with general knowledge, the difficulty and cost associated with the transmission of information will increase with the number of decision-makers to whom information needs to be communicated. These costs are therefore significantly reduced in a deliberative democratic system where decisions are taken by a handful of empowered institutions. Even if democratic bodies are decentralized to a more local level—something which would be generally beneficial for accessing local knowledge—the number of decision-makers would be only a very small fraction of the number of consumers in the marketplace.

It is worth pausing to note the novelty of this result, and how it essentially turns the Hayekian case for the market on its head. While Hayek argued that market mechanisms are epistemically valuable in allowing individuals to make the best use of their local knowledge, this at best holds for self-regarding decisions concerning a consumer's own interests. When it comes to decisions which concern justice and the common good, for which individuals require the local knowledge of others, markets are in fact in a worse position than democratic bodies in accessing dispersed information. Having to communicate this information to large numbers of individuals spread throughout the economy, a market system will struggle to utilize this knowledge for decisions which concern the common good. The ability to utilize local knowledge therefore becomes a reason to value democratic institutions, rather than the market. Collective democratic institutions play an important role in a deliberative system's division of epistemic labour, in that they reduce the number of actors to whom relevant local and general

DEMOCRACY AND THE DIVISION OF KNOWLEDGE   91

information needs to be communicated, therefore reducing the difficulty and cost of transmissions.

For similar reasons, a deliberative democratic system also increases the quality of these transmissions. Given the costs involved in communicating information to a vast number of individual consumers, this often leads to weak transmission mechanisms which can only communicate limited amounts of information in overly simplified forms. Transmissions in such a system commonly take the forms of advertising, public information campaigns, product labelling, and branding. As discussed in the previous chapter, when these communication methods are utilized by private firms there is often an incentive to provide misleading or false information, and trust in them is low as a result. Even leaving such issues aside, however, these transmission mechanisms can only provide consumers with limited amounts of information to make their decisions and require that often complex information be greatly simplified. Product labelling, for instance, which is a common tool for informing consumers, can only communicate information which can fit on a single label, and which can be easily and quickly understood by consumers. Labelling can therefore provide some necessary and important information, but it is very limited with respect to the amount and complexity of information consumers require to make decisions about the common good. The information relating to how a product may affect a consumer's personal health is already significant and complex, let alone the information needed to judge the varied ways that any one product may impact the common good. Similar things are true of advertising in magazines, television, and new media which often compress information into slogans or sound bites.

The task facing transmission mechanisms in a deliberative market system is also made more difficult by the fact that consumers have little incentive to listen or pay attention to such information. As argued in the previous chapter, individual consumers face an incentive problem when it comes to decisions about justice and the common good, meaning that they have little motivation to acquire or consider information relevant to how their market transactions affect others. Much of the work which goes into branding and advertising is therefore directed not at communicating nuanced information, but rather at simply capturing a consumer's limited attention. Again, this is not to say that consumers cannot learn anything from such transmission mechanisms, or that policies which mandate certain kinds of product labelling are useless. What it does mean is that these methods of communication can only communicate limited and often highly simplified forms of information, when

92 INTELLIGENT DEMOCRACY

compared to the knowledge required to effectively account for one's effect on the common good. As the empirical evidence of consumer knowledge cited in the previous chapter suggests, these mechanisms have not led to a consumer base which is well informed about the implications of their market transactions, and consumers often report finding it difficult to make such decisions as a result.

A deliberative democratic system, alternatively, can provide higher quality transmission mechanisms because information only needs to be communicated to a smaller number of more centralized empowered bodies. Scientific advisory committees, expert panels, policy advisers, research reports and briefing materials, parliamentary committees, citizen juries, public inquiries, public consultations, town hall meetings and many other mechanisms allow for much higher quality information to be communicated to empowered democratic bodies than could ever be communicated to consumers in the market. These forms of transmission can provide much more knowledge than product labelling or advertising but can also communicate it in a manner which is fitting for the complexity, uncertainty, and often technical nature of much socially relevant knowledge.[32] Of course, when it comes to very specialized scientific knowledge, some simplification is inevitable for those without particular training (an issue returned to in the next chapter). In comparison to the transmission mechanisms available to a deliberative market system, however, those available to a democratic system allow for a much richer communication of relevant knowledge. Even the most informal and unstructured transmissions in a democratic system, such as protests and petitions, are still often better at providing information given that they can be directed at a more limited number of empowered actors and institutions.

The first two advantages of a deliberative democratic system result from the lower number of decision-makers to whom knowledge needs to be communicated. Collective democratic institutions therefore play a role in the systems division of labour as they reduce the cost and increase the quality of transmissions from public space. A third advantage possessed by such as system is that it reduces the cognitive and epistemic burden placed on decision-makers. The problem for the market is that by placing decisions in the hands of consumers, it makes unreasonable demands of individuals. Each consumer will engage in a host of market transactions, each of which

---

[32] Slovic (1987, 2000).

will have consequences for others, and each of which will therefore create demands for information. Each purchase a consumer makes can affect a range of issues important to judging the common good—from labour conditions, to discrimination practices, to environmental quality—about which they will need to become informed. Individual market actors therefore confront a sizeable cognitive and epistemic burden. The time and energy needed to overcome this burden is significant, particularly for individuals who will face many other demands (working hours, care for dependants, need for leisure time, etc.).

The reverse of Oscar Wilde's quip that socialism would take up too many evenings with meetings is that free markets would take up too many evenings with research. Individual consumers will be required to spend unreasonable amounts of time and energy acquiring and understanding information about the impact of the many market transactions they engage in. In a deliberative democratic system, alternatively, these cognitive and epistemic burdens fall on collective political institutions which have a much greater capacity to deal with large amounts of information. No one individual within these empowered bodies needs to acquire and possess all forms of knowledge relevant to the common good, as this burden falls on the institutions as a whole. Individuals can therefore have specialized roles within these institutions, unlike a consumer who must consider information relevant to all of the effects of their market transactions. The empowered space of a deliberative democratic system also allows for the possibility for divisions of labour among political institutions along the lines of different policy areas (i.e. economic, health, or environment) and different geographical jurisdictions. The epistemic burden falling on any one institution can therefore be reduced through this specialization. Of course, too analytic or fragmented an approach may run the risk of missing important ways in which social problems are connected.[33] Where it is possible, however, divisions of labour can reduce the epistemic load placed on a single institution.

Through this comparison with markets, we can see that collective democratic institutions actually play an important role in a deliberative system's ability to gather knowledge. Having a deliberative system terminate in the decisions of democratic bodies reduces the costs associated with transmissions of information from public space, increases the quality of transmissions between these spaces, and reduces the cognitive and epistemic

---

[33] Dryzek (1987).

94 INTELLIGENT DEMOCRACY

burden placed on decision-makers. A system perspective therefore not only shows that collective democratic bodies can overcome Hayek's division of knowledge, but that they are themselves important to solving this problem, and that they provide democratic system with advantages over the market. If we were to reduce the scope and power of democratic institutions and leave more decisions to the market, as the Hayekian democratic sceptics recommend, then the division of knowledge Hayek identified would actually be more difficult to overcome.

Knowledge Gathering in the Deliberative System

This chapter has focused on replying to a central critique of democracy coming from the Hayekian brand of the new democratic scepticism. While the division of knowledge highlighted by Hayek and his successors appears daunting if one takes a unitary view of democracy as reducing to a single institution, taking a systemic perspective allows us to better understand democracy's ability to acquire the local and general knowledge necessary for addressing social problems. If democracy is understood as a broader deliberative system involving collective democratic bodies alongside an open and inclusive public sphere, then it can possess an ability for gathering information superior to that of even the market. So although Hayek's claims about the informational advantages of markets are widely accepted, even by those not sympathetic to his free-market prescriptions, I have argued that democracy is best placed to access dispersed and fragmented information. When it comes to second-order decisions concerning questions of justice and the common good then it is democracy which best realizes this epistemic ability. In other words, democracy is a more intelligent second-order institution than the market.

By replying to the objections of the Hayekian sceptics, this chapter has therefore produced a new systemic account of how democracy can come to acquire information. While epistemic democrats have often focused on the information provided by voters in elections, electoral mechanisms are likely to face many of the same problems as consumers. They would similarly require information to be communicated to vast numbers of individuals, increasing the costs and lowering the quality of transmissions, and would place a significant cognitive burden on lone individuals.[34] It is therefore the

[34] One possible solution to these problems is Ackerman and Fishkin's (2004) suggestion for a national day of deliberation, or Deliberation Day, where voters are brought together in small groups to

inclusion of collective institutions within a deliberative system, more than the use of elections as many epistemic democrats claim, which allows democratic decisions to become informed by the knowledge which emerges from the public sphere.

Of course, there are still many pressing questions confronting this model of a democratic system, and its capacity to explain democracy's intelligence. For instance, it is still not yet fully clear why the empowered institutions in such a system even need to be democratic. We have seen why it is important for public space to be open and inclusive, and how its democratic character is therefore important to its ability to gather information. The benefits of empowered democratic institutions, alternatively, have been argued to come from their collective character, a trait shared by many nondemocratic regimes such as epistocracy and political meritocracy. This chapter has not therefore established a complete argument for a deliberative 'democratic' system. To see why such a system should be fully democratic we will need to inquire more closely into the institutions of empowered space, and the benefits associated with democratic forms of decision-making. This inquiry will come in Chapters 6 to 8, where I turn to democratic sceptics who do not favour the market, but rather new forms of elite rule. Before this, however, I aim to further develop the systemic model of democracy introduced in this chapter. In the next chapter, I will consider the problems and imperfections which can afflict an open and inclusive public sphere and look to reply to those democratic sceptics who claim that democratic debate is dominated by the biases and prejudices of citizens, and that it is therefore little more than a machine for misinformation.

---

discuss issues and be provided with information. If conducted, such an event would help to raise the information level of the electorate and could offer a solution to the epistemic challenges confronting elections. The problem with this proposal, however, is the significant costs involved in providing detailed information to all or even most of an electorate. López-Guerra (2011), for instance, estimated that the price for running a deliberation day for the 2008 USA election would have been US$25 billion which is larger than the GDP of many countries. It is also difficult to see how a simpler proposal could even be applied to markets.

4

Bias, Misinformation, and the Democratic System

In the works of many of the new democratic sceptics, public deliberation is depicted as anything but informed, reasonable, or considered. Instead, we find a picture of the average citizen as dominated by political bias and motivated reasoning, and as being too wrapped up in their partisan identity to have any concern for the truth.[1] On these views, democratic citizens are little different from political 'sports fans', 'playing up evidence that makes their team look better and their rivals look bad', irrespective of its accuracy or reliability.[2] Their partisan biases and propensity for motivated reasoning are said to amount to 'hooligan characteristics', and the more that citizens engage with politics the more of a hooligan they become.[3] While this image of the average citizen is popular among democracy's most ardent critics, it has also increasingly entered mainstream discourse. Following the 2016 US presidential election and UK Brexit referendum, fears that politics is becoming awash with 'fake news' and misinformation have become widespread, and the blame is often laid at the feet of democratic citizens. Rather than considering political information in an impartial and reasonable manner, citizens are said to be accepting any false and misleading claim, as long as it supports their favourite political team.

This conception of democratic citizens, and the seeming prevalence of misinformation in contemporary politics, sits uneasily with the image of a democratic system painted in the previous chapter. How can an active public sphere be thought to gather the information relevant to political problems, if it is dominated by the partisan biases and social prejudices of citizens? As mentioned in the last chapter, I am alert to the fact that any deliberative system, and any democratic public sphere, will involve imperfections. They

---

[1] Brennan (2016a); Achen and Bartels (2017); Somin (2016); Bell (2016).
[2] Somin (2016, p. 79).
[3] Brennan (2016a, p. 41).

Intelligent Democracy. Jonathan Benson, Oxford University Press. © Oxford University Press 2024.
DOI: 10.1093/oso/9780197767283.003.0005

BIAS, MISINFORMATION, AND THE DEMOCRATIC SYSTEM   97

will not involve flawless deliberators nor will they only produce consistent and reliable claims to knowledge. After all, democratic debate will include the claims of NASA and the IPCC, but also climate deniers and flat earthers. To remain epistemically functional, then, a deliberative system must not only be able to gather information as argued in the previous chapter but must also be able to weed out the reliable from the unreliable. To be an intelligent system it must be able to evaluate, as well as acquire, information. If the new sceptics are correct that democracy is filled with citizens who are no different from political hooligans, then it seems unlikely that it will possess this epistemic ability.

While evaluating information is a necessary epistemic task for any political institution, it has received less attention among epistemic and deliberative democrats than the ability to gather or pool information. In fact, I will argue in this chapter that many prominent approaches to democratic theory offer little in helping us understand how democracy can determine the reliability of politically relevant information. Privileging impersonal forms of reasoning about truth, these approaches fail to recognize that the truth-value of much political information cannot be directly determined through public deliberation. Politics often requires knowledge which cannot be understood, verified, or even expressed by all deliberators, and as a result cannot possibly have its truth-value discovered by a deliberative process. Assessments of political information, I will argue, must therefore be primarily concerned with the trustworthiness of actors and institutions. When we cannot directly determine the truth of a claim, we are faced with a choice of whether to trust those who make it. If a deliberative system is to function epistemically, then, it must involve not only impersonal forms of reasoning about truth, but also appeals to trust.

The first part of the chapter is mostly theoretical, and is aimed at showing that the problem of evaluating political information is really a problem of determining trustworthiness. The second part then returns to the new democratic sceptics and their claims about hopelessly biased citizens. While on their view citizens will only ever trust that information which reaffirms their existing prejudices, I survey recent empirical research and argue that the evidence that democratic debate is dominated by bias is far less definitive than the sceptics would have us believe. In fact, much research supports the idea that democratic deliberation can help reduce forms of bias and motivated reasoning. The chapter therefore ends by considering how a democratic system can be best structured to do this and I identify another important

98　INTELLIGENT DEMOCRACY

division of epistemic labour within such a system. While the burden of gathering relevant information falls mostly on the open and unstructured public space, the burden of evaluating information falls mostly on the formal and structured institutions which allow for transmissions between public and empowered spaces. It is therefore only through taking a systemic approach, and looking at the interaction of its different spaces, that we can find a reply to the critiques of the sceptics and understand how democracy can both gather and evaluate information. Understanding democracy's intelligence again requires a systemic perspective.

Failing to Find the Truth

The previous chapter highlighted how the openness and undirected nature of a democratic public sphere is important to its epistemic value. Empowered institutions cannot possibly be aware of all the knowledge relevant to social decisions, and an overly directed public space will therefore fail to gather certain kinds of information. If left mostly undirected, however, public space institutions can search out and discover that knowledge they see as most valuable. While its openness can therefore produce benefits, the structure of the democratic public sphere can also introduce many flaws and imperfections into a deliberative system. If public space is undirected, for instance, then institutions will be free to organize themselves as they wish. While one institution may select members based on relevant expertise and training, another may employ nonexperts without technical know-how. Competence will therefore be spread unevenly across the different institutions of an open and undirected public sphere. Some of these bodies may also bring their own interests and biases which can influence the way they gather and communicate information. Although some institutions will be more impartial, others—like business associations or unions—will have vested interests in presenting their claims in certain ways or in drawing certain conclusions.

Given an uneven distribution of competence and interest, the reliability of the claims produced by public space institutions will vary significantly. A deliberative system will include the rigorous scientific claims of NASA and the IPCC, but also those of climate denial groups and the flat earth society. There is also no reason to think that voice will necessarily correlate with the reliability of claims in an unstructured public sphere. Well-funded groups can have greater access to the means of communication purely because of their economic resources, and irrespective of their competence. The ability to amplify claims will not therefore depend solely on their reliability.[4] So while the unstructured and undirected nature of public space is crucial to its ability to discover and gather information, this brief survey should be enough to recognize that it will also produce many imperfections. The information which emerges from any realistic public space cannot be taken as given, and a functional deliberative system must therefore have the ability to evaluate or filter knowledge claims in terms of their reliability. If it lacks this ability, and false knowledge claims pass from public space into the decisions of empowered institutions, then a democratic system will be unlikely to produce good decisions in respect of the common good.

How, then, should deliberators in such a system evaluate the quality of knowledge claims? According to one influential form of deliberative democracy, knowledge claims should be evaluated through a process of impersonal reasoning, and this approach has been endorsed by some leading epistemic democrats.[5] Sometimes referred to as Type 1 theories, such approaches emphasize logical argument and believe deliberation should exclude or minimize appeals to rhetoric or emotions. The 'first and most important characteristic' of deliberative democracy is therefore 'its reason-giving requirement.'[6] Deliberators are 'required to state their reasons for advancing proposals', and the reason they give should be *impersonal*.[7] They should not appeal to speakers or individuals, but rather to the value of the abstract propositions under discussion. Deliberation is therefore concerned with whether there are 'inherently' good reasons for supporting one claim over another—reasons which 'could convince anyone irrespective of time and space.'[8]

This focus on impersonal reason is often justified in terms of autonomy. Deliberators should 'attempt to convince each other that there are inherently good reasons' for an action, because their interlocutors are 'autonomous agents whose capacity for rational judgement must be respected.'[9] Providing reasons therefore treats them as 'autonomous agents' rather than merely

---

[4] Even if voice and competence are evenly distributed, an unstructured public space would still produce conflicting knowledge claims due to the different ways information can be analysed and aggregated. Two research centres may, in good faith, believe that the available evidence leads in different direction simply due to the techniques, theories, or normative assumptions they employ.

[5] Bächtiger, Niemeyer, Neblo, Steenbergen, and Steiner (2010); Landemore (2013b, p. 94).

[6] Gutmann and Thompson (2009, p. 3).

[7] Habermas (1975, p. 108).

[8] Habermas (1994, p. 52).

[9] Chambers (1996, pp. 99–100).

100   INTELLIGENT DEMOCRACY

'objects of legislation'.[10] This link with autonomy is closely connected to the classical distinction between reason and power.[11] While people may exercise their power to coerce others to support their ends, reason supplies an impersonal force of persuasion. Reasons convince others not as a result of the authority or position of the speaker, but through the force of those reasons themselves. They offer a force of persuasion independent of any individual or institutional power because they appeal to abstract propositions as opposed to persons. Deliberation based on impersonal reason therefore involves only 'non-coercive persuasion' which gives protection against 'manipulation and domination'.[12] It involves 'no force except that of the better argument'.[13]

While the focus on impersonal reason over rhetoric is often based on concerns for autonomy, it also has an epistemic appeal. The validity of the claims a deliberator makes is not determined by their position, power, or authority, but rather by whether there are inherently good reasons to support those claims. The truth or falsity of a statement should therefore be seen as independent of whether it is expressed by a commoner or a king. A consideration of persons therefore risks leading deliberation astray as it allows social positions and relationships of power to come to influence one's assessment of the truth, and distracts us from the inherent strength of the arguments being made. An epistemically rigorous form of deliberation would therefore subject all claims, whether they be to moral rightness or to empirical truth, to a critical process of impersonal reasoning. Discussion within a deliberative system should then be primarily concerned with the content of the knowledge claims produced by actors in the public sphere. It should consider these claims abstractly, and use standards of accuracy, consistency, and correctness to determine if there are inherently good reasons to accept them as true. Those knowledge claims which are determined as having high truth-values would then be accepted by deliberators and could come to influence empowered democratic decisions, while those determined as having low truth-values would be rejected.[14]

While Type 1 theories have been influential in democratic theory and among some epistemic democrats, this approach would fail to evaluate much of the knowledge relevant to political decisions. This is not simply because

---

[10] Gutmann and Thompson (2009, p. 3)

[11] O'Neill (2002).

[12] Chambers (1996, p. 152).

[13] Habermas (1975, p. 108).

[14] Some absolute threshold of quality may also have to be met. It is possible that the knowledge claims with the highest relative trust-value will still be of too low to be useful for decision-making.

BIAS, MISINFORMATION, AND THE DEMOCRATIC SYSTEM   101

of the cognitive limitations facing deliberators—although such issues may arise—but rather a deeper problem with the nature of the knowledge relevant to social decision-making. The issue facing these approaches is that much of this knowledge is either *specialized, tacit,* or *situated,* and cannot therefore have its truth-value discovered by public deliberation.[15]

Consider *specialized knowledge,* the key feature of which is that it is only produced by, and accessible to, those with very particular training and experience. The field of climatology, for example, is made up of several specialized subdisciplines including atmospheric science, earth science, oceanography, and biogeochemistry. To evaluate the truth of the claims produced by climatology requires a working understanding of these subdisciplines, their research methods, technical vocabulary and assumptions, standards of proof, and the current state of their research literatures. A claim about the mean global temperature over the next fifty years, for instance, is based on alternative climate models, and determining its reliability requires an understanding of the statistical methods and physical assumptions upon which these models are based. Such an understanding, however, is not even possessed by those with training in other scientific fields, let alone those in the democratic system who lack any scientific expertise. Specialized knowledge is also not confined to the natural sciences. It can be found in the social sciences, as well as among lawyers, accountants, environmental managers, or civil servants, all of whom have their own vocabularies and practices which require training and experience to understand.

There is not, of course, a simple binary between knowledge which is either nonspecialized and accessible, or specialized and inaccessible. Instead, there will likely be a spectrum between two polls. Climatology would be an example of highly specialized knowledge which is opaque to outsiders, while knowledge of different voting systems may not be common knowledge but is still accessible to most nonexperts with some reasonable investment of time and effort. The problem for Type 1 approaches to deliberation, however, is that the knowledge relevant to social decisions includes knowledge which is on the highly specialized side of the spectrum. Fields of environmental science, medical science, law, public health, epidemiology, economics, and political science can all produce information crucial to understanding certain social problems and their solutions. To evaluate their truth-value

---

[15] I discussed the issue of tacit knowledge and deliberation in a previous paper in *Politics, Philosophy and Economics.* See Benson (2019a).

102 INTELLIGENT DEMOCRACY

through impersonal reason, however, often requires an understanding of the methods, assumptions, vocabulary, and state of the art of these fields, which only a small minority with special training can possess. Importantly, this is not a problem of individual intelligence on the part of citizens, but rather the fact that no person can possibly be experienced in all areas of specialized knowledge. It therefore affects experts confronted with claims outside of their field, as well as lay citizens.

Thomas Christiano, however, has argued that specialized knowledge can be communicated through a deliberative system because there are overlapping areas of understanding.[16] If 'P knows about intellectual disciplines a, b, and c, and Q knows about disciplines b, c, and d', then the areas of overlapping understanding allows 'Q to understand some of a because P can translate the ideas of a into b and c'. Chains of overlapping understanding can therefore allow specialized knowledge to be translated throughout the system. The first issue with this solution is that there is no guarantee that these chains can connect all or even most deliberators. There may, for instance, be no chain of overlapping understanding which links a medical scientist to an economist to a civil servant, to a local resident. Secondly, translating specialized knowledge into the language of another discipline, so it can be understood, does not provide the skill needed to evaluate its truth-value. A talented popular science writer may be able to explain a debate in quantum physics to nonspecialists, but this is a long way from allowing nonspecialists to effectively evaluate the positions in that debate. Chains of overlapping understanding do not necessarily allow others to evaluate knowledge claims, then, as this requires a higher order of training and experience. The truth-value of specialized knowledge claims will not therefore be discovered in a deliberative system based on impersonal reasoning, as the reasons supporting them can only be understood by a small portion of deliberators.

The second form of knowledge which is problematic for Type 1 approaches is *tacit knowledge,* which is embodied in practical skills and know-how.[17] Unlike explicit knowledge, which is abstract and can be stated linguistically or statistically, tacit knowledge is contained within particular social practices, and can only be learned through participation within them. It cannot,

---

[16] Christiano (2012, p. 38).

[17] I follow Michael Polanyi (2013) in distinguishing tacit from explicit knowledge. This distinction has similarities to Gilbert Ryle's (1945) distinction between 'knowledge what' and 'knowledge how', Michael Oakeshott's (1991) distinction between 'technique' and 'practical' knowledge, and James Scott's (1998) use of the concept of 'metis' which includes tacit forms of knowledge. Polanyi's distinction was also taken up by Hayek (1978).

BIAS, MISINFORMATION, AND THE DEMOCRATIC SYSTEM   103

therefore, be easily expressed even by those who possess it. Michael Polanyi, for instance, points to our ability to recognize a face among thousands of others despite our inability to explain exactly how or why we are able to do so, as an example of tacit knowledge.[18] Perhaps a better example is our inability to fully articulate and explain all the rules of grammar and language which we abide by in our everyday conversations, or the knowledge required for many occupations, which cannot be learnt by reading a manual, but rather requires participation in the occupation itself.

The relevance of tacit bodies of knowledge for social and political decisions is often recognized.[19] Work on environmental governance, for instance, has pointed to how the practical knowledge of on-the-spot managers and local communities can greatly inform decision-making.[20] A large and detailed understanding of an ecosystem can be learnt through extended time living and interacting within it, and such practical understandings can allow people to recognize important but subtle changes or emergent properties within ecosystems, and even make reliable predictions. When individuals are called upon to explain how they do these things, however, they are often unable to fully articulate it.[21] These forms of tacit knowledge are often important to policymaking when explicit scientific knowledge is unavailable or incomplete, or when such knowledge is too general to be confidently applied to a context-specific decision. It should also be recognized, however, that scientific knowledge also has a critical tacit component. A scientist's ability to derive conclusions from large bodies of data, for instance, involves a practical component which cannot be expressed propositionally or taught to a student in a lecture or book. Instead, such skills are developed through engaging in the practices of science itself.

---

[18] Polanyi (2015).

[19] This has often come from a wider range of political positions. Hayek (1978), for instance, believed tacit knowledge undermined economic central planning as it could not be communicated in propositional or statistical form, and therefore that it favoured market mechanisms which left decisions to individuals. Scott (1998) similarly saw such knowledge as undermining of state planning but pointed to its utilization by local communities rather than markets. Oakeshott (1991), alternatively, argued that such knowledge gives us reason to support traditional political elites who had experience in the practice of politics.

[20] Fazey, Fazey, and Fazey (2005); Fazey, Fazey, Salisbury, Lindenmayer, and Dovers (2006); Raymond et al. (2010).

[21] As this example demonstrates, the tacit knowledge relevant to political decision-makers is not confined to a political elite but is much more widespread. A recognition of the need for tacit practical knowledge does not therefore lead to the acceptance of an elitist politics of the kind Oakeshott defended.

104 INTELLIGENT DEMOCRACY

Those with politically relevant tacit knowledge are therefore likely to include, among others, environmental managers, scientists, civil servants, care workers, street level bureaucrats, police officers, and community organizers. The reason such knowledge presents a problem for impersonal forms of deliberation, however, is that it points to a large body of knowledge which cannot be expressed linguistically. Deliberation involves a verbal form of communication which requires that all reasons must be communicated in propositions. The reasons supporting tacit knowledge claims simply cannot be offered up in verbal deliberation.[22] While the truth-value of specialized knowledge claims could not be determined because the reasoning supporting it could not be understood by all deliberators, the truth of tacit knowledge cannot be determined because the reasons supporting it cannot be expressed. As Polanyi succinctly put it, the existence of tacit knowledge entails that we 'know more than we can tell'.[23]

Of course, deliberation may be able to make certain kinds of tacit knowledge explicit. Through conversation and argument, the assumptions and foundations of certain claims can come to be articulated when they were previously left nonexplicit. This has, for instance, been found to be the case for environmental managers who through conversation with each other can articulate more of their knowledge than they could alone.[24] This is not, however, a workable solution for all the tacit knowledge in a deliberative system. Firstly, there are some forms of practical knowledge, such as how to ride a bike, which may have an irreducible tacit component.[25] Secondly, and perhaps more significantly, some forms of practical knowledge may simply be too complex to be fully articulated. It may be conceptually possible, for instance, to express all the rules of language and grammar, but this does not mean that I will be able to do so through conversation with others. Similarly, an environmental manager may not be able to fully propositionalize their knowledge of a complex ecosystem, even if it is conceptually possible for them to do so. Impersonal deliberation will therefore fail to discover the truth of tacit knowledge claims, as the reason supporting them will often be inexpressible.

A third and final form of knowledge which will evade evaluation by Type 1 deliberation is *situated knowledge*. This knowledge is not specialized in the

---

[22] Benson (2019a); Pennington (2003).
[23] Polanyi (1997, p. 136).
[24] Fazey et al. (2005); Fazey, Proust, Newell, Johnson, and Fazery (2006).
[25] Ryle (1945).

BIAS, MISINFORMATION, AND THE DEMOCRATIC SYSTEM 105

sense that it requires certain training to understand, nor is it tacit in the sense that it cannot be put into propositional form. Rather, it is situated in the sense that its truth is only known to certain individuals or groups given their particular position and is often difficult to verify by third parties.[26] The best example of this kind of knowledge is the reports of eyewitnesses or affected parties who, whether in a courtroom or a policy committee, often have relevant information for solving a given problem. As David Hume argued, 'there is no species of reasoning more common, more useful, and even necessary to human life, than that which is derived from the testimony of men and the reports of eyewitnesses and spectators'.[27] The trouble, however, is that we are often at a loss when it comes to directly evaluating the truth-value of these reports, at least in the practical world of politics.

Consider, for instance, an individual citizen who testifies that rising crime levels have left them with feelings of anxiety and stress, or that they are too scared to go outside at night. In such a case, other deliberators are often simply at a loss when it comes to evaluating the truth of these claims. Short of putting sensors on the person's head, others will struggle to verify the feelings of anxiety, stress, or fear, and short of monitoring all of this person's activities, they will struggle to verify how often they leave their home. Similarly, if a care worker claims that after a hospital reform, they have had less time to spend with patients, and since the reform is recent there is no independent research on the topic, it will be difficult for others to verify the truth of their statements. While these kinds of claims are common to political debate, and often the means by which the experience of affected parties is expressed, it is often difficult for third parties to directly evaluate their truth-value. This is, of course, not true of all eyewitness reports. If a witness in an environmental policy committee claims that they have health condition x as a result of pollutant y, but it is known through rigorous scientific studies that y simply cannot cause x, then their claim can be falsified. Unlike specialized and tacit knowledge which cannot be evaluated due to some necessary feature, situated knowledge presents a more practical problem. The issue is not that the truth-value of the reports of witnesses and affected parties cannot in principle be evaluated by all deliberators, but that in the practical world of

---

[26] I therefore use the term situated knowledge differently to Anderson (2006), who uses it to refer to what I have called local knowledge (following Hayek). While much local knowledge is also a form of situated knowledge, this is not necessarily the case as there are some claims to local knowledge which can be easily verified by third parties.

[27] Hume (2007, p. xiv). For a wider discussion of the importance of trust in testimony, see Coady (1994).

106 INTELLIGENT DEMOCRACY

politics there often is no independent evidence to help a third party evaluate the situated knowledge claims of eyewitnesses or affected parties. In these common cases, the truth-value of situated knowledge will go undetermined by a process of public deliberation based on impersonal reasoning.

Trust in the Deliberative System

A deliberative system based on impersonal forms of deliberation will fail to be epistemically functional, as it will struggle to evaluate much of the information relevant to political problems. It would therefore lack an epistemic ability important to the intelligence of any system. I will argue in this section, however, that this problem can be overcome if we expand the forms of reason seen as legitimate in deliberation. While many deliberative democrats have already moved away from a narrow focus on impersonal reason to consider the inclusion of things such as emotions and self-interest, I claim that an epistemically functional deliberative system must also include reasoning about trust.[28] When we cannot directly determine the truth of a claim, we are forced to rely on judgements of trust when choosing what to believe. Deliberation must therefore include reasons which apply to sources of knowledge claims and to the *ethos* of a speaker, alongside impersonal forms of reason.[29]

Impersonal forms of reasoning focus on first-order considerations about the content of knowledge claims and attempt to directly determine their validity. That is, they try to discover if there are inherently good reasons to support the truth-value of a knowledge claim, something which is often not possible when knowledge is specialized, tacit, or situated. A trust-based approach, alternatively, does not focus on the content of claims but rather makes second-order considerations about the sources of these claims.[30] It looks at whether individuals and institutions possess qualities which make them a trustworthy source of information. Do they, for instance, have the expertise or position to know what they claim to know, and do they have the character or incentives to suggest they will communicate this knowledge truthfully? If they do then we can accept what they are claiming as true, and if not, we can reject it. What is important about these second-order considerations

---

[28] Bächtiger et al. (2010); Mansbridge et al. (2010).

[29] Consideration of the character of a speaker were important considerations in Aristotelian or classical accounts of deliberation alongside reason and emotions. See Remer (2008); Yack (2006).

[30] The distinction between first and second-order considerations is based on Anderson (2011).

BIAS, MISINFORMATION, AND THE DEMOCRATIC SYSTEM 107

is that they require one to consider the characteristics of individuals and institutions rather than the content of their claims. They are distinct from impersonal forms of reasoning as they attend not to abstract propositions but to the ethos of speakers. As John O'Neill puts it, evaluations of trust 'attend to persons, not propositions'.[31]

This focus on persons will appear problematic from the perspective of Type 1 theories.[32] On these views we should be principally concerned with the truth-value of the claims made in public deliberation, and the characteristics of speakers will offer only distractions from considerations of truth. After all, whether a claim is made by a commoner or a king should have no bearing on the truth of that claim. This view, however, does not recognize that there is a relationship between truth and trust. As Neil Manson and Onora O'Neill argue, in 'placing trust in others' truth-claims, we aim to place it where 'their words accurately match the way the world is (or comes to be) and to refuse it where their words do not accurately match the way the world is (or comes to be)'.[33] If someone is evaluated to be trustworthy, then this provides us with good reason to accept what she is saying as true. In other words, trust is a proxy for truth. Type 1 theorists may still worry that a consideration of speakers will only introduce opportunities for relationships of power to corrode deliberation. However, judgements of trust should be based on the epistemic authority of a speaker rather than their social or political authority. While it would be problematic to trust the claims of your boss simply because they have social authority over you, trusting their claims because they have years of experience in the field is not. Similarly, we may choose to trust a commoner over a king, if we have good reason to think they are more of an epistemic authority on a particular topic. Appeals to epistemic authority do not necessarily distract us from a concern for truth, but rather allow us to track the truth of claims through the proxy of trust.

It is exactly this truth-tracking nature of trust which makes it an indispensable concern of democratic deliberation. Although the content of many political knowledge claims cannot be understood, expressed, or verified by all deliberators, judgements of trust move our attention away from their content to towards their source. One does not therefore need to engage with the content of specialized, tacit, and situated knowledge in order to evaluate its

[31] O'Neill (2002, p. 256).
[32] Type 1 deliberative democrats may also reject concerns for trust and ethos as inconsistent with autonomy. For a reply to such objections, see Benson (2019a).
[33] Manson and O'Neill (2007, p. 160).

108   INTELLIGENT DEMOCRACY

reliability. Consider a nondeliberative example of a doctor and patient. When a doctor diagnoses a patient and recommends a treatment, she draws on specialized knowledge acquired through her medical training, as well as the tacit knowledge she acquired through practising medicine itself. The doctor draws from knowledge which she cannot fully explain or express to her nonexpert patient and the patient is therefore in no position to evaluate the truth-value of the doctor's claims. Similarly, to make her diagnosis, the doctor often requires the situated knowledge of her patient, such as the patient's claims about the kind and intensity of pain they experience, or the length of time they have experienced symptoms. The doctor and patient relationship therefore involves knowledge which is specialized, tacit and situated.

The reason that this relationship does not break down, however, is that the parties accept claims based on trust. Although the patient cannot always understand the knowledge and reasons supporting the doctor's diagnosis and recommendations, they are able to accept and act on such knowledge by trusting the doctor. By considering the doctor's expertise and honesty, the patient is able to accept their knowledge claims based without needing to directly evaluate their content. Likewise, if the doctor trusts the claims of the patient, she can base her diagnosis on the patient's reports without directly evaluating their truth-value. Knowledge is therefore communicated and evaluated in this relationship through the proxy of trust. Conversely, communication within this relationship can also break down if trust is absent. If the patient is a known hypochondriac, for instance, then it can become difficult for the doctor to make an accurate diagnosis, while a patient may reject a doctor's prescriptions if they feel the doctor has an economic interest in offering a certain treatment over others.

The same logic can be applied to the communication and evaluation of knowledge in a deliberative system. Public space institutions will make knowledge claims based on specialized, tacit, and situated knowledge, which cannot be directly evaluated by most deliberators. Deliberators can, however, engage in second-order considerations about the trustworthiness of these knowledge sources. They could look at whether they should accept the claims of a climatologist, for instance, given their relevant expertise and training, with no need to fully understand the very specialist knowledge on which these claims are based. Similarly, they can consider whether or not to reject the knowledge claims of a fossil fuel employee not based on an impersonal evaluation of the content of their claims, but given their lack of expertise or economic interest. Changing the subject of deliberation from truth

BIAS, MISINFORMATION, AND THE DEMOCRATIC SYSTEM   109

to trust, therefore, allows a deliberative system to evaluate claims based on specialized, tacit, and situated knowledge. It shifts the focus from first-order considerations of the truth of propositions, to second-order considerations about the trustworthiness of speakers, and therefore removes the need to evaluate the content of knowledge claims. For a deliberative system to remain epistemically functional, then, deliberative democrats must expand the forms of reason they see as legitimate to include evaluations of the *ethos* of speakers.

On what basis, however, are deliberators in a deliberative system meant to determine the trustworthiness of individuals and institutions? Evaluations of trustworthiness are often considered to involve two main factors: *expertise* and *honesty*.[34] Expertise considers the extent to which an individual or institution can be expected to have the knowledge they claim to have, while honesty refers to the extent to which they can be expected to express this knowledge truthfully. For Aristotle these factors represented the epistemic and the normative components of trustworthiness, and he thought both were essential.[35] Someone who is ignorant but honest, or knowledgeable but dishonest, cannot be trusted. Evaluating trust within a deliberative system will therefore most commonly involve a consideration of the different social markers of expertise and honesty.

Expertise requires one to consider whether individuals and institutions have relevant experience or training in a particular area. This is most straightforward in respect to formal scientific knowledge, where formal qualifications or positions are normally an effective marker of knowledge. These include relevant PhDs, academic appointments and honours, and having a track record of publishing in respected journals. At the institutional level we can also look at the qualifications of those an institution includes and promotes. The fact that a scientific body or think tank determines their membership in line with experience and training, for instance, is a marker of its expertise. In less formal domains of knowledge these formal markers may be absent. A campaign group, for instance, may have knowledge of the effectiveness of local public services, but no qualification to prove it. In these cases, an individual's or group's experience in a particular social or

---

[34] Anderson (2011); Collins and Evans (2008); Fricker (2007); Goldman (2001); Guerrero (2016); Sperber et al. (2010). Goldman (2001) argues that dialogical ability is a relevant factor in determining expertise, but it is excluded here due to problems of distinguishing the true argumentative ability from rhetorical skill or showmanship.

[35] Aristotle (1991).

110 INTELLIGENT DEMOCRACY

professional practice may therefore be the main marker of their expertise. Long-term participation in a campaign group is an indicator of knowledge about local public services, just as a long-term career in environmental management is an indicator of knowledge about a particular ecosystem. Similarly, the inclusivity of informal institutions will be important. A campaign group or movement which includes only the wealthy and more educated, for instance, may be deemed not to have knowledge about the general impact of a social problem. In other situations, an organization's exclusiveness may be a marker of certain kinds of expertise. A women's movement, for example, may possess knowledge of the gendered effects of a social problem which may be marginalized by other parts of the deliberative system. The extent and form of a group's inclusivity can therefore also be an indicator of expertise.

Assessing honesty will similarly involve a consideration of certain social markers, such as those indicating an individual's or institution's character, intentions, and incentives. Do they, for instance, have any vested interests in presenting information in certain ways, do they have any explicitly partisan motivations, or do they have a history of making biased, misleading, or false claims? A research institute concerned with the effects of acid rain, for instance, may be evaluated as having expertise if it is made up of appropriately qualified individuals. However, the research institute may be found untrustworthy if their funding comes exclusively from big polluting industries or if they have a record of misusing data or plagiarizing the work of others. Key indicators of honesty therefore include evidence of vested interests, partisan bias, or track-records of malpractice. Another marker is whether an individual or organization is open and transparent. Do they, for instance, commit themselves to processes of scrutiny, such as peer-review or public debate, or do they make their evidence and data publicly available?

Elizabeth Anderson refers to these latter issues as an actor's 'epistemic responsibility', which she defines as the extent to which they are willing to hold themselves 'accountable to the demands for justification made by the community of inquirers'.[36] Adhering to higher standards of transparency and being accepting and responsive to scrutiny are markers of honesty, while secrecy and evasion of criticism are markers of dishonesty.[37] Epistemic responsibility can also include the way individuals and institutions respond

[36] Anderson (2011).

[37] Anderson considers epistemic responsibility to be a separate category from honesty, although I see the former as simply evidence for the latter. If a person is transparent and open to criticism, for instance, then that is evidence that they are honest.

BIAS, MISINFORMATION, AND THE DEMOCRATIC SYSTEM 111

to mistakes or errors. The extent to which a newspaper offers corrections, retractions, and apologies, for instance, is important to our judgement of their honesty. An actor's epistemic responsibility will be particularly important when they have a clear political leaning. Unlike parts of the natural sciences which may be more neutral, organizations such as think tanks, business associations, or unions may have a clear political or partisan association which raises the issue of bias. An important factor in considering their honesty will therefore be whether they are open about their political views, associations, and sources of funding; whether they allow their claims, methods, and data to be scrutinized by others with alternative political views; and whether they are responsive to their critics. A political association is not therefore a disqualifying factor in the assessment of trust.[38] However, it is important that these associations are transparent so that deliberators can assess trustworthiness clearly.

Evaluating political information based on trust will therefore commonly involve attending to the different social markers of expertise and honesty. These second-order considerations can allow information to be assessed in a democratic deliberative system, even if it cannot be understood, expressed, or verified by all deliberators. Of course, accepting claims based on trust is not foolproof. The social markers of expertise and honesty are not unfailing, and trusting another always involves a risk that one's trust will be misplaced. In fact, without this risk, trust would not be required in the first place. If I knew for sure that what someone was saying was true, then I would not need to trust them. Trust is exactly required when there is uncertainty. The work of the new democratic sceptics, however, suggests that citizens are dominated by bias and motivated reasoning, and that they will therefore be poor judges of political information and the trustworthiness of its sources. Such sceptics therefore point to the possibility of systematic errors in a deliberative system's evaluations of trust.

A Politics of Bias and Misinformation

When we talk of the ability of a deliberative system to evaluate information, we are really talking about the ability of the system to determine the

---

[38] In fact, when it comes to the normative issues of politics an actor's partisan identification may actually be a reliable way of assessing trustworthiness (Rini, 2017).

112 INTELLIGENT DEMOCRACY

trustworthiness of different individuals and institutions which claim to be sources of political knowledge. For many of the new democratic sceptics, however, most democratic citizens are simply not up to this task. According to them, the average citizen is little different from a political sports fan, rooting for their favourite team. They are said to act like 'hooligans' who 'play up evidence that makes their team look better and their rivals look bad', irrespective of its accuracy or reliability.[39] Far from evaluating the trustworthiness of alternative knowledge sources in an impartial and dispassionate manner, on this view democratic citizens are highly motivated political reasoners who will accept any information as long as it is favourable to their side. A democracy filled with these political sports fans will therefore be a bad judge of politically relevant information and will look more like a machine for generating misinformation than a reliable epistemic system.

In defending this view of democracy, the new sceptics often lean on research from social and cognitive psychology on motivated reasoning. Connected to many cognitive biases—such as confirmation bias, desirability bias, and in-group bias—motivated reasoning occurs when an individual looks to accept what they want to be true rather than what is true. In the political domain in particular, individuals are said to engage in 'identity-protective cognition', according to which people's political identities have a strong bearing on their acceptance of new information.[40] Conservatives and liberals, for instance, will assess information relating to climate change differently, because one will see it as a threat to their sense of political identity and their conception of a preferred social order. On this account of political psychology, then, democratic citizens are unlikely to evaluate information based on the trustworthiness of its source. They will instead seek out information which confirms their pre-existing political views and identities, while rejecting out of hand any information which contradicts them. Like hooligan sports fans, their main concern will be to find that evidence which allows their side to win and to look most favourable.

Consistent with these accounts, empirical work finds that people with differing partisan identifications tend to accept different kinds of information, with people generally more likely to accept information which is consistent with their pre-existing political views.[41] They are also found to resist

---

[39] Brennan (2016a, p. 41); Somin (2016, p. 79).
[40] Kahan (2012).
[41] Pereira, Van Bavel, and Harris (2023); Strickland, Taber, and, Lodge (2011); Vegetti and Mancosu (2020).

BIAS, MISINFORMATION, AND THE DEMOCRATIC SYSTEM   113

factual corrections which they challenge their incorrect partisan beliefs.[42] An extreme and often discussed example of these findings is known as 'the backfire effect', according to which individuals actually become more confident in their false partisan beliefs after receiving factual corrections. For instance, indicating that President Obama is a Christian or that the Affordable Care Act did not involve 'death panels' was found to lead Republicans to more strongly believe that Obama was a Muslim and that such panels existed.[43]

These partisan accounts of political psychology are commonly endorsed by many of the new democratic sceptics and are cited as evidence of the hooligan nature of the average citizen. They have also started to receive wider attention as popular explanations for the prevalence of fake news and other forms of misinformation.[44] Fake news refers to blatantly fabricated information which presents itself as credible news content, but without the normal procedural standards of news, and has attracted much concern particularly following their perceived prevalence during the 2016 US presidential election and UK Brexit referendum.[45] Those concerned include not only those already sceptical of the quality of democratic discourse, but also many deliberative democrats, who see this misinformation as a threat to public debate.[46] According to partisan accounts of psychology, however, the acceptance and sharing of this content is not only unsurprising, but to be expected. Placing more value in their political identities than in concerns for truth or trustworthiness, citizens are thought to be only too happy to endorse fake news which favours their political team.

If these depictions of democratic citizens are correct, a democratic system will therefore fail to effectively evaluate political information in terms of the trustworthiness of its sources. In fact, encouraging more deliberation in a political system may even make problems of misinformation worse. According to one influential theory of motivated reasoning, known as Motivated System 2 Reasoning, greater reflection only increases an individual's propensity to engage in self-justification.[47] This is because the more an individual engages in explicit reflection, the more they are able to find reasons to accept only that information which supports their political team. Some empirical work,

---

[42] Nyhan and Reifler (2010); Nyhan, Reifler, and Ubel (2013).
[43] Berinsky (2017); Nyhan et al. (2013).
[44] Kahan (2017); Taub (2017); The Economist (2018); Van Bavel and Pereira (2018).
[45] Lazer et al. (2018); S. Ryan (2017) Allcott and Gentzkow (2017); Persily (2017).
[46] Chambers (2021); Curato, Hammond, and Min (2019); Dryzek et al. (2017); Forestal (2021); McKay and Tenove (2020).
[47] Kahan (2012).

114 INTELLIGENT DEMOCRACY

for instance, has found that increased analytical thinking leads to greater political polarization over topics such as gun control and climate change.[48] A democratic system which promotes deliberation over politically relevant information may therefore even increase the spread of fake news and other forms of misinformation, as it only encourages citizens to engage in greater motivated reasoning.

Not So Biased After All

The possibility that partisan biases may adversely influence a deliberative democratic system must be recognized. While such a system can absorb individual or sporadic errors in the evaluation of trust, the presence of systematic errors could undermine its ability to acquire accurate information. Such errors are particularly worrisome in the case of transmissions from public to empowered space, as failures in this part of the system could lead to misinformation influencing binding democratic decisions. If democratic citizens are hardwired partisan reasoners, however, then systematic errors are to be expected. While the new democratic sceptics therefore point to important problems, the evidence supporting their views is much more controversial than they would have us believe. A survey of the empirical research coming from social psychology actually gives us reasons to question the influence of bias at the individual level, as well as its effects at the level of group deliberation.

Starting at the individual level, much evidence for partisan bias comes from the association between political identification and the acceptance of new information. It is important to see, however, that partisan bias is not the only possible explanation for this association. Alternative accounts have, for instance, drawn on a Bayesian view where the rational acceptance of information should be based on one's prior beliefs. This therefore suggests that it is only rational for those with differing political views to accept different information, as their prior beliefs are also likely to differ. Such reasoning has, for instance, been shown to explain differing beliefs over things such as climate change.[49] One cannot therefore simply move from an association between one's political positions and the acceptance of new information, to the claim

---

[48] Kahan, Peters, Dawson, and Slovic (2017); Kahan et al. (2012).
[49] Gerber and Green (1999); Tappin, Pennycook, and Rand (2020); Druckman and McGrath (2019).

BIAS, MISINFORMATION, AND THE DEMOCRATIC SYSTEM 115

that individuals are necessarily biased. Furthermore, empirical work has also found that partisanship does not necessarily remove a concern for the truth, as the democratic sceptics often imply. For instance, it has been found that people are more likely to accept true news stories which conflict with their political views than untrue news stories which support them.[50] Similarly, recent studies have failed to replicate the backfire effect, finding that people are generally willing to revise even their partisan beliefs when provided with factual corrections.[51]

One large and recent study directly questions the strong influence of political commitments on the evaluation of information and its sources. Thomas Wood and Ethan Potter conducted five studies involving more than 10,000 subjects and tested how individuals evaluated information from partisan and nonpartisan sources.[52] Not only did this research observe no evidence of the backfire effect, but participants all along the ideological spectrum were found to be capable of following factual corrections and changing their beliefs across the fifty-two political issues they considered. This was true even in those cases where the information directly challenged their prior political commitments. In fact, this study supports the ability of individuals to make effective trust evaluations even in the presence of strong political factors. Subjects were presented with false statements made by partisan political figures, such as Donald Trump or Hillary Clinton, in a mock news article which also gave a factual correction by an independent source, such as a government statistical body. The subjects were therefore given the task of determining which of these two knowledge sources to trust. The result was that participants generally accepted the claims of the independent sources rather than the partisan political source, even when the latter shared their political identity. They did not therefore act like political sports fans rooting for their team no matter what, but rather judged independent sources to be more trustworthy and changed their beliefs accordingly. As the researchers of this study concluded, citizens 'choose just the facts, ahead of their ideology'.[53]

If citizens are willing to put the facts before their partisanship, however, then what explains the emergence of political misinformation, such as fake news? In addressing this question it is firstly important to recognize that

---

[50] Bago, Rand, and Pennycook (2020); Pennycook et al. (2021); Pennycook and Rand (2019).
[51] Guess and Coppock (2020).
[52] Wood and Porter (2019).
[53] Wood and Porter (2019, p. 143).

116 INTELLIGENT DEMOCRACY

the phenomenon of fake news is much less widespread than often feared.[54] Instead, this kind of content tends to be consumed and shared by only a small fraction of the population. One study of fake news on Twitter, for instance, found that just 1% of users in their sample were responsible for 75% of all links to fake news sites, and 11% were responsible for *all* such links.[55] This compared to the top 1% of real news sharers who accounted for only 30% of real news sources. It is simply not the case that democratic citizens on a whole are falling victim to these forms of misinformation, as the views of the new democratic sceptics would suggest.

Secondly, those who do consume and share fake news may not be doing so as a result of their political bias, but rather a lack of attention and reflection. Gordon Pennycook and David Rand, for instance, argue that the consumption of fake news is better explained by classical views of reasoning rather than accounts of partisan bias.[56] Classical views follow dual-process theories in distinguishing between System 1 forms of reasoning which are more automatic, immediate and intuitive, and System 2 reasoning which is more controlled, deliberate, and considered.[57] When someone takes a decision slowly and carefully, they are engaged in System 2 processing, and they would be engaged in System 1 if they make it quickly and unreflectively. While the Motivated System 2 account mentioned in the previous section suggests that System 2 processes only involve greater self-justification, the classical view sees it as correcting for the mistakes of the faster and less deliberate System 1. In other words, while we may make mistakes when acting automatically and intuitively, we can perform much better when taking our time and being more considered. On classical accounts, then, fake news is not so much a problem of political bias and motivated reasoning, but rather of a lack of reflection and deliberation.

Consistent with this view, it has been found that people who are more reflective are less likely to accept fake news and a more likely to distinguish reliable content from that which is biased and misleading.[58] Asking people to rate the accuracy of news headlines is also found to reduce the sharing

---

[54] Grinberg, Joseph, Friedland, Swire-Thompson, and Lazer (2019); Guess, Nagler, and Tucker (2019).

[55] Osmundsen, Bor, Vahlstrup, Bechmann, and Petersen (2021).

[56] Pennycook and Rand (2019, 2021).

[57] Kahneman (2011).

[58] Bago et al. (2020); Bronstein, Pennycook, Bear, Rand, and Cannon (2019); Pehlivanoglu et al. (2021); Pennycook and Rand (2019); Ross, Rand, and Pennycook (2021). Belief in fake news is also associated with other factors linked with analytical thinking, such as dogmatism, religious fundamentalism, and openness to bullshit. See Bronstein et al. (2019); Pennycook and Rand (2020).

of false content, while altering individual levels of deliberation (e.g. through time constraints) finds a link between more deliberation and a lower belief in false but not true news. Analytical thinking has similarly been linked to a reduction in the intention to share fake and highly partisan content through both survey experiments and sharing behaviour on Twitter.[59] According to this research, the small number who do accept and share fake news stories may be doing so not because they are hopelessly biased reasoners, but because they are not giving it enough consideration. It also suggests that if they were to engage in greater reflection, then they would be much more discerning in respect to the content they choose to believe and share.

None of this is to say that the empirical evidence is definitive, or that there is no evidence supportive of the view that partisan bias can have an influence on democratic citizens. As it stands, however, the evidence is far from conclusive or uncontroversial as the new democratic sceptics often present it. In fact, much of the evidence we do have does not clearly point in favour of the partisan account of psychology, and instead supports classical views where individuals have an ability to distinguish false from true information when they are engaged and reflective. There is also evidence that the spread of much discussed forms of misinformation, such as fake news, are far less prevalent than often feared, and less than the work of the new democratic sceptics would suggest. The vast majority of democratic citizens therefore appear to be effectively avoiding this content. The claim of the new democratic sceptics that democratic citizens are ruled by political biases and prejudices is therefore far from uncontroversial, and we have a range of evidence suggesting that individual citizens can be trusted to evaluate political information.

The Benefits of Group Reasoning

While the last section questioned the evidence supporting strong claims about the political biases of democratic citizens, it could not rule out their influence at the individual level. Another important question, however, is the extent to which any individual biases affect group deliberation. Studies pointing to such biases tend to be conducted at the individual level, looking at how individuals accept or reject information. There is, however, a growing

---

[59] Arechar et al. (2022); Mosleh, Pennycock, Arechar, and Rand (2021); Pennycook, McPhetres, Zhang, Lu, and Rand (2020); Ross et al. (2021).

118   INTELLIGENT DEMOCRACY

literature which suggests humans are much better group reasoners than they are individual reasoners.[60] According to these views, it is wrong to see human reasoning as an individual process, as it is best understood as a process conducted between groups. While cognitive biases may lead to errors at the individual level, this literature suggests bias can be corrected by engaging in reasoning with others. Firstly, deliberating with others can encourage greater reflection, prompting individuals to engage in more considered System 2 forms of cognition. Secondly, group deliberation may allow those with opposing biases to correct one another, so that they reason more effectively as a group than as individuals. As John Rawls put it, 'the exchange of opinion with others checks our partiality and widens our perspectives' as it makes us 'see things from their standpoint' and recognize 'the limits of our version.'[61]

The connection between these understandings of group reasoning and the views of deliberative democrats has been recognized.[62] Deliberative democrats reject views of democracy based on the aggregation of isolated individual preferences, and instead focus on the importance of public deliberation between citizens. They therefore endorse a conception of democracy based on group forms of reasoning where bias and cognitive failures are less likely. Rather than being undermined by claims of individual level partisan bias, then, deliberative democracy may in fact be the solution to such problems by encouraging group forms of political reasoning. Both lab experiments with citizen deliberation and the experience of deliberative mini-publics, such as deliberative polls and citizen assemblies, offer support for this idea. There is now a significant amount of evidence that the influence of individual biases can be reduced through deliberation, as well as a good understanding of the kinds of deliberation which can do this most effectively.

Empirical work on mini-publics, for instance, finds that people's prior positions do not completely dominate their acceptance of reasons, and that people do change their positions as a result of deliberation, mostly due to being introduced to new information.[63] These results are often attributed to the diversity of deliberators, as this increases the range of reasons and opinions which are heard, and allows deliberators to correct one another's political biases. While a left-wing individual and a right-wing individual may have their own sets of biases, it is by engaging with each other that they can

[60] Mercier and Sperber (2011, 2017); Sloman (2017); Sperber et al. (2010).
[61] Rawls (1971, p. 358).
[62] Chambers (2018); Landemore and Mercier (2010, 2012).
[63] Fishkin (2011); Goodin and Niemeyer (2003); Luskin, Fishkin, and Jowell (2002).

BIAS, MISINFORMATION, AND THE DEMOCRATIC SYSTEM   119

check one another. In fact, these biases can make deliberation productive, as each individual will be more alert to the argumentative flaws and confirmation biases of others. For this reason, politically diverse deliberation is less likely to result in the acceptance of dominant group positions than deliberation between politically homogeneous groups.[64]

Factors other than diversity are also likely to play an important role in controlling bias. Empathy within the group, for instance, can make people less likely to see things through only their own viewpoint and more likely to accept views and information which contradict their political commitments.[65] Forms of deliberation which include storytelling or the testimony of effective parties could therefore be effective at counteracting bias by means of empathy. Repeated deliberations may reduce the influence of bias as well, as it makes it easier for deliberators to accept new information and even change their position on a topic.[66] Laboratory experiments have also found that clear rules and the presence of moderators can reduce the influence of pre-existing political positions, even among like-minded groups.[67] Diversity among deliberators may not, therefore, be necessary to control partisan bias as long as other structural features are in place.

These forms of group deliberation may also help to reduce social biases based on gender, ethnicity, or class. Although less discussed among the new democratic sceptics, Lynn Sanders and Miranda Fricker have argued that a person's social position can significantly affect how people evaluate their credibility or authority as a source of knowledge.[68] Prejudicial stereotypes about certain groups can explicitly or implicitly affect how the source is perceived, leading to marginalized groups being seen as less credible than the socially privileged. A female scientist's claims about the effects of a public health policy may, for instance, be seen as less authoritative than the same claims made by an equally well qualified male scientist. The influence of prejudice represents a 'deliberative wrong' or 'epistemic injustice' to those whose testimony is undermined, but they also undermine the epistemic ability of a system which must evaluate information via trust.[69] Rather than tracking the truth, trust judgements would instead track social privilege.

---

[64] Chappell (2011); Fishkin (2018); Fishkin and Luskin (2005); Luskin, Sood, Fishkin, and Hahn (2022).

[65] Morrell (2014).

[66] Mackie (2006).

[67] Grönlund, Herne, and Setälä (2015).

[68] Sanders (1997); Fricker (2007).

[69] Owen and Smith (2015); Fricker (2007). One may argue that these problems are greater if deliberation considers trust and therefore characteristics of persons and not just propositions. Bias and

120 INTELLIGENT DEMOCRACY

While unlikely to be eradicated, there is again evidence suggesting that certain kinds of group deliberation can help reduce these social biases. While Sanders points to studies finding the presence of these dynamics in criminal juries, other forms of deliberation have had more success. A study of deliberative polls, for instance, found that that there was no particular pattern or movement towards the positions taken by advantaged or privileged groups, compared to those of the underprivileged.[70] In half the cases studied, deliberators moved in the direction of the positions of advantaged groups (white, male, and educated), and in in the other half they moved away from them. Another study of twenty-one deliberative polls produced similar results, finding 'only irregular and feeble' attitude shifts towards the views of the socially advantaged.[71] James Fishkin argues that these results are again explained by the structure of deliberative polls which, compared to criminal juries, involve trained moderators, place less emphasis on consensus, and include more diversity among deliberators.[72] Disproportionately including minority groups may also help to counter social biases, although according to this work on deliberative polls, this may not be necessary.[73]

While the new democratic sceptics focus on the individual level biases of democratic citizens, this runs counter to an understanding of human reasoning as group reasoning. The evidence from studies of citizen deliberation lend support to the idea that individual level partisan biases do not necessarily influence group level deliberation, and that collective reasoning can work to counter their influence. It is by reasoning with others that we check our partiality, consider issues from alternative perspectives, and therefore defend against the cognitive failures from which we may suffer when reasoning alone. This evidence does not, however, support group deliberation without caveats. Instead, it suggests that the structure of group deliberation is important to the successful controlling of individual biases. Structural features of

prejudice, however, can be powerful and yet unconscious, and therefore the credibility of a speaker may be significantly undermined even though deliberators aim to evaluate only the content of their claims. In fact, making the evaluation of sources explicit may even lower their effect as they force deliberators to consciously evaluate a person's credibility and question otherwise unconsidered judgements.

[70] Siu (2009).
[71] Luskin et al. (2022, p. 1222).
[72] Fishkin (1997, 2011).
[73] Oversampling certain groups may, however, have other nonepistemic benefits such as symbolic value for those historically marginalized, changing perceptions of minority groups, and helping to correct past injustices. See Mansbridge (1999b).

deliberation such as group diversity, clear rules, and moderation therefore play an important part in achieving the benefits of group reasoning.

Error Correction in the Deliberative System

While the new democratic sceptics place much emphasis on problems of political bias, the last two sections have questioned their prevalence at the individual level, as well as the extent to which individual bias is likely to adversely affect collective deliberation. As we saw, however, the kind and form of deliberation is likely to play an important factor in controlling for the impact of bias. The evidence suggests that individuals alone may be more prone to bias than those in groups, and that unstructured groups may be more prone than structured groups with clear rules and diversity. The influence of bias may therefore be less significant than the new sceptics often claim, but the likelihood that trust evaluations will be free of biases will vary depending on the form that deliberation takes. On a unitary view of democracy this would introduce a dilemma, requiring one to choose between structured and unstructured deliberation. A systemic perspective, alternatively, allows us to consider many sites of deliberation taking different forms and connecting in ways which benefit each other.

Deliberative features such as clear rules, group diversity, and moderation tend only to be possible on small scales and within more formal institutions. The open deliberations of public space, alternatively, are subject only to vary broad rules of freedom of speech and associations, as well as general norms of civility. Certain components or institutions within public space can, of course, involve highly structured deliberation. Scientific organizations often have rigorous procedures for discussion; newspapers can have clearly defined editorial standards; and many social movements have developed strong norms governing their members' deliberations, allowing time for all to speak. While individual components may therefore produce areas for structured deliberation, the public sphere as a whole cannot possibly be subject to rules ensuring group diversity or equal speaking time. It involves the interactions of large numbers of institutions and individuals which cannot be tightly controlled. In fact, even if it were possible, enforcing such a structure on public space would be epistemically unwise given that its openness and undirected nature is part of what makes it effective at discovering and gathering knowledge.

122 INTELLIGENT DEMOCRACY

Not all of a deliberative system will involve the forms of deliberation best suited to controlling bias, and certain parts of the system will therefore be more open to their influence than others. This is not necessarily a problem, however, as long as one takes a systemic view. As we have seen in the previous chapter, many of the advantages of deliberative systems come from their ability to create divisions of epistemic labour which distribute tasks and responsibilities across different components of the system. Although some areas of the system may be less able to control for bias, others may compensate for these deficits. One component of the deliberative system which is important in this respect are transmissions. Transmissions are important because they determine which of the knowledge claims produced by the public sphere can come to influence the binding decisions of empowered space. While errors in transmissions pose significant risks to the epistemic functioning of deliberative systems, this also happens to be an area where greater amounts of formal deliberation can take place. Advisory committees, commissions, parliamentary committees, public consultations, citizen juries, and public inquiries all allow for more controlled and structured deliberations which are less open to bias. Even more informal mechanisms of transmission, such as lobbying or even protest, require information emanating from the public space to pass into more empowered institutions, which again allows for more structured forms of deliberation. The transmission of information to empowered space can play a role in filtering the knowledge claims emerging from the public sphere, correcting for the errors produced by bias, and determining which claims should come to influence binding democratic decisions.

The parts of the deliberative system where errors in trust evaluations create the most problems are therefore also the parts of the system which can be best organized to prevent such errors. Before knowledge claims come to influence the binding decisions of empowered institutions, they pass through transmissions which can offer more structured forms of evaluation. This does not mean that all forms of bias will be eradicated in these parts of the system, nor does it mean that other parts, such as public space, will inevitably be riddled with bias and error. As we have seen, many studies question the strength of political bias at the level of the individual or in nondiverse deliberative groups, and public space can also include many sites of formal deliberation. However, it does mean that transmissions and empowered spaces will be less susceptible to errors in trust evaluations due to political and social

BIAS, MISINFORMATION, AND THE DEMOCRATIC SYSTEM 123

bias, and that they can therefore play an important role as an epistemic filter within the wider deliberative system.

The fact that not all deliberation within the system can be structured is not, therefore, necessarily problematic. To the contrary, as long as there is a functional division of labour it can be an advantage. We do not judge a democratic system by looking only at the performance of one of its areas or components in isolation, but rather by looking at how different parts of the system work together in a division of labour. We can look at how the different parts of the system provide their own advantages, and how they can compensate or correct for the deficiencies of others. One of the reasons public space can be effective at gathering dispersed knowledge is that it is open and undirected, giving institutions the autonomy they need to search out and aggregate information which is otherwise inaccessible. While this openness is productive to knowledge-gathering, it creates weaknesses for knowledge evaluation as it leaves individuals more susceptible to the forms of bias in the evaluation of trust. These latter faults can, however, be compensated for by other parts of the system. While the structured nature of transmissions and empowered space limit their capacity to gather information, it increases their ability to evaluate it. Claims produced in public space therefore pass through a more structured and rigorous process of deliberation before they can come to influence binding democratic decisions. They pass through an epistemic filter which can help correct the errors produced by more open spheres of deliberation (see Figure 4.1).

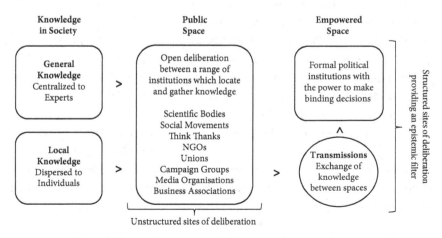

Figure 4.1 Knowledge evaluation in a deliberative democratic system

124   INTELLIGENT DEMOCRACY

It is the interaction between these different sites, then, which allows the deliberative system to both discover and gather information, as well as evaluating it before it enters empowered democratic decision-making. A division of labour therefore exists not only within the public sphere as highlighted in the previous chapter, but also between the different spaces of a deliberative democratic system. The open and unstructured nature of public spaces allows them to locate and gather diverse forms of knowledge, while the structured nature of transmissions and empowered space allows them to evaluate knowledge claims more effectively. This epistemic view of a deliberative system is therefore analogous to Habermas's formulation of a deliberative democracy.[74] Instead of public opinion being laundered and clarified as it moves from the open public sphere to more rigorous forms of justification at the centre, however, it is trust claims which are subject to more demanding forms of deliberation as they approach empowered space. It is the two spaces working together which then produces a system which has the ability to both gather and evaluate information, two abilities which these spaces could not possess when considered on their own.

Knowledge Evaluation in the Deliberative System

Deliberative systems are imperfect. They will produce knowledge claims with varying levels of reliability, and they will include rigorous scientific expertise alongside bad faith incompetence. Such systems, however, have the ability to limit or manage their imperfections. Deliberation, when it includes reasons which appeal to the trustworthiness of persons and institutions, has the ability to filter and evaluate the claims produced by public space. Although public space may be open, unstructured, or even wild, other parts of the system can provide more rigorous deliberation which can more accurately determine the information which should influence empowered democratic decisions. It is the divisions of labour between different parts of the deliberative system, then, which allow it to act as both a system for knowledge gathering and a system for knowledge evaluation. This chapter has therefore again used the systemic perspective to provide a greater understanding of democracy's epistemic abilities, and in doing so also replied to the new democratic sceptics who claim that democracy will be ruled by

---

[74] Habermas (2006a, 2015).

bias, motivated reasoning, and misinformation. It shows that the intelligence of democracy includes the ability to evaluate, as well as gather, information. The next chapter turns to another set of concerns coming from the new democratic scepticism. It will consider another variant of this scepticism which, like the Hayekian one, is deeply critical of the centralized nature of democratic politics. Rather than advocating for a system of free markets, however, these sceptics claim that we need to make politics itself more like the market.

5
Polycentricity For and Against Democracy

I started my defence of the intelligence of democracy by engaging with those new democratic sceptics who wish to reduce the role of politics altogether. By shrinking the overly centralized democratic state, Hayekian sceptics wish to replace much of politics with the free market. There is another brand of democratic scepticism, however, which is also highly critical of collective forms of democracy. These new sceptics do not appeal to Hayek and the free market, but to the work of Elenore and Vincent Ostrom and the idea of polycentricity. Rather than a single democratic authority, these new sceptics argue for more diverse systems of governance where there is competition between a mix of private, public, and third-sector institutions. Both Europe and the United States have seen a significant growth in the privatization of public services, quasi-independent agencies and public-private partnerships, and the outsourcing of goods provision to charities, NGOs, and regimes of private governance. These sceptics claim that further reforms of these kinds could help produce a more polycentric and more intelligent form of governance compared to the monopolistic democratic state. Like those who favour the market, these new sceptics do not reject democracy outright, as they see democratic institutions playing a role within this competitive regime. They do, however, wish to dethrone the democratic state, reducing it to just another actor in a wider polycentric network.

A key motivation for this polycentric view is to make politics 'more like the market'. By increasing the range of public, private, and third-sector actors, citizens are given the freedom to 'vote with their feet' as they enter and exit institutional alternatives. Citizens can act like consumers as they pick and choose their preferred providers of goods, services, and regulations. A polycentric form of governance is therefore said to allow for greater forms of experimentation and self-regulation than could be achieved by a monocentric democratic state. By trying to make politics more like the market, however, I will argue that advocates of this polycentric approach end up replicating the market's epistemic problems in the political arena. By relying on individual exit as a bottom-up mechanism for institutional selection, these polycentric

Intelligent Democracy. Jonathan Benson, Oxford University Press. © Oxford University Press 2024.
DOI: 10.1093/oso/9780197767283.003.0006

approaches confront the same incentive and informational problems Chapter 2 identified as afflicting markets. Rather than merely repeating the problems discussed in previous chapters, however, I look to expand the information problem by showing how it can affect a range of self-regarding exit decisions, and not only those which concern justice and the common good. I then argue that a priority of democracy can overcome these problems as it introduces top-down forms of institutional selection which have a capacity to monitor and evaluate alternatives. Once again, then, we find that democracy is a more intelligent second-order institution.

The first half of the chapter therefore questions the polycentric approaches offered by the democratic sceptics. The second half, alternatively, argues that prioritizing democracy does not necessarily imply the forms of monopoly and monocentricity criticized by the sceptics. While it grants democracy a privileged role among social institutions, democracy does not need to take the form of a single centralized authority. In fact, once democracy is understood in systemic terms it can be seen to possess all the defining features of polycentrism as well as its main advantages. Although the concept of polycentricity is not often discussed by deliberative democrats, I argue that the systems perspective offers a highly polycentric understanding of democratic politics which looks very different from the centralized administrative state which is so often the target of the sceptics' disapproval. I then go on to consider how a deliberative democratic system can be arranged to best realize its polycentric benefits and endorse greater forms of political and democratic decentralization. This chapter therefore rejects the interpretation of polycentricity advocated by democratic sceptics but ends by using the concept to better understand the intelligence of democracy and the epistemic benefits of deliberative systems. By increasing political decentralization, democracy can expand its ability to engage in experimentation and self-regulation.

The Polycentric Critique of Democracy

The concept of polycentricity was originally proposed by Michael Polanyi but has received a revival of interest after being taken up and further developed by Elenore and Vincent Ostrom, the former being awarded the Nobel Prize in Economics in 2009.[1] Although the idea has an intuitive appeal, it is

---

[1] Polanyi (2013); Ostrom (1972, 2009, 2010); Ostrom and Ostrom (1965); Ostrom, Tiebout, and Warren (1961).

128 INTELLIGENT DEMOCRACY

often difficult to define due to the range of fields which have adopted it, and the range of institutions which have been labelled as polycentric. In one of the clearest conceptualizations of the concept, Paul Dragos Aligica and Vlad Tarko argue that there are three necessary features of any polycentric system:

(1) *A Multiplicity of Decision-Making Centres*: there are a number of distinct but overlapping sites of authority which compete and interact with each other.
(2) *An Overarching System of Rules*: there is a universal set of rules determining how sites of authority interact, their respective jurisdictions, and the boundaries of the system.
(3) *Spontaneous Orders*: orders and regularities emerge from interaction and competition between decision centres which are not the product of intentional design.[2]

The first feature is the presence of multiple decision-centres and contrasts polycentric governance with monocentric governance involving a single source of authority. So while an administrative state is monocentric in implementing a single policy for the whole of society, a polycentric governance system disperses authority across 'many centres of decision-making which are formally independent of each other'.[3] Goods are not therefore provided through a single body, nor is there a single regulatory framework. Instead, multiple but overlapping authorities provide alternative goods and regulations which can be opted in and out of by individuals. Governance systems do not possess either one or many decision centres, of course, and there is therefore a broad spectrum between monocentricity and polycentricity. More polycentric systems include a wider range of decision centres, whether they be state and government agencies, private companies, nonprofit organizations, public-private partnerships, or voluntary associations.

Decision centres in a polycentric system are not, however, completely free to do as they wish. Instead, they are subject to the second feature of polycentricity, which is an overarching system of rules. Although these rules may be open to revision, it is the presence of these rules which distinguish polycentricity from unordered anarchy. Such rules govern the terms of interaction and competition between different authorities and their respective

---

[2] Aligica and Tarko (2012).
[3] Ostrom et al. (1961, p. 831).

POLYCENTRICITY FOR AND AGAINST DEMOCRACY   129

jurisdictions, as well as the boundaries of the polycentric system itself. System 'insiders' can be defined as those actors subject to the general rules of the system, while 'outsiders' are classed as those not subject to them.[4] These overarching rules do not predetermine the interactions of the different decision centres, however, and this makes space for the third feature of polycentricity; spontaneous orders. Such orders or regularities are 'spontaneous' in the sense that they emerge from the unplanned processes of competition and cooperation between actors rather than being the outcome of some intentional designer of the system. As Adam Ferguson put it, they are a result of human action but not human design.[5] Polycentric systems can therefore possess forms of self-regulation and self-correction which do not require outside intervention.

The concept of polycentricity has been used to describe and understand a range of institutional systems, from markets to organized science. The Ostroms, for instance, were particularly interested in metropolitan governance. They claimed that the coordination of actors in metropolitan areas does not always 'rely exclusively upon bureaucratic command structures controlled by chief executives' but rather 'interorganizational arrangements' that created 'self-regulating tendencies'.[6] They also argued that more polycentric metropolitan areas were more efficient than those which were centralized and hierarchically structured. A number of scholars, most notably Paul Dragos Aligica and his colleagues, have argued that such findings should lead us to question the monopoly on governance which is often granted to the democratic state.[7] While the work of the Ostroms allows for many interpretations and has been utilized by those on both the political left and right, these authors come from a more classically liberal perspective and argue that this work should lead us to give polycentricity priority over democracy.[8]

Adopting Jack Knight and James Johnson's distinction between first- and second-order institutions, Aligica argues that the second-order task of monitoring and adapting society's institutional mix should be assigned to

---

[4] Aligica and Tarko (2012, pp. 254–256).

[5] Ferguson (1996). Ferguson was often quoted by Hayek (2011, 2013) in his discussion of market orders.

[6] Ostrom and Ostrom (1965, pp. 135–136).

[7] Aligica (2014, 2018); Aligica and Boettke (2009); Aligica et al. (2019).

[8] I restrict my focus in the first half of the chapter to those who use polycentricity to make a critique of the democratic state and who are often classically liberal or libertarian in their political commitments. For an example of how Ostrom's work can also be utilized by the political left, see Wall (2018).

130 INTELLIGENT DEMOCRACY

a polycentric process of competition between public authorities and a host of other institutional forms, from private firms and charities, to community groups and commons arrangements.[9] On this priority of polycentricity view the respective role of these different institutions is not determined by a higher democratic authority but rather by an open and ongoing process of competition between these decision-making units. Questions of whether a good should be provided by a private company or a government agency should therefore be answered through competition and negotiation between these institutional models. Similarly, there would not be a single regulatory framework for areas of health or finance determined democratically, but many competing sets of regulations which can be opted in and out of as people wish, and competition would then select the best on offer.

Public or state institutions can still play a role in providing goods, services, and regulations on this view.[10] Like the free-market sceptics considered earlier in the book, and unlike the epistocrats and political meritocrats to come, these sceptics do not therefore reject democracy outright. They do, however, wish to restrict its power and scope. Public institutions should not be seen as the only providers, nor should they be given any kind of priority. Instead, emphasis is placed on nonhierarchical and competitive relationships, and on the restriction of centralized bodies, including those which are democratic. While these centralized bodies may be needed to help create and maintain the system of rules necessary for a polycentric system to function, the second-order task of institutional selection is primarily determined by competition between this system's different actors. A priority of polycentricity therefore takes a unique 'bottom-up perspective' on the task of institutional selection which sees individual choice and association as the 'main normative guidelines', and 'requires us to shift focus from the modern administrative state as the unique and pre-eminent form of public administration'.[11] Selection between first-order institutions is therefore predominantly decided by an open competitive process on this view, while a priority

---

[9] Polycentricity is a very broad concept and the idea of a priority of polycentricity can allow for approaches different from Aligica's. Markets, for instance, are often described as polycentric, so one interpretation of a priority of polycentricity is the free-market positions discussed in Chapters 2 and 3. I will also endorse my own approach to polycentricity based on deliberative systems later in this chapter, showing that it can also play a role in a priority of democracy.

[10] The state may also be needed to resolve certain market failures on this view, but only where government failures are likely to be smaller, and where there is no civil society or third-sector alternative. These are conditions which are believed not to be often met. See Aligica et al. (2019, p. 21).

[11] Aligica et al. (2019, pp. 21, 63).

Table 5.1 A Priority of Democracy and Polycentricity

	A Priority of Democracy	A Priority of Polycentricity
Second-Order	Democracy	Polycentric Competition (with little democratic or political interference)
First-Order	Institutional Diversity (including arrangements which are competitive)	Institutional Diversity

of democracy would give democratic institutions a significant power to intervene and select a winner (see Table 5.1).

A priority of polycentricity is thought to possess two key benefits: *self-regulation* and *experimentation*. Both of these advantages are directly linked to the key features of polycentricity and are therefore said to show its distinct advantages over the more democratic approach. The first advantage is eloquently explained by Elinor Ostrom:

> While all institutions are subject to takeover by opportunistic individuals and to the potential for perverse dynamics, a political system that has multiple centers of power at differing scales provides more opportunity for citizens and their officials to innovate and to intervene so as to correct maldistributions of authority and outcomes. Thus, polycentric systems are more likely than monocentric systems to provide incentives leading to self-organized, self-corrective institutional change.[12]

The problem with monocentric systems is that they put all their eggs in one basket. If a single centre of authority is corrupted or makes mistakes, then the whole system must bear the costs of their bad decisions. If authority is dispersed, however, then corruption and mistakes in one unit of authority do not necessarily spread to others, preserving the wider system. Decision centres can then learn from the mistakes of others, but also take advantage of these mistakes by providing the goods and services no longer available. Individuals can then use their exit rights to shift to these institutions allowing the system to spontaneously correct over time. This dispersal of

[12] Ostrom (1998).

132 INTELLIGENT DEMOCRACY

authority therefore allows for self-correction. It can also help prevent errors from occurring in the first place by creating incentives for monitoring and checking others. In public-private partnerships, for instance, each party in the relationship has an interest in the other performing their duties effectively, and therefore each has an incentive to check the other and punish any malpractice. Polycentric systems therefore create self-regulating tendencies which can prevent and correct errors by individual components.

The second advantage of polycentricity is that it increases the scope for experimentation. While the past two chapters have focused on the importance of knowledge gathering, we cannot assume decision-makers can have complete information. It is therefore crucial that new information can be produced over time about how different institutional arrangements work in practice and under what conditions. As Knight and Johnson argue, a central task of any second-order institution is therefore to maintain an 'experimental environment'.[13] Aligica, however, argues that 'one can hardly think of a better arena for experimentation than polycentricity'.[14] Unlike a monocentric system where a central authority implements a single solution for the whole system, polycentric orders can implement and test many more experiments at any one time. A range of private, public, and third-sector institutions are allowed to test out alternative solutions simultaneously, therefore increasing the scope of experimentation and knowledge production, as well as innovation.[15] Because decision centres have the opportunity to 'go their own way', polycentric systems provide a more effective environment for entrepreneurial activity. Actors can therefore invent and test out novel solutions to social problems without needing to have them agreed to by some central authority.

If it is the multiplicity of decision centres in a polycentric system which allows for greater experimentation, it is bottom-up competition and individual exit which allows for its benefits to be realized. Running many experiments is one thing, but some kind of selection mechanism is required if a system is to learn from these experiments and produce better solutions over time. For Aligica and his colleagues, this mechanism should be individual exit. As decision centres offer alternative solutions, individuals move between them in order to find the best on offer. They learn about the alternatives available to them and 'vote with their feet' as they move between institutions.

[13] Knight and Johnson (2011, pp. 12–19).
[14] Aligica (2014, p. 66).
[15] Aligica (2018); Aligica et al. (2019); Boettke and Coyne (2009).

POLYCENTRICITY FOR AND AGAINST DEMOCRACY   133

If a private firm offers better transportation than the public provider, or an association of banks provide more effective self-regulation than state regulation, then individuals can make use of their exit rights. Monocentric governance, alternatively, restricts exit opportunities by granting authority to a single institution and therefore makes voice the sole mechanism for selection. A priority of polycentricity therefore advocates for limiting the democratic state in order to make greater room for more private and third-sector organizations, and greater space for bottom-up selection via individual exit.

The Limits of Bottom-Up Selection

The focus on competition and individual exit among advocates of polycentricity is often motivated by a desire to 'make politics more like the market'. By allowing private and third-sector institutions to compete alongside public agencies, polycentric approaches allow citizens to 'vote with their feet' just as consumers select between firms in the marketplace. While this is done with the hope of replicating the benefits of markets in the political arena, it can just as easily replicate their failures. A key problem facing those who favour a priority of polycentricity is this: that by relying on individual exit they end up reproducing many of the epistemic problems which we have already found to afflict markets.

On both the polycentric and the free-market view, the task of monitoring, evaluating, and selecting alternatives is predominantly left to single individuals. Just as it is the role of the individual consumer in the market to select between competing firms and their products, it is the task of individual citizens in a polycentric system to select between the goods, services, and regulations offered by a range of private, public, and third-sector alternatives.[16] As we have seen, this focus on individual exit is thought to be crucial to realizing many of the benefits of polycentricity, but it also introduces the same epistemic problems faced by markets when it comes to second-order decisions which must account for concerns of justice and the common good. For bottom-up selection to be effective at promoting the common good, individuals must be able to evaluate competing institutions

---

[16] To the extent that it relies on individual decision-makers, this polycentric approach is also similar to elections. I will focus on the comparison with markets because supporters of polycentricity often explicitly aim to replicate market mechanisms, and because both approaches focus on individual exit rather than voting.

134   INTELLIGENT DEMOCRACY

in terms of their effect on a large number of distant others. They need to be able to recognize when an experiment in the provision of a good, service, or regulation has been a success or a failure in terms of the broader public interest, and not only their own self-interest.

As Chapter 2 argued, however, individuals will often struggle to make informed decisions when they must account for other-regarding concerns. Firstly, individuals will tend to face an *incentive problem* when making such decisions, given the very small impact of their exit choices on the common good. Just as a consumer's choice to exit one private firm has minimal consequences for aggregate demand, a single citizen's choice to exit a private, public, or third-sector institution will have only minimal consequences for the wider polycentric system. This exit decision is just one vote, so to speak, among possibly millions of exit votes. Individual exit decisions therefore have a very low probability of being decisive when it comes to second-order decisions which must account for justice and the common good, and individuals will face the problem of rational ignorance. Secondly, individuals in a polycentric system will also face an *information problem*. While they may possess relevant local knowledge and learn through experience when it comes to their own self-interest, information about their own specific conditions will not reliably inform them about how alternative private, public, and third-sector institutions affect a large range of distant others. Instead, they will face a sizeable burden for information about the effect of the alternatives available to them in terms of the common good, a burden that they will have little incentive to overcome.

The focus on individual exit in the priority of polycentricity leads it to replicate the same epistemic problems as confront markets when it comes to second-order tasks. While both approaches prioritize individual exit decisions in determining a society's institutional mix, individuals will generally lack the knowledge needed to effectively evaluate alternatives in terms of other-regarding values. If exit decisions are not informed, however, then polycentric competition will not effectively select between the results of institutional experimentation, nor will these choices drive the system's self-regulating or self-correcting tendencies. As was the case with the invisible hand of the market, then, a system of polycentric competition will struggle to realize its epistemic benefits when it comes to other-regarding values concerning justice and the common good. Polycentric advocates could, of course, argue that polycentric competition best fosters the common good because it best promotes individuals' self-interested preferences. Even if the approach did best advance these preferences, and I will offer some reasons to be pessimistic below, this argument cannot ground second-order priority because it relies on a controversial conception of justice (i.e. a form of preference utilitarianism). As argued in Chapter 1, people reasonably and persistently disagree over justice and any argument for second-order priority must therefore remain neutral on this question.

Making politics more like the market, therefore, reproduces the epistemic problems of markets in the political arena. Rather than further rehearsing the discussions of previous chapters, however, I will instead use this section to expand on the information problem. So far, I have focused on how other-regarding decisions introduce particular epistemic challenges for individual decision-makers, a focus which was justified given the importance of justice and the common good to second-order tasks, and to the conception of intelligence adopted in this book. However, while other-regarding decisions certainly produce epistemic issues not confronted by most self-regarding decisions, bottom-up selection can also face challenges in respect a range of self-regarding decisions in both market and polycentric systems. That is, the information problem can extend to certain self-regarding decisions and therefore further limit the intelligence of regimes which rely primarily on individual exit.

One well recognized issue is the problem of exit costs. Even if an individual determines an alternative to be superior in terms of their self-interest, they may be limited in their ability to select this alternative if the costs of doing so are significant. This would in turn reduce the ability of bottom-up selection to push the system towards better alternatives. This problem is greatest in the case of interterritorial exit where individuals have to move between different geographical areas, and larger monetary expenses are combined with the possible loss of community and family relationships. Recognizing this, defenders of a priority of polycentricity argue that we should encourage intraterritorial forms of competition, pointing to private and third sectors as examples.[17] However, intraterritorial competition is limited in the case of public goods which must be provided geographically, and even private goods can involve significant costs of entry if they are provided by private suppliers.[18] While the problem of exit costs are important, it should also be

---

[17] Aligica et al. (2019, p. 151).They refer to the distinction between interterritorial and intraterritorial exit as the distinction between political and functional decentralization.

[18] A possible reply to this problem is to allow centralized political institutions to redistribute resources. This is the strategy of Jeffrey Friedman (2019), who argues that the state should follow a

136 INTELLIGENT DEMOCRACY

recognized that certain self-interested decisions also face an information problem similar to that facing decisions about justice and the common good.

To see this, it is useful to first consider a case where individual exit is likely to be effective. In a market for smartphones, for instance, private firms experiment with alternative solutions to our communication and other problems by providing different products. Typically, the success and failure of these products is easily observable by individual consumers, at least in terms of their own self-interest. They can see which performs faster, has the best sound, takes the best photos, or is the most aesthetically pleasing, and they can make their decisions accordingly. As Samuel DeCanio argues, it is the ability to easily observe the outcomes of the different phone designs which stops these decisions from being epistemically demanding.[19] If individual consumers could not easily observe such outcomes, then they would need to make predictions about the likely results of alternative phone designs, and this would require a significant amount of knowledge on their part. They would, for instance, need to be familiar with often very technical information about how the screens, cameras, software, and processors of different phones produce alternative outcomes. Having direct access to the outcomes themselves, however, means that consumers will not require any of this information. They can simply observe which phone produces the best image quality, for instance, and therefore do not need any knowledge of how its technical design produces this result. So, although the internal workings of these alternative smartphones are likely to be opaque to the vast majority of consumers, individuals can still make effective decisions simply by observing their results.

This example involves only private firms, but we can easily extend the principle to a polycentric system which incorporates nonprofits and public bodies. The point is that the epistemic burden facing individuals is reduced by having access to the outcomes of the alternatives available. Individuals require no further technical knowledge about the design and production of the alternatives on offer, as they have direct feedback about the outcomes of these designs. In other words, they are able to learn easily through their experience with such products and draw on the resulting local knowledge. The epistemic burden facing exit decisions will therefore be smallest and

---

version of the Rawlsian Difference principle with the aim of maximizing the exit opportunities of the worst off. For a critique of this view see Benson (2020) and for a reply see Friedman (2020).

[19] DeCanio (2014).

POLYCENTRICITY FOR AND AGAINST DEMOCRACY   137

least troubling when individuals can easily observe the outcomes of the alternatives available to them. Conversely, this suggests that the epistemic burden will be greatest and most troubling when the results of experimentation are less forthcoming. In cases where individuals cannot easily observe the results of competing alternatives, they will require a larger amount of additional information in order to evaluate and rank options. This is the case when it comes to other-regarding decisions about justice and the common good. The outcomes of alternatives in terms of the common good are not easily observable, as they concern effects on a large number of very distant others, disconnected from any one individual making their exit decisions. As a result of this disconnect, the local knowledge of individuals will be less informative, and they will require large amounts of additional information about how competing alternatives affect others.

While true of other-regarding decisions, there is also a range of self-interested decisions which create a similar problem for market and polycentric systems. Consider, for instance, decisions concerning one's personal health. The products we consume can impact our health in any number of ways due to the chemicals, toxins, and pollutants they contain, or the risks associated with their use. These impacts, however, are often not easily observable at the point of making an exit decision. There can, for example, be significant time lags or delays between the consumption of a good and any negative health effect being felt. Alternatively, the options available may only increase the background risk of health problems, or may be only one among several difficult to distinguish potential causes. Each of these complicating factors produces a disconnect between the individual making the exit decision and the potential outcomes of the alternatives available to them.[20] Just as individuals are often disconnected from the impacts of their decisions on the common good, they can be similarly disconnected from the impacts of their decisions on their own health. This disconnect is not geographical, but rather introduced by significant time lags, complex causal chains, and effects on background uncertainty. So while decisions about one's personal health are purely self-regarding, it can still be difficult to observe the outcomes of alternatives at the point of decision-making.

---

[20] I have elsewhere referred to goods possessing such a disconnect as 'low feedback goods' as it limits the feedback individuals can receive about the outcomes of their decision to select one good over another. See Benson (2019b).

138   INTELLIGENT DEMOCRACY

Even greater problems are introduced when we consider the ability of individuals to determine how their self-interest is impacted by structural risks and alternative regulatory frameworks. Take, for instance, the financial sector. Individual financial products can certainly have effects which are not easily observable at the point of decision-making, such as the results of a teaser rate on a mortgage. However, the systemic risks associated with individual banks or banking systems are even more difficult for individuals to identify. Even if one was aware that one's bank will likely combine their mortgage with others and sell it to other financial institutions, one cannot simply observe the systemic risks such a practice will produce, and the consequences these risks may have for their interests. The same is true for different regimes of financial regulation. On a polycentric view there should not only be competing financial products, but also competing public and private regulatory frameworks which individuals can move in and out of. How such regulations incentivize certain kinds of behaviour among both consumers and financial institutions, and how this can impact an individual's interests, is not, however, as self-evident as the performance of different smartphones.

Instead, many of the effects of regulatory frameworks are indirect, involve the behaviour of others, occur over long time periods, involve complex causal chains, or simply increase background risks of certain harms. Individuals cannot therefore simply observe the outcomes of alternative regulatory frameworks and make their exit choices accordingly. As the experience of the financial crisis suggests, consumers are often unaware of complex financial regulations and industry practices, the systemic risks they create, and the dire consequences this may have for their personal finances. This is also not a problem which only afflicts the financial sector. The outcomes of regulatory frameworks more generally—whether they are regulating the production of medical products, energy production, or insurance policies—produce outcomes which impact the interests of individuals in ways that cannot be immediately observed. Instead, there is a disconnect between the individuals making exit decisions and the potential outcomes of alternatives for their own self-interest.

The result of these disconnects is that individuals will face a significant burden for information. Remember that the reason why individuals do not need to understand the design of different smartphones is that they could simply observe the results of their alternative designs. If these results were not observable, then the consumer would need to understand the internal workings of each smartphone, in order to make a prediction about their

POLYCENTRICITY FOR AND AGAINST DEMOCRACY   139

possible results. This would, however, require technical knowledge and know-how which is not available to the average individual. Although this is not the case in markets for smartphones, analogous problems do confront our above examples. Given that individuals cannot easily observe the outcomes of alternative financial products or regulatory frameworks, for instance, they will instead require a significant amount of information about these alternatives and their likely effects. How do different financial products, services, and regulations work in practice, what incentives do they produce for consumers and financial institutions, and what systemic risks do they possibly contribute to? Answering these questions is likely to be as difficult for the average consumer or citizen as answering questions about how different cameras and processor designs produce better smartphones. Such questions require a significant amount of often technical information as well as an ability to draw conclusions from this information about the likely outcomes of alternatives.

When it comes to self-interested decisions such as these, then, individuals will face an information problem similar to that confronting other-regarding decisions about justice and the common good. Just as there is a separation or disconnect between the individual decision-makers and their effects on others, in these cases there is a separation or disconnect between the individual decision-maker and their effects on their own interests. In both cases, the result is that individuals cannot directly observe the results of institutional experiments, and they will therefore face an information problem. In a couple of respects, this information problem may be less damaging than that which faces decisions about other-regarding values. Firstly, while other-regarding decisions also confront the problem of rational ignorance, these self-interested decisions still provide individuals with some incentive to acquire further information. Secondly, self-interested decisions only require enough information to judge what is best for one's own interests, while decisions about justice and the common good require enough information to determine an option's impacts on the interests of and the relations between a very large number of others.

The epistemic and cognitive burden facing other-regarding exit decisions is, therefore, likely to be significantly larger in many cases. Nevertheless, the epistemic burden associated with many self-regarding decisions can still be overly burdensome even for the well-motivated, and can therefore undermine bottom-up forms of selection in both markets and polycentric systems. The size of this burden can be recognized when we consider the number

140   INTELLIGENT DEMOCRACY

of exit decisions individuals must engage with. A priority of polycentricity in particular expects individuals to select between a whole range of private and public goods, social programmes, and regulatory frameworks, many of which will require a large amount of additional information. While an individual may acquire the information needed for any one of these decisions, effectively navigating all of these choices is a task which is likely to overburden even well-motivated individuals, particularly given other restrictions on the average citizen's time and energy (working hours, care for dependants, need for leisure time, etc.). Increasing the number of decision centres in a system can, therefore, sometimes worsen the ability of a system to make good decisions. While defenders of a priority of polycentricity and markets focus on the experimental benefits of having large numbers of good providers, they fail to recognize that in many areas of social life this increases the epistemic and cognitive burden facing individuals. It increases the epistemic load associated with effectively monitoring and selecting institutional alternatives. This suggests a tension in polycentric and pro-market forms of the new democratic scepticism which want to increase the scope for institutional experimentation, while also relying predominantly on bottom-up forms of institutional selection. Increasing the number of experiments increases the epistemic and cognitive burdens placed on individuals, reducing their ability to make effective assessments of institutional alternatives, and thereby reduces the ability of bottom-up selection to realize the benefits of that very experimentation.

The Benefits of Top-Down Selection

When decisions concern only self-interested preferences, when exit costs are low, and when results of alternatives are easily observable, bottom-up mechanisms of individual exit may well be effective. They will face significant epistemic problems, however, when it comes to decisions concerning justice or the common good, and even a range of purely self-interested decisions where the results of alternatives are less forthcoming. These problems challenge the intelligence of a priority of polycentricity—as well as a priority of markets—as we cannot expect them to produce epistemic benefits if individuals cannot tell the difference between alternatives. The abilities of experimentation and self-regulation require that individuals can identify the successes and failures of first-order institutions. In a whole host of cases, including all important decisions about justice and the common good, individuals will likely lack the knowledge necessary to do this.

Where bottom-up selection and individual exit are limited, top-down forms of selection offer an alternative. While individuals in a market or polycentric system are unlikely to possess the large amount of often technical knowledge necessary to make certain kinds of decisions, we saw in Chapters 3 and 4 that acquiring such knowledge is a central ability of more collective democratic institutions. When situated within a broader deliberative system, empowered democratic bodies are able to access and evaluate much more information than individual citizens or consumers. A democratic approach which assigns second-order tasks to these more collective institutions is therefore in a much better position to make decisions not only about the common good, but also a range of decisions concerning only self-interested preferences. Such an approach would allow for forms of top-down institutional selection which are better at dealing with epistemically and cognitively burdensome decisions.

Top-down selection can take several forms. Democratic bodies can, for instance, directly mandate or prohibit certain institutional models which have been evaluated as successful or unsuccessful, or they can merely incentivize or disincentivize them through subsidies and awards. They can also focus on helping to reduce the epistemic and cognitive demands placed on individuals, allowing them to make more effective exit decisions for themselves. If the reader was not convinced in the previous section that some self-interested decisions come with a significant epistemic burden, this may well be because we currently make our decisions in highly regulated environments. More centralized institutions prohibit particularly harmful products and services, and this unburdens us of many of the most epistemically demanding work. Lisa Herzog refers to this as part of the broad 'epistemic infrastructure' which surrounds markets and which can allow individuals to make better decisions than they could with only the information provided by market prices.[21] When I walk around a supermarket, for instance, I do not need to consider all the ways each product may kill me or seriously undermine my health, as political institutions have relieved me of this cognitively demanding task through regulation. Top-down forms of selection can therefore promote better exit decisions as they allow individuals to make choices in those areas

---

[21] Herzog (2020).

142 INTELLIGENT DEMOCRACY

where they can be most effective, such as decisions about which of the safe supermarket products best meet their particular culinary preferences.

Defenders of a priority of polycentricity may object that introducing top-down selection will inevitably cut off future opportunities for experimentation, and that prioritizing democratic institutions therefore does more harm than good. If democratic institutions select the best first-order solution from those currently available and mandate this solution for the rest of the system, then this would seem to stop other decision centres from experimenting and discovering even better solutions. Hayek mounts an argument along these lines when critiquing state intervention in the market.[22] He claimed that even if the state could make the best use of the current set of solutions, its monopoly would 'prevent the emergence of more effective alternatives' into the future. This objection is strongest when considering mandates by democratic authorities. If a democratic authority provides only incentives to adopt certain alternatives, such as through the tax system, then this would not stop others from 'going their own way' if they wished. Furthermore, even when solutions are mandated, democracies allow for forms of dissent and resistance which can allow for alternatives to emerge. The resistance of 'sanctuary cities' to the national enforcement of immigration laws in many countries would be one such example.

The objection can be modified, of course, to say that while top-down selection does not stop future experimentation, it does reduce it. Taxes or subsidies, for instance, do not prohibit new innovations, but they may disincentivize them. This modified objection, however, simply highlights a trade-off between creating opportunities for future experimentation and reaping the benefits of current experimentation. I see no reason why future experimentation should always be preferred in this trade-off given that bottom-up selection may be ineffective at picking successes. More experimentation does not lead to general improvements if successes are not selected and promoted. So even if top-down forms of selection decrease future experimentation among first-order institutions, they increase the system's ability to evaluate and select from their results, and therefore increase the extent to which we can benefit from the experimental environment. In other words, top-down selection can increase the overall benefits realized from experimentation, even while decreasing the total number of experiments. This endorsement of top-down selection does not therefore reject the importance

[22] Hayek (2011, p. 377).

of experimentation. Decision-makers do not have complete information, so it is important that new knowledge can be produced through a process of trial and error. What this argument does question, however, is that bottom-up mechanisms of individual exit are always best suited to evaluating and selecting between the results of such experimentation. In a large range of cases, most significantly those which concern justice and the common good, individuals will struggle to acquire the knowledge needed to determine which institutional experiment produces the best results, and top-down selection by more knowledgeable democratic institutions is therefore likely to be more effective.

Polycentricity within Democracy

The last two sections defended democracy against the polycentric alternatives favoured by one brand of the new democratic scepticism. In the rest of this chapter, however, I will argue that this does not necessarily imply a defence of monocentrism. Although much of the polycentric critique of democracy focuses on its supposed monocentric features, this is somewhat misleading given that democracy and polycentricity are not conflicting concepts. While polycentricity concerns the number of decision centres in a system, democracy is concerned with the egalitarian nature of decisions. Whether something is egalitarian and democratic tells us nothing about the number of decision centres involved. Advocating for democracy does not therefore entail an endorsement of monocentrism.

In fact, the systemic approach to democracy I have been developing in this book possesses all of the defining features of polycentrism, and recognizing this can help improve our understanding of its epistemic value. Unitary approaches to democracy found among many deliberative and epistemic democrats invite the objections of polycentric sceptics because they focus on single democratic institutions or mechanisms. A systemic perspective, alternatively, directly rejects a monocentric understanding of democratic politics, focused as it is on the interactions of many institutions and spaces within a deliberative network. The systemic approach argues that values of inclusion, participation, and epistemic competence cannot be fully realized by just one democratic authority and must therefore be distributed across a network of different actors. Although the concept of polycentricity is not often encountered in the literature on deliberative democracy and

144 INTELLIGENT DEMOCRACY

deliberative systems, this approach is highly polycentric in its conception of democratic politics.[23] Consider, for instance, the following passage from Jane Mansbridge and her coauthors describing a deliberative democratic system:

> A system here means a set of distinguishable, differentiated, but to some degree interdependent parts, often with distributed functions and a division of labour, connected in such a way as to form a complex whole. It requires both differentiation and integration among the parts. It requires some functional division of labour, so that some parts do work that others cannot do as well. And it requires some relational interdependence, so that a change in one component will bring about changes in some others.[24]

This passage does not depict a singular democratic authority, but rather a conception of democracy which involves all the defining features of polycentrism. Firstly, deliberative systems involve multiple but overlapping decision centres and units of authority. Within empowered space, for instance, decision-making authority can be distributed vertically between local, state, national, and international bodies, as well as horizontally between executive, legislative, and judicial branches. There are also nonterritorial distributions of authority, as can be seen in the distribution of different policy areas (e.g. health, education, or environment) between government departments or agencies. Empowered space is not therefore monocentric but includes parliaments, courts, citizen juries, and bureaucratic agencies, among many others. It also does not represent the whole of the system, with public space offering an even greater range of actors. The public sphere includes 'journalists, bloggers, social movements, activists, advocates for different causes, politicians, public relations professionals, corporate spokespeople and citizens', all of whom play a role in influencing empowered decisions as well as taking certain decisions of their own.[25] The latter refers to informal decisions over such things as what should be the subject of debate or what should or should not be settled through the state.

On a systemic approach to democracy, then, 'the entire burden of decision-making and legitimacy does not fall on one forum or institution but is distributed among different components in different cases'.[26] Such a

---

[23] In Parkinson and Mansbridge's (2012) much cited collected volume on deliberative systems, for instance, the terms polycentric and polycentricity do not appear.

[24] Mansbridge et al. (2012, pp. 4–5).

[25] Stevenson and Dryzek (2014, p. 28).

[26] Mansbridge et al. (2012, p. 5).

POLYCENTRICITY FOR AND AGAINST DEMOCRACY   145

system is not anarchic, however, as these different components interact under an overarching set of rules. Formal constitutions and laws, along with informal norms and customs, govern the relationships between empowered institutions within a democratic system. These rules determine the respective jurisdictions or units of authority, their powers, who is included within them, how they relate to other units, and the boundaries of empowered space in respect to the other areas of the system. Public space institutions, alternatively, act under the rule of law and within formal rights to freedom of speech and association. They are also governed by social and cultural norms, such as general rules of civility. The institutions of both empowered and public space are not therefore free to do as they wish, as they are subject to broader sets of overarching rules.

Such rules do not wholly determine the interactions within a democratic system, however, therefore allowing for the emergence of spontaneous orders. Such orders are perhaps most recognizable in public spaces which are more unstructured and unpredictable. For instance, 'emergent decisions' can occur within such spaces as a result of the unplanned interaction of many individuals and organizations. These decisions can create new norms governing such things as the legitimate role of the state or which issues take priority on the policy agenda. They also work to produce and reproduce rules of civility and good conduct. These nonbinding decisions are not planned by any one individual or institution, but rather involve decision by 'accretion', where norms and practices change spontaneously over time as the result of many different actions.[27] Other spontaneous orders include the emergence of new organizations, communities, and associations within public space, which are not predetermined by rights of speech and association but are produced through the free interaction of individuals. Spontaneous regularities and outcomes can also occur within more structured empowered spaces. As Gus diZerega has argued, formal democratic institutions manage actors with diverse and often competing ends through a set of procedural rules.[28] These interactions between actors are not directly planned or controlled by any one designer but are rather the spontaneous outcome of a process of deliberation, bargaining, and compromise within a set of general procedural guidelines. The outcome of any democratic procedure therefore emerges as the outcome

[27] Mansbridge (1986).
[28] diZerega (1989, 2011).

146 INTELLIGENT DEMOCRACY

of individuals and organizations interacting under an overarching system of rules.

While the last section defended democracy from the forms of polycentric governance imagined by certain new democratic sceptics, it did not reject all kinds of polycentrism. We need top-down forms of selection by democratic institutions, but this does not presuppose a monocentric political authority. As long as a priority of democracy is interpreted as a priority of a democratic system, then it also possesses all the defining features of polycentricity. To endorse a systemic approach to democracy is to endorse a particular form of polycentrism.

Realizing the Polycentric Benefits of Deliberative Systems

While deliberative systems are polycentric, not all polycentric systems are born equal. Possessing the defining features of polycentrism does not necessarily entail that a deliberative system can achieve all their advantages. The question, then, is: How can a democratic system be arranged in order to best realize the benefits of experimentation and self-regulation which can come from its polycentric features? These benefits can be most readily achieved in public space. This more open part of the system involves a large and diverse range of mostly undirected institutions, which create significant opportunities for experimentation. Public space institutions are free to experiment in the ways they represent certain groups or interests, influence empowered institutions, and acquire different forms of knowledge. They can even experiment with ways of providing certain goods or services, as in the case with certain community organizations, NGOs, and social movements. Low barriers to entry in public space further increase the chances of innovation as new organizations and associations can form and try out alternatives. There are also significant opportunities for self-regulation and self-correction in this area of a democratic system. As Mansbridge and her coauthors argue:

> We expect that a highly functional deliberative system will be redundant or potentially redundant in interaction, so that when one part fails to play an important role another can fill in or evolve over time to fill in. Such a system

POLYCENTRICITY FOR AND AGAINST DEMOCRACY 147

will include checks and balances of various forms so that excesses in one part are checked by the activation of other parts of the system.[29]

If any public space institution does fail in its role, this does not necessarily affect the rest of the system as each institution possesses a high level of independence and may organize themselves in a diversity of ways. If a community organization or NGO fails to communicate the knowledge and interests of those they aim to represent, then this does not necessarily impact other organizations. It also leaves opportunities for other institutions to offer representation for these groups, allowing the system to self-correct. It has been argued, for instance, that the emergence of social movements following the financial crisis was in part due to the failures of traditional unions to represent the interests of working people.[30] Low entry costs then increase the potential for self-correction, as it allows new institutions to take advantages of opportunities. Self-regulating tendencies can also emerge in public space, as institutions which cooperate or compete have incentives to check the operations of others. Competing think tanks or scientific bodies, for instance, have an incentive to review and scrutinize each other's claims, and so do those who aim to represent competing interests. Self-regulating tendencies can therefore be found in public space, alongside experimentation.

The ability to benefit from polycentrism, however, appears to be more limited in empowered spaces. While this area of a deliberative system is critical to second-order tasks given their power to make binding decisions, it is also more rigidly structured, involves fewer units of authority, and has much greater barriers to entry. Such limitations are well illustrated by federalist systems which have often been argued to represent a form of political polycentricity.[31] While a federal system allows individual states the opportunity to experiment with alternatives and learn from one another, the limitations of realizing the benefits of polycentricity should be clear. The number of states in a federation is limited and there are significant barriers to entry. A significant cap is therefore placed on the amount of experimentation within a federal system, and the potential for self-regulation is also limited as each state is still responsible for a significant proportion of the system.

---

[29] Mansbridge et al. (2012, p. 5).
[30] Las Heras and Ribera-Almandoz (2017).
[31] For further discussion, see Wagner (2005); Bednar (2009).

148   INTELLIGENT DEMOCRACY

The deliberative systems approach, however, does not prescribe any one set of institutional arrangements, but instead allows us to consider alternative ways of distributing political authority. While traditional federalism is limited by its low number of decision centres, the number of political authorities in a deliberative system can be increased through further decentralization. Rather than having a single democratic authority or small number of states conducting second-order tasks for the whole system, political units at multiple levels can be given the power to engage in institutional selection. Decentralizing the power to make binding decisions to not only states, but also to regions or cities, could therefore increase the range of authorities and the scope for experimentation and self-regulation. Experimentation at these levels would increase the number of trials which could take place at any one time. This would then multiply the number of institutional mixes or institutional arrangements one can observe and learn from at any moment, increasing our knowledge of the conditions under which alternatives are successful. Opportunities for self-regulation would also be increased with greater decentralization. Just as any first-order institution can make mistakes in addressing a social problem, second-order political institutions can make errors in adjusting the first-order mix. More widely dispersing political authority, however, confines such mistakes to smaller jurisdictions, and allows others to learn from and correct these mistakes.

Increased political decentralization with empowered spaces could therefore help a deliberative system benefit more greatly from its polycentric features, by increasing the number of jurisdictions and units of authority. Political decentralization can therefore produce epistemic benefits. Chapter 3 already noted one such benefit, in that decentralization brings political decisions closer to individuals, therefore reducing the difficulties which come from gathering local knowledge. This chapter's engagement with the concept of polycentricity, however, has identified further advantages. By increasing the level of polycentricity within empowered space, political decentralization creates greater opportunities for experimentation and self-regulation. This does not require that we do away with centralized democratic authorities, which may still have an important role to play. However, this approach would allow more decentralized units such as regions, cities, or communities greater autonomy in determining their own institutional mix.

A question which arises, however, is what selection mechanisms would a deliberative system involve in order to spread the benefits of experimentation at the second order? Decentralizing political authority increases the

POLYCENTRICITY FOR AND AGAINST DEMOCRACY   149

amount of experimentation taking place, but if the system is to learn from these experiments and promote their successes, then some mechanism is needed to evaluate and select among their results. One possible mechanism is individual exit. Julian Müller, for instance, advocates a polycentric political system based on free cities and places much emphasis on the ability of individuals to move between political jurisdictions, and many supporters of federalism similarly focus on political exit.[32] We have already seen, however, why such an approach is unlikely to be effective. Firstly, exit costs are likely to be high in cases of political decentralization, as they tend to involve territorial distributions of authority. Individuals must therefore move geographically, combining financial costs with the loss of community and family networks. Secondly, individuals are likely to confront informational problems when making exit decisions. Consider, for instance, just the limited forms of experimentation found in federal systems. To make an effective exit decision an individual will need to become informed about the range of public programmes and regulations provided by different states, as well as their results. Which state provides the best unemployment insurance, in-work benefits, financial regulation, environmental quality, consumer protection, market competition, tax system, and infrastructure provision not only in terms of one's own interest but also in terms of the public interest? Individuals are therefore likely to face too great an epistemic burden to effectively make use of their exit rights, and they will also lack the incentive to acquire such information when it comes to concerns for justice and the common good. A deliberative system can therefore allow for exit between political jurisdictions—and should do so for reasons of freedom and autonomy—but this is unlikely to provide an effective selection mechanism.

In Chapter 2 we also saw why individual voters are not in the best position to determine the effectiveness of alternative institutional arrangements, at least when it comes to questions of justice and the common good. Popular views of democratic experimentation, such as Elizabeth Anderson's Deweyan approach, see elections as playing a key role in determining the success and failures of policy experiments.[33] Citizens are said to experience the results of public policy and then provide feedback to policymakers through voting. When the results of policy experiments are not easily or directly observable, however, individual voters will struggle to identify successes and failures in

---

[32] Müller (2019). Also see Pincione and Tesón (2006); Somin (2016).
[33] Anderson (2006).

150 INTELLIGENT DEMOCRACY

a similar way to individuals tasked with making exit decisions. While this chapter's systemic approach differs from Anderson's in highlighting the benefits of polycentricity and decentralization, it therefore also requires a different understanding of the selection mechanism used to evaluate and promote the results of democratic experimentation.

Selection is more likely to occur, on the systems approach, through two different mechanisms: emulation and top-down selection. Both of these mechanisms involve selection by political institutions, rather than individuals, and therefore by bodies which have a greater capacity to acquire information. The first involves lower-level political authorities monitoring each other and identifying successes and failures. Each decision-making unit, whether it be a state, city, or local authority, can evaluate the performance of others in order to produce a better understanding of the conditions under which institutions produce desired consequences. Receiving both general and local knowledge through the information-gathering function of the public sphere, each empowered institution can learn from the experience of others, avoiding their mistakes and emulating their successes. To the extent to which this process is competitive, then, it involves yardstick competition rather than the exit-based competition favoured by advocates of polycentricity discussed earlier. The different democratic authorities provide points of comparison which allow them to be ranked and judged relatively. The multiple decision centres in a deliberative system can therefore benefit and learn from one another through comparison and emulation.

The second mechanism involves selection by higher-level political authorities. As mentioned above, the call for political decentralization with empowered space does not rule out higher and more centralized democratic bodies. These more centralized political authorities can then perform a range of functions aimed at aiding experimentation and selection among lower political units. The least interventionist of these functions would involve the supply of information to lower units about the success and failure of alternatives, aiding them in their processes of emulation. Centralized bodies can also support lower-level institutions through redistribution and therefore the provision of resources necessary for experimentation. More interventionist functions, however, would include regulating the scope of experimentation, or what Müller helpfully refers to as the 'search space'.[34] That is, democratic institutions can determine the limits of what lower-level

---

[34] Müller (2019).

political authorities can experiment with. Although these limits will differ depending on the conception of justice or the common good endorsed, there will always be some reasonable restrictions on experimentation. Obvious examples would be experiments with slavery, low ages of sexual consent, or other basic rights, which higher-level institutions can remove from the acceptable search space. On a broader conception of justice, however, there may also be limits to the amount of experimentation which can be conducted around levels of inequality, the provision of basic needs, access to education, and so on.

While regulating the acceptable search space within which lower units can try out alternatives, more centralized democratic authorities can also directly determine the selection of institutions at lower levels. This most interventionist function would do more to limit the number of experiments performed by lower units, but may be appropriate when lower units experience large-scale failures in their role as second-order institutions. In these cases, intervention by more centralized bodies may be necessary to achieve correction. This kind of direct intervention may also be appropriate when the decisions of lower units are likely to produce large externalities for others, or where addressing a social problem requires joint action across many or all political authorities. Climate change may be one such example. While addressing climate change may benefit greatly from experimentation in how to cut emissions, it at least requires targets or limits to be set by higher-level authorities in order to achieve coordination. While the decentralization of democratic authority is therefore helpful in expanding the scope of experimentation which can occur in a deliberative system, there can still be an important role for more centralized bodies in aiding the experimentation process and acting as a possible selection mechanism.

On a systemic approach to democratic experimentation, then, the task of evaluating the success and failure of empowered institutions will not predominantly fall on mechanisms of individual exit as it does in market and polycentric approaches, nor primarily on individual voters as it does in Anderson's Deweyan model. Instead, this task will be conducted by forms of emulation between political authorities, or top-down selection by more centralized democratic units. What is important about both of these mechanisms is that they give the task of monitoring and selecting alternatives to political institutions which have the ability to acquire much greater amounts of information about the success and failures of these alternatives. The systemic perspective therefore produces a view of the experimental

152　INTELLIGENT DEMOCRACY

process which differs in important ways from that of democracy's polycentric critics, but also from common views of democratic experimentation among epistemic democrats which emphasize the role of elections in institutional selection.

Who Should Make Empowered Decisions?

If one takes a unitary view of democracy as existing in a single institution or mechanism, then the intelligence of democracy appears vulnerable to the critiques of those new democratic sceptics who favour a priority of polycentricity. On a systemic perspective, however, democracy can itself be seen to possess functional forms of polycentrism which not only provide it with the epistemic abilities of experimentation and self-regulation, but also allow it to perform these abilities better than the polycentric systems favoured by the sceptics. The systemic approach has also allowed for a new understanding of democratic experimentation, focused not on elections and single democratic bodies, but on decentralization and mechanisms of emulation and top-down selection. I have therefore used the systemic approach to reply to another form of the new democratic scepticism but also applied the concept of polycentricity to better understand democracy's epistemic value. A polycentric analysis of deliberative systems suggests that we can improve the intelligence of democracy by increasing forms of political decentralization within empowered spaces.

Important questions concerning the structure of empowered institutions still remain. Over the previous chapters we have seen many reasons why the institutions of empowered space should be collective, why they should be connected to a free and open public sphere, and why they can benefit from being decentralized. I have so far said very little, however, about why these empowered institutions should take a democratic form. To fully understand the intelligence of a deliberative 'democratic' system, then, we need to inquire more directly into the institutions of empowered space. We need to ask how these institutions should make their political decisions, and what mechanisms should be used to select their members. Should elections still play some role in the appointment of empowered actors, for instance, or are there alternative democratic or nondemocratic mechanisms which can do a better job and allow for more intelligent political decisions? Answering such questions requires us to consider an alternative brand of the new democratic scepticism; not one which wishes to shrink the scope of collective politics in favour of markets or polycentrism, but one which wants to transform politics in a more elitist direction. Advocates of epistocracy and political meritocracy also see the benefits of more collective forms of politics but wish to reserve them for those with knowledge, ability, and virtue. The remaining chapters therefore turn to these more elitist forms of the new democratic scepticism and the challenges they present to the intelligence of democracy.

6
Diversity and Political Problem-Solving

Whether it be in favour of free markets or polycentric systems, many new democratic sceptics argue that the ills of democracy should lead us to shrink the scope of politics. They claim that we can achieve more intelligent decisions if only we were willing to limit democracy and grant more power to the private or third sectors. While we have seen the shortcomings of these views, they only represent a portion of the new democratic scepticism. Alongside those who wish to shrink politics are those who wish to transform it in a more elitist direction. Historically the most common objections to democracy are to its inclusiveness and come from those who believe politics should be reserved for a more able and knowledgeable elite. Aristocracy was traditionally defended on the grounds that only a certain social class had the education and experience to rule, while it was the wisdom of philosopher kings which was thought to justify their power. Similar arguments can still be found in the work of the new sceptics, although they are now exercised in defence of systems of epistocracy or political meritocracy, rather than aristocracy or monarchy. I have so far offered little defence of democracy against these kinds of arguments. While the previous chapters showed that a deliberative system can gather and evaluate knowledge and engage in experimentation and self-regulation, they said very little about why the final decisions of such systems should be taken democratically, rather than by some wiser and more able elite. The remainder of this book will therefore focus on more elite forms of the new democratic scepticism, and on the question of whether 'rule by the few' is really more intelligent than 'rule by the many'.

As a starting point, this chapter considers a popular strategy for defending democratic forms of deliberation and decision-making which appeals to their diversity. Hélène Landemore has produced the most prominent and sophisticated version of this argument, and her work is of particular interest for two reasons.[1] Firstly, it rejects the central claim supporting elite forms of rule: that political decisions are most epistemically reliable when taken by

---

[1] Landemore (2013a, 2013b).

Intelligent Democracy. Jonathan Benson, Oxford University Press. © Oxford University Press 2024.
DOI: 10.1093/oso/9780197767283.003.0007

the most able among us. This view, Landemore argues, underestimates the contribution of cognitive diversity to collective intelligence, and therefore fails to recognize the epistemic value of democratic inclusion. It overlooks the fact that diverse deliberators can outperform high-ability deliberators. Secondly, Landemore argues that the best mechanism for achieving such diversity is the use of random sortition or lotteries. Given that I have already questioned the epistemic abilities of elections in Chapter 1, Landemore's focus on random selection offers an alternative approach to collective democratic decision-making.[2]

The central claim of this chapter is that cognitive diversity is insufficient to defend the democratic character of empowered political institutions.[3] When it comes to the formal bodies of empowered space, diversity brings many benefits, but it does not necessarily outweigh the value of individual ability. My argument advances in two steps. The first considers Landemore's account—which is based on the *diversity trumps ability theorem*—and argues that it is not fully convincing due to its reliance on an 'oracle assumption'. While others have objected to this assumption on grounds of value pluralism, I claim that the greater challenge is that it underestimates the complexity of political and social problems, and therefore struggles to apply to the political domain. The problem of complexity is not limited to Landemore, however, but is shown to afflict many idealized accounts of deliberation which implicitly accept an oracle assumption by appealing to 'the force of the better argument'. I therefore use a discussion of Landemore's account to draw attention to the more general challenges complexity creates for epistemic approaches to democratic deliberation.

The second step of the argument then considers what value cognitive diversity may still bring to deliberation, even under conditions of complexity. I utilize a simple model—based on *the relationship between cognitive diversity and diminishing returns to cognitive type*—which draws on the insights and logic of Landemore's contributions but does not require an oracle assumption and is therefore better placed to deal with complexity. The conclusions which can be drawn from this model, however, are far more modest than those of Landemore and other epistemic democrats. While cognitive diversity is

---

[2] This is also an approach I will myself endorse in Chapter 8, although I do this for different reasons and claim that it must be combined with elections if it is to support the intelligence of democracy.

[3] A version of this chapter was first published in a paper in *Synthese*. See Benson (2021). Note that this paper and this chapter are focused on cognitive forms of diversity and their contribution to face-to-face deliberation. They do not, therefore, consider the value of other forms of diversity to the democratic public sphere, as discussed in Chapter 3.

156 INTELLIGENT DEMOCRACY

certainly shown to have value, the new model also shows us that this value will not necessarily trump the contributions of individual ability. In other words, the empowered deliberations of epistocrats or political meritocrats may well outperform democratic forms of deliberation. I therefore argue that when it comes to the binding decisions of empowered space, cognitive diversity is insufficient to defend the epistemic superiority of democratic decision-making. Although it has been a central concern of epistemic democrats, a full defence of democracy's intelligence must look beyond cognitive diversity.

Can Diversity Trump Ability?

Landemore interprets deliberation as a process of collective problem-solving where participants aim to arrive at the best possible solutions to social and political problems. She then looks at how fully inclusive forms of deliberation (democracy) compare at this problem-solving task, to forms of deliberation involving only a subset of the demos (aristocracy, oligarchy, epistocracy, etc.). In making this comparison, Landemore assumes that both levels of knowledge about the problem, and levels of motivation to solve it in the common interest, are equal across forms of deliberation. While the ability to gather knowledge has been the concern of the last few chapters, and the question of motivations will be the subject of the next two, Landemore's approach focuses on problem-solving. She also assumes that there is an accurate and uncontroversial method for selecting high-ability deliberators, and that levels of individual ability can therefore differ between forms of deliberation. These assumptions are generous to supporters of elite rule, as they allow for the creation of an epistocracy of the more able who are equally well-motivated towards the public interest (a possibility I challenge in the next chapter).

In this problem-solving context, it is normally thought that the most important factor in selecting a deliberative group would be individual ability. The best problem-solving group is the group that consists of those individuals who would alone produce the best solutions to the problem. Landemore, however, argues against this conventional wisdom on the grounds that it fails to see the role of cognitive diversity in the 'emergence of collective intelligence'.[4] It is not only important that deliberators are of high ability, but also

---

[4] Landemore (2013b, p. 69).

DIVERSITY AND POLITICAL PROBLEM-SOLVING   157

that they think differently from one another. Cognitive diversity refers to the 'variety of mental tools that human beings use to solve problems or make predictions in the world'.[5] It refers not to differences in knowledge but rather differences in the 'cognitive toolboxes' that individuals use to approach problems and come up with different solutions.

Landemore illustrates the importance of cognitive diversity through an example of New Haven residents, public officials, and police deliberating about the problem of recurring muggings on a local bridge. The first round of these deliberations ended with a police officer's suggestion to post a police car in the area, but this was found ineffective as the muggings simply occurred when the car was absent. After deliberating some alternative strategies, someone suggested installing streetlights to deter muggings after dark. This suggestion 'struck everyone as far superior' and 'quickly garnered a consensus'.[6] A city technician, however, argued that the high voltage railroad track under the bridge ruled out electric lighting. Another deliberator then inquired about the use of a solar-powered light. While a city accountant explained that this would be much too expensive, a resident asked if the city could apply for stimulus money to cover the costs. The problem was finally solved. Landemore points to how it was the different problem-solving approaches of these diverse deliberators that allowed this group to move from the suboptimal solution of the police car to the optimal solution of the solar powered streetlight.

Using the technical work of Lu Hong and Scott Page, Landemore then provides a formal and generalizable explanation of these insights.[7] According to Hong and Page's diversity trumps ability theorem (DTA), under certain conditions, a group of cognitively diverse problem solvers are better than a set of high-ability problem solvers. The logic behind the DTA is that a group of high individual ability problem solvers will think in similar ways and will therefore reach only their highest common local optima (the solutions of each individual deliberator after considering the problem). They look for solutions in the same places and therefore get stuck on their best common solution, rather than achieving the global optima (the best solution). If only the police were involved in the New Haven deliberations, for instance, then they would have got stuck on their shared local optima of policing strategies.

---

[5] Landemore (2013b, p. 89). Landemore takes her definition of cognitive diversity from Page (2008).

[6] Landemore (2013b, p. 101).

[7] Hong and Page (2004); Page (2008).

158 INTELLIGENT DEMOCRACY

A homogeneous group therefore performs little better than any one individual within the group. A diverse group, alternatively, thinks very differently and will search for solutions in different places. Their local optima therefore differ and this creates the possibility of guiding one another beyond their local optimum and towards the global optimum. It was the alternative suggestions of the other deliberators, for instance, which allowed the New Haven group to move past policing strategies and to eventually solve the problem.

According to the DTA, then, a random selection of diverse problem solvers can outperform a group of the best individual problem solvers due to their cognitive diversity. Of course, not all kinds of cognitive diversity are beneficial to solving all kinds of problems. As Page has put it, 'we cannot expect that adding a poet to a medical research team would enable them to find a cure for the common cold'.[8] However, Landemore argues that political problems are far too diverse and unpredictable for us to determine the relevant cognitive skills in advance. We cannot therefore 'tell in advance from which part of the *demos* the right kind of ideas are going to come'.[9] When it comes to a general political assembly which will face diverse and unpredictable problems going forward into the future, we simply want as much cognitive diversity as possible.

In order to select deliberative groups with as much diversity as possible, Landemore advocates for the use of sortition. Sortition involves the selection of deliberators through a random lottery, as are commonly used in the selection of juries for criminal trials or the selection of participants for citizen assemblies or other mini-publics. Elections are likely to favour certain kinds of people over others, such as those with wealthy or a Type A personality, and therefore retain an 'aristocratic flavor'.[10] Random sortition, alternatively, avoids these biases. Instead, it aims at producing a 'descriptive representation' of the population to ensure a 'statistical similarity between the thoughts and preferences of the rulers and the ruled'.[11] In other words, sortition looks to create a statistical representation of the cognitive diversity which exists in the wider population. Using the DTA, Landemore is therefore able to argue that a randomly selected group of citizens will outperform a group of high-ability aristocrats or epistocrats. Even if we could create a political elite of the

---

[8] Page (2008, p. xxix).
[9] Landemore (2013b, p. 112).
[10] Landemore (2013a, p. 1218).
[11] Landemore (2013b, p. 108).

DIVERSITY AND POLITICAL PROBLEM-SOLVING   159

most able political problem solvers, we should still prefer a democratic group of deliberators due to their greater cognitive diversity.

Deliberating with Oracles

For the DTA to hold, four conditions need to be met. These are that (1) the problem being faced is difficult enough; (2) all problem solvers need to be relatively smart or 'not too dumb'; (3) problem solvers should think differently from each other but should still be able to recognize the best solution; and finally (4) the population from which problem solvers are taken should be large and the group of problem solvers should not be too small.[12] Although Landemore claims all these conditions hold in the political domain, this section argues that the complexity of political problems frustrates a straightforward application of the DTA.[13]

The important condition in this respect is condition 3.[14] This assumption states that while deliberators must think differently enough to ensure diversity, these differences do not stop them all being 'capable of recognizing the best solution when they are made to think about it'.[15] The second part of this assumption, which Landemore and Page have referred to as the 'oracle assumption', is a highly demanding condition.[16] It assumes the existence of an oracle which is a 'machine, person, or internal intuition that can reveal the correct ranking of any proposed solutions'. The assumption requires that if the true value of solution y is greater than the true value of solution x, then each individual deliberator will recognize that y is ranked higher than x. That is, the 'best solution must be obvious to all'.[17] This is an important assumption in Landemore's argument, as it allows a diverse group of decision-makers to move from worse to better solutions. As deliberators with different cognitive skills offer up new solutions, it is the oracle assumption which allows them to recognize when a better solution has been offered, and therefore move past their local optima towards the global optima. This was the case in the New Haven deliberation where new solutions 'struck everyone as far superior' and

[12] Landemore (2013b, p. 102).
[13] Although the mathematics supporting the DTA has been debated its internal validity is assumed here. For the mathematical debate, see Kuehn (2017); Thompson (2014).
[14] Gunn (2014); Quirk (2014).
[15] Landemore (2013b, p. 220).
[16] Landemore and Page (2015, p. 6).
[17] Landemore (2013b, p. 102).

160   INTELLIGENT DEMOCRACY

therefore allowed for the generation of a 'consensus'.[18] If this is not the case, then a diverse group may get stuck below the global optima and possibly below the common local optima of a high-ability but low-diversity group.

The issue, however, is that many political problems are much more complex than that faced by the residents of New Haven. Consider, for instance, a move from the problem of muggings in a single site to the more general problem of crime in New Haven. This larger problem of crime is much more complex as it involves not only many alternative policing strategies but also the social determinants of crime, such as education, housing, welfare, and areas of public health. The answer to which combination of these varied policies is likely to be most effective is not as clear or as obvious as the solution to the muggings on a single bridge. Even if the best policy combinations are suggested during deliberation, this will not necessarily lead to a 'eureka' moment where everyone recognizes the best policy.[19] This is because complex political problems allow for multiple plausible and reasonable interpretations, which can lead even well-intentioned deliberators to disagree on what the best solution would be. Consider environmental problems as another example. Landemore and Page argue that everyone will agree that an 'environmentally sustainable solution is better than a costly and dangerous one'.[20] This may well be true. However, there is likely to be much reasonable disagreement about which solution is actually the most environmentally sustainable given the complexity surrounding such problems. There is often uncertainty about the magnitude of the effects of environmental problems, their possible courses, and the effectiveness of alternative policy options. These features allow for multiple plausible interpretations of the problem so that there is no reason to think that everyone will necessarily recognize which solution is best for the environment.

The problem here is not one of value disagreement. Previous critics have objected that Landemore downplays the problem of moral pluralism, which can lead deliberators to disagree over the best solution.[21] On these objections, deliberators can have a complete and agreed understanding of the nature of a political problem but disagree due to conflicts over fundamental values. On the objection pursued here, alternatively, disagreement comes

[18] Landemore (2013b, p. 101).
[19] Note that this problem is not simply overcome by including more knowledge. Even with all currently available information many political problems will still allow for alternative interpretations and more information can often increase complexity.
[20] Landemore and Page (2015, p. 9).
[21] Ancell (2017); Levinson (2014); Muirhead (2014); Stich (2014).

not from values but from a lack of a complete and agreed understanding of the problems deliberators are attempting to solve. We can therefore have agreement on the values of 'environmental sustainability' and 'efficiency', for instance, and yet still disagree about which policy is best in terms of these criteria. The oracle assumption, therefore, seems to either underestimate the complexity of political problems, or the ability of deliberators to deal with this complexity.

My challenge of complexity may also be more difficult to address than previous challenges based on value pluralism. Landemore has argued that value pluralism may be less concerning than often feared, as democracies often possess a consensual background of basic values which can be appealed to during political problem-solving.[22] In those cases where common values happen to be absent, value disputes can also be solved procedurally (e.g. by a deliberative compromise or majority vote) before collective problem-solving begins, so as to produce a set of common values which all must accept (at least until the next election). Neither of these replies, however, does anything to weaken the problem of complexity. Even if there is complete consensus over basic values, the underline complexity of political problems can still allow for many reasonable interpretations of the best solution, while any attempt to solve disputes over the correct understanding of a problem in advance would seem to undermine the process of problem-solving itself. The DTA's relevance to politics is therefore more greatly limited by complexity than by value pluralism.

Landemore and Page have attempted to defend the application of the oracle assumption to politics.[23] Firstly, they argue that perfect oracles are not required for the DTA to hold. Suppose there are five possible solutions to a problem with true values of 1, 2, 3, 4, and 5, and that each deliberator is able to assign values with an error of less than 0.5. In this case, everyone would arrive at the correct ranking even without a true oracle. This defence, however, does not appear to get us very far in the case of complex political problems. Essentially it still requires that deliberators can make the correct ordinal ranking of policies, which itself seems very unlikely in the political domain where problems are complex. Problems such as crime and environmental sustainability can produce disagreement not only over the precise value of alternative solutions, but also their ordinal rankings.

---

[22] Landemore (2014).
[23] Landemore and Page (2015).

162 INTELLIGENT DEMOCRACY

Secondly, they argue the oracle assumption does not require that problems are trivial or their solutions clear, as it is through the giving of arguments and reasons that deliberation renders previously unnoticed and unrecognized solutions obvious. It may well be possible that deliberation can do this, and it may be that once a complex solution is explained it becomes more obvious than it was before. This does not, however, give us reason to think that an oracle will always, or even mostly, be possible for political and social problems where the outcomes of alternative policies are themselves debatable and contested. Even if the best combination of policies designed to deal with crime in New Haven is offered up in deliberation, this may well not be recognized by all.

Thirdly, Landemore and Page argue that developments in technology will increase the likelihood of oracles, claiming that improvements in data, information, and modelling will lead to improvements in oracles. This final reply may also be true. As Landemore's New Haven example illustrates, there are political problems which are small and simple enough that there can be agreement over the best solution when it is introduced, and over time technology may increase the number of such problems. There may even come a time when technology has advanced to such an extent that the solutions to even our most challenging political problems are easily recognized. The issue, however, is that for the foreseeable future many of our political and social problems will remain complex, and the oracle assumption and DTA will be unlikely to hold.

We can therefore conclude that for political problems which are simple enough to assume the existence of an oracle, and those which may be made simple enough in the near future, Landemore's use of the DTA helps us understand the benefits of cognitive diversity and the superiority of democracy over elite rule. However, for the many political problems which are likely to remain complex for the foreseeable future—and I suspect that these represent the majority—the DTA fails to provide a convincing account of the benefits of cognitive diversity. While Landemore's use of the DTA is therefore certainly not without insight or application, it is limited in showing the epistemic merits of democratic deliberation when it comes to a broad range of pressing political problems.

How Forceful Is the Force of the Better Argument?

While our focus in the previous sections has been on Landemore, this discussion actually highlights the more general issue that complexity creates when defending the epistemic value of democratic deliberation. As Landemore and Page have noted, one way of thinking about the oracle assumption is that it represents a version of the deliberative democratic ideal of 'the force of the better argument'.[24] In the ideal of deliberation or in an ideal speech situation, deliberators are said to be led by 'the forceless force of the better argument' to accept the best and only the best reasons put forward, and therefore to select the best proposal offered up in deliberation.[25] In the ideal of deliberation, then, deliberators behave just like oracles. Many approaches to deliberative democratic theory which focus on idealized conceptions of deliberation therefore implicitly accept a version of the oracle assumption. Complexity is not therefore just a problem for the application of the DTA but any account of democratic deliberation which makes strong or idealized claims about the force of the better argument or the ability of reason-giving to lead to agreement on the most valid claims.

Of course, considering idealized versions of deliberation is often productive and can help in identifying its epistemic merits. The problem, however, is that it also obscures the difficulties of applying these merits to the realities of politics. When we consider the complexity of many real world problems we cannot assume highly competent deliberators who can, like oracles, always recognize the best argument or the best solution on offer. The problems facing the oracle assumption do not therefore point only to the limitations of Landemore's view, but highlight a much more general difficulty in explaining the value which diversity brings to less ideal forms of political deliberation. The question, then, is can cognitive diversity still produce epistemic benefits when problems are complex and the 'force of the better argument' imperfect? Or even more important for my purposes, does cognitive diversity still possess enough value to trump the value produced by empowering a higher ability elite?

The rest of this chapter aims to address these questions. In doing so, it is first important to recognize that deliberation can still benefit political problem-solving even in less idealized conditions. While 'the force of the

---

[24] Landemore and Page (2015, p. 6).
[25] Chambers (1996); Cohen (1986, 2005); Estlund (2009); Habermas (1984).

better argument' can be seen as one example of the oracle assumption, this is only true in the context of an ideal speech situation where open deliberation leads everyone to accept the best reasons. More general appeals to the benefits of argument do not need to take such a strong form and can bring benefits to much less ideal forms of deliberation. In an academic seminar, for example, participants exchange arguments and counterarguments for different positions, helping them to further refine their work and form better solutions to their research problems. It can help them recognize the limits of their proposals and lines of reasoning, eliminate the weakest parts of their paper, and update or strengthen others. These are all benefits of 'the force of the better argument' but they do not imply a strong oracle assumption. These are benefits of discussion and argument which can be recognized without assuming academic seminars will end, given enough time, in a consensus.

The same can be said of political deliberation. Deliberators can help correct misinterpretations and bad forms of reasoning, lead people to account for previously unaccounted for factors, weed out bad or inappropriate solutions, and improve more promising ones, even if it will not end with a consensus over the one best solution. Particularly weak or poorly constructed crime or environmental policies may, for instance, be eliminated, and more promising ones improved, all while there exists disagreement over the best overall solution. Political deliberation can therefore still allow a group to come up with a better solution or set of solutions (which can then be voted on) than they would have otherwise, even when problems are complex and the force of the better argument is far from perfect. What value, then, if any, does cognitive diversity contribute to deliberative problem-solving under conditions such as these? The following sections develop a new and simple model of cognitive diversity which draws on the insights and logic of Landmore's account, but which does not include an oracle assumption. This model builds on the relationship between diversity and diminishing returns which has been recognized in other domains, but is used here to understand the epistemic benefits of cognitive diversity to democratic deliberation.[26] While this model shows that such diversity can have value even for complex problems, it also tells us, contrary to past work, that this diversity will not necessarily make democratic deliberation superior to all forms of elite rule.

---

[26] I build on Page's (2010) more general discussion of this relationship.

An Alternative Model of Cognitive Diversity

To remind us, cognitive diversity refers to the 'variety of mental tools that human beings use to solve problems or make predictions in the world'.[27] It points to the different 'cognitive skillsets' or 'cognitive toolboxes' that individuals use to approach problems and produce solutions. These cognitive toolboxes or skillsets include a 'diversity of perspectives (the way of representing situations and problems), diversity of interpretations (the way of categorizing or partitioning perspectives), diversity of heuristics (the way of generating solutions to problems), and diversity of predictive models (the way of inferring cause and effect)'.[28] A particular cognitive toolbox therefore represents a particular set of cognitive skills and the cognitive diversity of a group represents the range of different cognitive skills included within it.

The new account of deliberation put forward here also draws on the underlying logic of the DTA: that cognitively diverse groups include individuals who think differently from each other and can therefore contribute different things to problem-solving. It spells out this benefit, however, through the relationship between cognitive diversity and diminishing returns to cognitive type. The logic behind this relationship is that while cognitively diverse groups have individuals who think differently—they can, for instance, contribute different reasons and solutions in the process of problem-solving— the benefits of these contributions reduce as the number of deliberators with the same cognitive skills increases. When we add a mathematician to a problem-solving group, for instance, this produces a great benefit. They offer a whole new set of cognitive skills to the table which was not there before. They bring whole new ways of thinking about the problem, and whole new solutions. When we add another mathematician to the group, this is again a benefit. Two mathematicians are certainly better than one. The contribution they make, however, is less than the first as those particular cognitive skills are already represented. They will certainly add to problem-solving, but they will not be bringing a whole new set of cognitive skills the group did not have before. Every additional mathematician makes a positive contribution (at least until the group becomes too large and impractical), but there will be diminishing returns to these contributions.

---

[27] Landemore (2013b, p. 89).
[28] Landemore (2013b, p. 102); Page (2008).

166 INTELLIGENT DEMOCRACY

The value of cognitive diversity emerges from its ability to exploit the presence of these diminishing returns. Consider, for instance, Landemore's New Haven example. The diverse deliberators offered alternative reasons and solutions to the problem. The police contributed policing solutions, a resident streetlighting solutions, the electrician objections to lighting solutions, and the accountant arguments about costs. However, once these individuals were included in deliberation there would be less value in including other similarly minded people. Once representatives of the police were present and able to offer policing solutions, less benefit would be produced by having more police included in deliberation. Policing strategies were already on the table and found to be ineffective. There would therefore be diminishing returns to including more police in deliberation, and it was more valuable in this case to have other deliberators who thought very differently and could offer alternative kinds of solutions. The technician from the city also added much to deliberation by pointing out the problems of using electric lighting which helped the group to arrive at the final solution of a solar-powered light. However, once that technician was included and able to point out this problem, a second technician was not required to do so. A second technician would not, therefore, have provided as great a contribution to solving the problem as the first. Of course, a second technician may have been able to contribute in other ways, so their contribution will still be positive. However, their value to problem-solving would diminish compared to the first. It was therefore beneficial to have others, such as residents and the city accountant, who thought differently and could offer alternative reasons and solutions.

The New Haven case therefore illustrates the logic behind the relationship between cognitive diversity and diminishing returns. A more formal explanation of this relationship, however, can be made through the use of a simple example, adapted from Page for our purposes.[29] In this simple example, we have a political community who, unbeknownst to them, is about to face a novel political problem that will have to be dealt with through their main political institution, a small deliberative assembly. For simplicity, let us assume that there are only four kinds of cognitive skillsets present in this community so that each member of the community either has cognitive toolbox A, B, C, or D. Of course, any actual community will have a much greater range of cognitive skills, and they will not neatly fall into clearly defined categories.

[29] Page (2010).

DIVERSITY AND POLITICAL PROBLEM-SOLVING 167

Table 6.1 Diminishing Returns to Cognitive Skills

Cognitive Toolbox	Person #1	Person #2	Person #3
A	50	20	10
B	30	20	10
C	20	20	10
D	20	10	10

However, these simplifying assumptions are helpful to our example and do not undermine its applicability to more realistic situations.

Table 6.1 shows numerical values for the contributions made by each cognitive toolbox to the problem-solving group. These numerical values represent the extent to which adding a person with a particular cognitive skillset increases the ability of the group to improve its solutions. Not all cognitive skills are equally useful for all problems, so we can assume that they will make different contributions to this novel problem. In this case, toolbox A makes the greatest contribution and D the smallest. The table also breaks the contributions down for each additional person with the same toolbox. Importantly, the value of these contributions decreases with every additional person with the same cognitive skills. The first person with toolbox A, for example, makes a contribution of 50, the second of 20, and the third of 10. There are then diminishing returns to cognitive skills.

We can now ask which kind of deliberative assembly this political community should prefer given their situation as it is described. Let us say that there are three possible deliberative assemblies which the political community could have. The first is a *Diverse Assembly*, which involves the most cognitive diversity as it is made up of three people each with a different cognitive toolbox. The second is a *Moderate Assembly*, which is less diverse as it contains three people with two different cognitive tool boxes between them. Finally, there is a *Homogenous Assembly*, which is the least diverse as it is made up of three people all with the same cognitive toolbox.

Consider calculating the overall problem-solving contributions which would be made by those in a *Diverse Assembly*. This would involve adding three numbers from the Person #1 column. An assembly involving three people with toolboxes A, B, and C, for instance, will have an overall problem-solving value of 100 (50+30+20). It is important to see that the Person #1

168   INTELLIGENT DEMOCRACY

column is the highest value column. Because of diminishing returns, the Person #2 and Person #3 columns will have lower values for any one particular cognitive toolbox than the Person #1 column. The contributions made by all of the deliberators in a *Diverse Assembly*, therefore, come from the highest value column, no matter which cognitive skillsets they have. Now consider calculating the overall problem-solving value made by those in a *Moderate Assembly*. This will involve adding only two numbers from the high-value Person #1 column and one from the lower value Person #2 column. For instance, an assembly made up of two people with toolbox A, and one with toolbox C will have an overall value of 90 (50+20+20). Finally, consider calculating the overall problem-solving value of a *Homogenous Assembly*. This involves taking only one number from the high-value Person #1 column and then one from each of the lower-value columns. For instance, an assembly consisting of three people with toolbox A will have a total value of 80 (50+20+10), while an assembly consisting of three people with toolbox D will have a value of 40 (20+10+10).

Through this simple example, we can see the explanation for why we should generally prefer a more cognitively diverse assembly to a less cognitively diverse assembly. Calculating the overall problem-solving contributions for a *Diverse Assembly* will always involve taking more numbers from the Person #1 column than it does for the less diverse assemblies. This is also true whichever toolboxes happen to be included in the different assemblies. Due to diminishing returns, however, this Person #1 column will be of higher value than the other columns. The contribution of cognitive skillsets diminishes with every additional person, so the first-person column will be of greater value to the second- or third-person column. As a result, a *Diverse Assembly* is more likely to have a higher total problem-solving value than a *Moderate* or *Homogenous Assembly*. Other things being equal, we are better off with a more diverse assembly. The epistemic benefits of cognitive diversity are therefore explained through the relationships between diversity and diminishing returns. Diversity can exploit the presence of diminishing returns to cognitive type in order to produce epistemic benefits.

Importantly, this account of the benefits of cognitive diversity holds only in cases where we do not know the problem in advance. If we knew the exact problem, then we might be able to make reasonable judgements about (1) the initial contribution of each cognitive toolbox and (2) the exact rate of diminishing returns these toolboxes exhibit. From these factors, we may be able to judge the relative contributions of each individual. We may find, for

DIVERSITY AND POLITICAL PROBLEM-SOLVING   169

instance, that the first deliberator with one cognitive skillset makes a lower contribution than the second, third, or even fourth deliberator with another cognitive skillset. If this is the case, then we would not necessarily want to select for diversity. For instance, if the small political community knew the exact contributions of each cognitive skillset (i.e. they knew the content of Table 6.1), then they would know that selecting an assembly involving two people with toolbox A and one with toolbox B, has the same total value as selecting a more diverse assembly involving three people with toolboxes A, B, and C.

It is not, therefore, always the case that a diverse group is preferable to a less diverse group for any and all problems. As Landemore has already argued, however, the unpredictability and diversity of political problems means we cannot, at least in the case of a general deliberative assembly, specify the exact political problem in advance. There is simply too great a variety of political problems and too much uncertainty surrounding them to specify them before they arise. When it comes to forming a general political assembly we do not know the exact problems it will have to confront, and we therefore cannot specify either (1) or (2). As a result, we will not know the content of Table 6.1.[30] What we do know, however, is that diminishing returns are present and therefore the first column of the table will be the highest value column for all cognitive toolboxes. The best thing we can do then is select a deliberative assembly with the largest amount of cognitive diversity. We should select for greater diversity as this will involve taking more numbers from the high-value column and, therefore, have the greatest chance of producing the highest value group. As a result, this argument holds under the same conditions as Landemore's. It applies to a general deliberative assembly where political problems cannot be specified in advance. In such a situation we would prefer a cognitively diverse group of deliberators, *ceteris paribus,* to a more cognitively homogeneous set of deliberators.

The fact that we cannot specify the problem in advance also addresses a possible objection to the new model. While it may be reasonable to assume that diminishing returns to cognitive skills will kick in at some point, it may not necessarily kick in from the very beginning. Cognitive toolboxes may not experience diminishing returns from the second person as is the case in our simple example but rather at some later stage. In fact, diminishing

---

[30] In fact, even knowledge of the problem may not be enough for specifying (1) and (2) as it can be difficult to specify cognitive skills into clear categories.

170 INTELLIGENT DEMOCRACY

returns may begin at different times depending on the particular problem that deliberation is attempting to solve. So according to this objection, diminishing returns to cognitive skills will be present after n people with a particular cognitive skillset are added to deliberation, but n may be greater than one and may differ from problem to problem. This objection does not, however, change our conclusion in favour of a more diverse assembly if we do not know the problem in advance. If we are not able to specify the problem then we will not have information about (1) the initial contribution of each cognitive toolbox and (2) the exact rate of diminishing returns. However, not knowing the problem in advance also means that we will not have information about the value of n. If we cannot specify the problem, then we will not be able to specify the point at which diminishing returns will begin for each cognitive skillset. What we do know is that there will be a general trend of diminishing returns for cognitive skills. Earlier columns in the above table are therefore still *more likely* to be of higher value than later columns. Assuming there will be some tendency to diminishing returns, then the first deliberators with a particular cognitive skillset are still *more likely* (although not necessarily) to have a greater contribution than later deliberators with the same skillset. More diverse groups, therefore, are still *more likely* to have a high problem-solving value than less diverse groups, *ceteris paribus*. The best thing the community can do, therefore, is select for a more diverse group.

The relationship between cognitive diversity and diminishing returns to cognitive type, therefore, explains the value of such diversity to political problem-solving. It is important to see that it does this without positing a strong oracle assumption. It assumes that deliberation and the force of the better argument can provide benefits to problem-solving, such as by weeding out bad forms of reasoning, eliminating poorly constructed solutions, and improving more promising alternatives. In other words, it requires that the introduction of more deliberators and new cognitive skills makes some positive contribution to the problem-solving process (as can be seen in the simple example above). What this new model does not require is a strong version of the oracle assumption, such as that found in the DTA, where all deliberators can recognize the true value of all proposed solutions. Deliberation needs to bring added value to problem-solving in order for the benefits of diminishing returns to be realized, but it does not need to lead all deliberators to follow the force of the better argument to the one best solution. While the latter

DIVERSITY AND POLITICAL PROBLEM-SOLVING 171

assumption is ruled out by political complexity, the more modest assumption can be retained. As long as deliberation contributes something positive to problem-solving, the benefits of diminishing returns can demonstrate the value of cognitive diversity within the deliberative group.

This new account can therefore continue to explain the value of diversity even when complexity leads to nonideal forms of deliberation where oracles are absent and the force of the better argument is imperfect. What this account cannot show, however, is that such diversity makes democratic deliberation superior to all forms of elite rule. The model shows how cognitive diversity can provide democratic deliberation with epistemic benefits not possessed by more homogeneous elites, and that these benefits do not vanish when problems become complex. It does not, however, show us that this diversity necessarily trumps individual ability. It only speaks to the benefits of diversity over homogeneity and does not include the value of individual ability—the values in Table 6.1 refer only to the added benefit of a deliberator's cognitive skillset and not their individual ability to solve the problem. This result is not necessarily surprising. As long as problems are complex and the force of the better argument imperfect, democratic deliberators cannot be assumed to always guide each other to solutions which are better than those found by groups of high-ability individuals. Perhaps they sometimes will, but the new model gives us no reason to think they always or mostly will. It is therefore unclear that democratic forms of deliberation will outperform elite forms of rule if the latter involves deliberators of higher ability who are equally well motivated towards the common good.

The conclusions which can be drawn from this account of cognitive diversity are therefore more modest than those of Landemore. When it comes to political problems which are not highly complex and for which oracles are likely, cognitive diversity may make democratic deliberation epistemically superior to deliberation between any subset of the demos, as the DTA suggests. However, when political problems are more complex and oracles are absent, cognitive diversity remains valuable but it is unclear if it makes democratic deliberation epistemically superior to more elite forms of deliberation involving higher ability deliberators. Given that many, if not most, political problems are likely to exhibit complexity, the benefits of cognitive diversity cannot alone establish the epistemic superiority of democratic deliberation, as earlier work has claimed.

How to Select for Diversity

Before moving to consider what epistemic value empowered democratic decision-making may possess above and beyond its diversity, it should be noted that even the more modest conclusions of this chapter are open to challenge. Firstly, one may reject the view that democratic forms of deliberation best achieve cognitive diversity, and secondly, one may argue that real world democratic debate involves epistemic failures which will likely overshadow diversity's benefits. In respect to the first, a number of Landemore's critics have challenged her claim that random sortition is the best mechanism for achieving cognitively diverse groups, and suggest nondemocratic mechanisms may do better. Importantly, we do not need to show that random selection is a perfect mechanism for promoting cognitive diversity but only that it is better at doing so than methods which try to engineer it more directly.

For instance, some have argued that diversity can be engineered by directly selecting for certain cognitive skills.[31] If we know we are going to face an economic problem, for instance, then we should directly select for cognitive diversity around that subject, by selecting people with a diversity of economic perspectives (e.g. neoclassical, Keynesian, Austrian, Marxist). Random selection, alternatively, may end up including less relevant cognitive skills, or overselecting those which are most common in the population (say neoclassical) while underselecting those which are less common (say Austrian). Directly selecting deliberators with particular cognitive skills would therefore produce more diversity than purely random selection, and lead to a form of epistocracy. Landemore, however, has argued that such an approach faces several challenges.[32] Firstly, the diversity and unpredictability of political problems frustrate attempts to specify problems in advance and, therefore, to specify which cognitive skills will be most relevant. Secondly, even if we do know the problem in advance, cognitive skills do not always fit into clearly defined and identifiable categories (such as neoclassical or Keynesian), making them difficult to directly select. Thirdly, even if it is possible to identify the relevant dimension of cognitive diversity in advance, there is no reason to think that this particular dimension (say economic) will be helpful and not counterproductive when it comes to other kinds of

[31] Kelly (2014); Quirk (2014).
[32] Landemore (2013b, 2014).

DIVERSITY AND POLITICAL PROBLEM-SOLVING   173

problems (environmental, health, education, crime, etc.). When it comes to a general purpose assembly, we are better off relying on random selection.

Aaron Ancell, however, suggests an alternative method of engineering cognitive diversity which uses random selection but in a nondemocratic manner.[33] He argues that individuals can possess different numbers of cognitive skills, and that cognitive diversity can therefore be increased by selecting for those individuals who have more cognitive skills than the average person. These could be individuals from particular professions which require a large number of problem-solving skills (i.e. doctors, behavioural economists, or climate scientists) or simply those with a university education which can increase the size of an individual's cognitive skillset. Ancell therefore suggests that cognitive diversity would be better achieved by randomly selecting from these more exclusive groups rather than the whole population, and that the benefits of cognitive diversity support a form of epistocracy rather than democracy.[34]

There are a number of problems with this more exclusive form of sortition. Firstly, we cannot always be certain that individuals from these more exclusive groups, such as the university educated, will necessarily have more cognitive skills than the average person. Cognitive skills are not necessarily additive, which means that acquiring new ones can come at the cost of losing old ones. A university education in economics may provide an individual with a useful new set of cognitive skills but can also lead an individual to think only in terms of a single model (i.e. a rational choice model) at the exclusion of others. Some types of education and training may therefore result in fewer or the same number of cognitive skills rather than more. Secondly, even if we can find a subset of the demos who can be reliably said to have more cognitive skills than average, we also need to be sure that this restricted section of the population does not compromise diversity. Increasing the number of cognitive skills only increases cognitive diversity if those skills are not already present in the group. We do not simply want more cognitive skills, but different ones. Selecting for particular groups in society, however,

---

[33] Ancell (2017).

[34] Ancell also argues that this kind of epistocracy would likely increase levels of individuals' ability. This is part of a wider critique of Landemore's claim that we should maximize cognitive diversity without concern for individual ability. This part of his argument is not discussed here as this chapter does not defend any such claim about superiority of diversity over ability. Instead, it provides a formal explanation of the epistemic benefits of cognitive diversity and argues that this provides democratic deliberation with a unique (although not necessarily superior) epistemic value. This chapter does not therefore directly dispute Ancells's claim that increasing individual ability and cognitive diversity would be better all things considered.

174 INTELLIGENT DEMOCRACY

can risk reducing the diversity of cognitive skills even while it increases the number of such skills.

This could arise for nonideal reasons. Background inequality means that certain groups in society are more likely to have a university education, or be a member of an elite profession, so that selecting these groups may reduce overall diversity, even if individuals in these groups have many cognitive skills. Even under more ideal circumstances, however, the university educated will have similar educational experiences and be more likely to enter certain walks of life. The result is that they may form similar cognitive skillsets and therefore become more cognitively homogenous than the general population (which includes the university educated and the nonuniversity educated). The same may be said of those in particular professions, such as behavioural economists or climate scientists. Those professions involve similar academic and professional training which may prioritize certain cognitive skills, such as statistical skills, while not including other skills which may be helpful to social problems. If the group of deliberators in the New Haven example included only the university educated, for instance, then it would have possibly excluded the representatives of the police, the city technician, and some local residents, all of whom contributed to solving the problem but may not have had university degrees. Narrowing the pool from which deliberators are randomly selected therefore runs the risk of increasing the number of cognitive skills while decreasing diversity compared to the whole population. So, although random sortition is not a flawless mechanism for selecting cognitive diversity, it is still preferable to its nondemocratic alternatives.

The Threat of Deliberative Failures

The second possible challenge to democratic deliberation's ability to realize the benefits of diversity concerns the issue of deliberative failures. The model of deliberation in this chapter—as well as Landemore's—makes an assumption that there are no negative synergies produced through deliberation.[35] Negative synergies refer to any dynamic which may cause the group to come

---

[35] The new model also does not assume the presence of positive synergies where individuals working together produce benefits above those of the sum of their individual parts, and it differs from Landemore's account in this respect. The new account does not, however, need to deny the potential for positive synergies. Rather, it shows that the diversity present in democratic deliberation has epistemic benefits even without positive synergies.

DIVERSITY AND POLITICAL PROBLEM-SOLVING   175

to worse decisions than they would as individuals. So while our example of the small community assumed that every deliberator made a positive contribution, the presence of negative synergies would mean that adding more deliberators may actually undermine problem-solving. Importantly, democratic deliberation can still have epistemic value even with the presence of negative synergies as the positive effects of diversity may simply cancel them out.[36] If the negative synergies are large enough, however, then they could outweigh the epistemic benefits of cognitive diversity.

A core claim of many new democratic sceptics is that public deliberation will face large synergies of this kind due to the likelihood of certain deliberative failures.[37] For instance, many sceptics claim that deliberation tends to produce both group homogenization and polarization. Homogenization refers to a tendency of deliberation to lead to the acceptance of dominant group opinions. If most of a group already prefers to increase public spending on healthcare, for instance, then group homogenization suggests that deliberation will lead to greater conformity around that view. Polarization, alternatively, refers to the tendency of deliberation to move a group towards more extreme versions of their shared or dominant positions. If a group is conservative-minded, for instance, then polarization suggests that they will become even more conservative after deliberating together. Both of these effects have been raised as concerns for democratic deliberation, and they both have some empirical support from lab experiments.[38] Of course, it may be that a group homogenizes or polarizes towards the correct position. However, such effects can take place irrespective of the group's pre-existing position, and therefore deliberation cannot be expected to lead to better decisions any more than chance.

Contrary to the claims of the new democratic sceptics, however, the empirical evidence suggests that citizens can deliberate without giving rise to these deliberative failures. The forms of democratic deliberation supported by this chapter are those based on random selection, and therefore find most similarity with deliberative mini-publics, such as citizen assemblies and deliberative polls. The evidence coming from studies of these deliberative institutions, however, is that failures of homogenization and polarization can be reduced or avoided through the structural design of group deliberation.

---

[36] Page (2010).
[37] Brennan (2016a).
[38] Sunstein (2000, 2002, 2009).

176 INTELLIGENT DEMOCRACY

As Cass Sunstein has pointed out, there are two main mechanisms behind these dynamics.[39] Firstly, the desire to be accepted by members of a group creates a social pressure to take up dominant group positions or endorse more extreme versions of them. Secondly, more reasons are likely to be given in favour of a group's dominant position, thus producing further support for that view. Both of these mechanisms, however, are much less likely if the group of deliberators is diverse, as such diversity reduces the pressure of social conformity and increases the range of reasons heard.[40] Deliberative groups selected by random sortition, like deliberative mini-publics, are therefore less likely to be affected by homogenization or polarization, a point noted by Sunstein.[41] Furthermore, Kimmo Grönund and colleagues have found that clear discussion rules, trained moderators, and the provision of information can also reduce the chances of polarization.[42] In fact, their study found that including these factors in the 'deliberative package' can reduce polarization even among like-minded groups, therefore suggesting that group diversity may not be essential to removing these negative synergies.

Another set of possible deliberative failures are associated with problems of social domination where individuals tend to favour the positions of the socially privileged (white, male, middle- or upper-class, etc.) over the socially underprivileged (nonwhite, female, working-class, etc.). Although such dynamics are paid less attention by the new democratic sceptics, they also represent negative synergies as deliberation would end up tracking domination rather than good reasons.[43] As discussed in more detail in Chapter 4, however, the effect of these social biases can also be significantly reduced by structural features of deliberation. Factors such as placing less pressure on consensus or increasing group diversity, for instance, are important in understanding the reduced influence of these effects in deliberative mini-publics compared to the deliberations of criminal juries.[44]

More generally, there are now numerous studies of structured forms of citizen deliberation which dispute the presence of one or more of these deliberative failures.[45] In one large study, for example, Robert Luskin and

---

[39] Sunstein (2002).

[40] Chappell (2011); Fishkin (2018); Fishkin and Luskin (2005); Min and Wong (2018); Morrell (2014).

[41] Sunstein (2000, p. 116).

[42] Grönlund et al. (2015).

[43] Fricker (2007); Sanders (1997); Young (2011).

[44] Fishkin (2011, 2018); Luskin et al. (2002); Siu (2009).

[45] Blais, Carty, and Fournier (2008); Fishkin, Kousser, Luskin, and Siu (2015); Fishkin, He, Luskin, and Siu (2010); Fishkin and Luskin (2005); Luskin et al. (2002); Smith (2009).

colleagues analysed 21 deliberative polls including 372 small groups and 139 policy issues.[46] They found that deliberation does not regularly homogenise or polarise attitudes, nor shift attitudes towards those of the socially advantaged, and where such effects were observed they were also found to be 'feeble' and not to significantly affect deliberation. Although their results cannot rule out all possible negative synergies, they do 'suggest a relatively deliberative discussion, involving considerable weighing of the merits', and are inconsistent with what would be expected from 'routine and strong homogenization, polarization, and domination'. So while this chapter's model of the benefits of cognitive diversity assumes the absence of significant negative synergies and deliberative failures, the empirical evidence suggests that such an assumption is not unrealistic for structured forms of deliberation based on random selection.

How Far Can Diversity Take Us?

While a popular strategy for defending democratic decision-making against elite forms of rule is to appeal to their cognitive diversity, this chapter has found this strategy to be insufficient. Sophisticated versions of this argument such as Hélène Landemore's may show the superiority of democratic deliberation when it comes to simple problems, but it is much more difficult to establish the relative merits of diversity when it comes to the wide range of political issues which are far more complex. When the force of the better argument is imperfect and oracles absent, we cannot necessarily assume that a diverse range of deliberators will be able to lead each other to solutions better than those which can be produced by a more able elite.

This is not to say that diversity's epistemic value vanishes in the face of complexity. The chapter has offered a new model which shows how diversity can exploit the presence of diminishing returns in ways which produce epistemic benefits not found in more homogeneous forms of political problem-solving. Cognitive diversity therefore remains a string in the bow of deliberative and epistemic democrats, and Landemore deserves much credit for drawing this to our attention. Contrary to the claims of earlier epistemic democrats, however, cognitive diversity is insufficient to ground the epistemic superiority of democratic deliberation over more elite alternatives, at

---

[46] Luskin et al. (2022, p. 1222).

178 INTELLIGENT DEMOCRACY

least when it comes to the formal institutions of empowered space.[47] It is insufficient to show that empowered democratic decisions are likely to be more intelligent than empowered epistocratic or meritocratic decisions, when the latter involves higher ability deliberators.

If the benefits of cognitive diversity are not enough to establish the superiority of democracy, then what can? Over the next two chapters, I will explore an alternative strategy based on motivations. While we have seen how deliberative systems can gather and evaluate knowledge, engage in experimentation and self-regulation, and now utilize cognitive diversity, a question remains over how we can ensure democracies use these various epistemic abilities to advance the public interest. For political institutions to be intelligent they must direct their powers towards the promotion of justice and the common good, rather than towards the self-interest of political leaders, or worse still the promotion of injustice and the common bad. In the following chapters, I argue that part of the intelligence of democracy is that it has a superior ability to motivate decisions towards the public good when compared to any of the elitist alternatives offered by the new democratic sceptics. Such an argument, however, requires us to again take a systemic perspective. Neither the democratic mechanism of elections nor that of random sortition can generate this epistemic ability on its own, and democracy's intelligence is instead derived from a combination of these different institutions within a broader democratic system.

---

[47] Diversity may also be an asset for the democratic public sphere, as discussed in Chapter 3.

7

Elections and Elite Rule

Political power can be exercised for many purposes, and not all of them have anything to do with justice or the common good. Political leaders can enrich themselves and their families, provide benefits to favoured social groups and classes, or punish and persecute their political foes. If democracy is to be intelligent, then, what ensures that empowered democratic institutions aim to promote the common good, rather than their own self-interests or perhaps even the common bad? While the previous chapters have argued that democratic systems can gather and evaluate information, engage in experimentation and self-regulation, and utilize cognitive diversity, a question remains over how we can make sure that they use these epistemic abilities to enhance the public interest. One does not need to look very far to find examples of political power being used for nefarious purposes, whether this be in democratic or nondemocratic regimes. How are we therefore to ensure that political decision-makers are motivated to solve social problems in the name of the common good?

In this and the following chapter, I will argue that democracy best solves this motivational problem, and this is a key factor supporting its intelligence over more elitist regimes. Such an argument, however, requires that we again take a systemic perspective. I aim to show that the motivational ability of democracy cannot be achieved by a single institution, but instead requires that we combine the democratic mechanisms of elections and sortition. Although these two procedures have their benefits and limitations, it is by connecting them within a broader democratic system that they can offset each other's faults and produce a system which is more intelligent than either on its own. This chapter begins by focusing on the strengths and weaknesses of democratic elections in overcoming the motivational problem when compared to its elitist alternatives; the next will argue that they must be combined with random sortition to achieve the full intelligence of democracy.

I begin with what I will call the *conventional democratic solution* to the motivational problem, according to which regular and competitive elections align the interests of political representatives with the public good. Although

Intelligent Democracy. Jonathan Benson, Oxford University Press. © Oxford University Press 2024.
DOI: 10.1093/oso/9780197767283.003.0008

180   INTELLIGENT DEMOCRACY

a popular defence of democratic politics, this conventional solution is only half right. I argue that elections can motivate decision-makers away from the worst abuses and misuses of political power, but struggle to motivate them to enact the very best policies for the common good. While the latter is often a much too epistemically demanding task given the limits of voter knowledge, the former is surmountable even for the uninformed. Democratic elections provide a certain *protective value* as defences against the worst political decisions, but lack *proactive value* in only moderately motivating the very best. I therefore show how elections can still play a productive role in a democratic system, and contribute to this system's intelligence, despite the problems of voter knowledge highlighted earlier in this book. The epistemic competence of elections may be less significant than many epistemic democrats believe, but can still act as effective guards against the worst abuses and misuses of political power.

After establishing what elections can and cannot do, I then consider whether the elitist alternatives advocated by the new democratic sceptics offer any improvements. Among the new sceptics, the favoured forms of elite rule are political meritocracy—which involves the selection of political leaders through examination and experience—and epistocracy—which involves the use of regular elections but with a restricted franchise that excludes the most ignorant. Drawing on previous critiques of elite rule, I argue that neither offers much promise in addressing the motivational problem. By removing inclusive elections both these systems will have less protective value than a representative democracy and are therefore more open to the worst misuses of political power. These misuses are also likely to include manipulations of the procedures used to select meritocratic leaders and epistocratic voters, so they come to reflect the interests of those in power rather than any reasonable conception of merit or competence. I therefore argue that the reduced protective value which comes from removing inclusive elections also ends up undermining any proactive value which may have come from empowering the more able.

This chapter will therefore chart a position between the epistemic democrats who see inclusive elections as highly epistemically reliable, and the elitist democratic sceptics who believe they should be removed. Instead, I claim that elections are highly imperfect but necessary guards against abuses and misuses of power. This does not mean that electoral democracy is the best we can do, however. A systemic approach need not rely on elections alone, and the next chapter will develop a new proposal for combining them with mechanisms of random sortition, a proposal which can further improve the motivational ability of democracy and therefore enhance its intelligence.

The Conventional Democratic Solution

Any epistemic approach to politics, whether it be democratic or otherwise, will need to deal with a motivational problem. If political institutions are to promote justice, then they will not only require knowledge and information, but also the motivation to take decisions in the name of the common good. Actors within empowered political institutions may aim only at the promotion of their own political or economic interests, the betterment of their favoured social class, or at the persecution of their rivals. Across the world, including in longstanding democracies, we can see political power being exercised to enrich the privileged and to further undermine the vulnerable, and one does not need to think political leaders are always self-interested or malevolent to recognize the importance of this problem. Even if many who hold public office care deeply about the public interest, this does not eliminate the damage which can be done by the minority with bad intentions, the potential for good motivations to weaken or become corrupted over time, or the structural incentives which can lead even the most well-meaning actors to take decisions against the general interest.

How then should political institutions be arranged so that they can best guard against abuses of political power and incentivize leaders to promote the common good in their political decisions? Many instrumental arguments for democracy claim that inclusive elections are the best answer to this question. The familiar argument, which I will refer to as the *conventional democratic solution* to the motivational problem, is that regular and competitive elections help align the interests of political representatives with the public good. The problem with dictatorships and other undemocratic regimes is that they leave political leaders relatively unconstrained in their use of political power. They lack strong forms of accountability and mechanisms for incentivizing those in power to take account of the needs and interests of the whole population. The opportunities for ruling elites to use their power in self-serving or nefarious ways are therefore significant. Of course, even authoritarian leaders must fear the prospects of revolution and therefore give some minimal consideration to the general interest in order to avoid regime change. Given the dangers associated with revolt and the significant power

182 INTELLIGENT DEMOCRACY

imbalance between rulers and the ruled, however, this provides only a weak source of motivation.

Representative democracy, alternatively, makes empowered actors accountable to the public sphere through regular and competitive elections which condition their political power on the consent of the governed. It grants all citizens the ability to both authorize political power by selecting those who hold public office, and the ability to punish political decision-makers for the decisions they take. A democratic system is therefore arranged so that gaining and retaining political power requires those who desire it to convince the wider population that they will use it to promote their interests and values. In other words, inclusive democratic elections work to broaden political leaders' *circle of concern*. While a dictator may for the most part take into consideration only their own self-interest and that of other members of the ruling elite, democratically elected representatives must concern themselves with the broader public interest if they wish to remain in power. The need to be elected and re-elected therefore provides representatives with incentives to take decisions which enhance the common good and gives them many fewer opportunities to use their power in self-serving or malicious ways.

The competitive nature of elections then strengthens this incentive and further reduces the space for self-serving behaviour. In an electoral democracy, political representatives do not only need to convince the population that they will promote their interests and values, but that they will do this to a greater extent than the political opposition. The incentive is therefore to find and promote the best possible policies for the general interest so that one has the best odds of staying in office. A peaceful but competitive struggle for power within democratic procedures therefore forces political leaders to promote the common good or risk being beaten by their rivals. These competitors will also highlight the failures and weaknesses of those in office at every opportunity, further reducing the scope for self-interested behaviour for fear that it will be weaponized come election time.

This presentation of the conventional democratic solution is, of course, somewhat idealized, and one is unlikely to find many democrats who believe that elections perfectly or always motivate representatives towards the common good. Democrats can and commonly do recognize that elections only occur every few years, that representatives can be influenced by such things as campaign funding and special interests, or that they may have some reasons for attending to certain sections of the population over others. However, they can still maintain that regular and competitive elections which are inclusive of the whole adult population create more of an incentive for empowered political leaders to consider the public interests than nondemocratic systems. As imperfect as they may be, elections still broaden the circle of concern for political decision-makers much more than unaccountable dictators or oligarchs. While it will be less idealized than presented above and will likely come with all the relevant caveats, many supporters of democracy will endorse some version of this conventional solution to the motivational problem. To understand the strength of this solution, however, we need to determine just how imperfect democratic elections really are, and how they stack up against the elitist alternatives offered by the new democratic sceptics. Although I think there is an important element of truth to the conventional democratic solution, I argue that it is less compelling than democrats often believe.

What Elections Can and Cannot Do

The difficulty with the conventional solution to the motivational problem is that it is only half right. My claim is that while regular and competitive elections can help to motivate decision-makers away from the worst abuses and misuses of political power, they will struggle to motivate them to take the best decisions and adopt the very best policies for the public interest. The reason that they are unlikely to do the latter relates to the limits of voter knowledge. If elections are to motivate political decision-makers to enact the policies which best promote justice and the common good, then voters need to be able to hold them accountable. They need to be able to punish political leaders for taking bad decisions and select between competing candidates in accordance with the quality of the policies they propose. It was the argument of Chapter 2, however, that voters are unlikely to possess the knowledge necessary to identify the impact of political decisions on the common good, or to rank and compare alternative policy proposals by this criterion. These kinds of evaluations, unlike those relating to their self-interest, require voters to consider the effects of public policy on a large number of distant others. In doing this, however, they will have little incentive to acquire relevant information (given the low probability that their vote will be decisive), they will struggle to learn through trial-and-error experimentation (as they are disconnected from the effects of decisions on others), and they can make

184 INTELLIGENT DEMOCRACY

little use of their local knowledge (as this knowledge concerns the effects of policies only on themselves).

The kinds of accountability required for elections to motivate political leaders towards the best policies therefore comes into conflict with the incentive and information problems identified earlier in this book. Voters are unlikely to reward political leaders for good decisions and punish them for bad ones, as they will generally lack the knowledge needed to tell the good from the bad. Empirical work finds that voters are not well informed about the alternative policies on offer at election time, and therefore also about their effects on the public interest.[1] In fact, the majority of voters are found not to have consistent or reliable policy preferences to which political parties can appeal during electoral competition. Instead they tend to vote not based on their assessment of the consequences of the alternative policies on offer, but rather on their social environment, sense of identity, and sense of belonging to a political party.[2]

This is not to say that there is no correspondence between the public's views and the policy choices of their representatives. Even those who are most pessimistic about voter knowledge concede that elected politicians must have some concerns for the views of the electorate.[3] While most citizens cast their votes based on their sense of identity rather than policy, there is also likely to be some connection between one's group identity and one's individual interests.[4] In a world where groups matter and often face a common set of problems, group identity will often be a reasonable heuristic for one's individual interests. If someone votes for the British Labour Party because they identify as working class or votes Democratic because they identify as an African American woman, then these votes may still track the voter's interests as long as their interests broadly align with these groups, and these parties are generally more supportive of these group interests. This is not to say that these parties are the best possible representatives for these groups—far from it—but that one's group identity can still act as an imperfect proxy for one's interests. Identity-based voting does not therefore simply represent irrational signals in the wind. Unable to evaluate policy directly, individuals can vote according to the association between parties and group identity,

---

[1] Bartels (1996); Campbell et al. (1980); Caplan (2011); Friedman (1998); Zaller (1992).
[2] Barber and Pope (2019); Broockman and Butler (2017); Lenz (2013).
[3] Achen and Bartels (2017).
[4] This point has been pressed in more detail by both Chambers (2018) and Lepoutre (2020).

ELECTIONS AND ELITE RULE   185

and this will provide political leaders with some incentive to appeal to these group interests.

Elections will remain a very blunt instrument, however. As long as political candidates can offer rhetoric and promises which appeal to voters' sense of identity or belonging, and have the ability to take decisions without much public attention, they will be relatively free to promote their own interests or those of the more economically privileged and politically connected. Without informed public scrutiny and accountability for the decisions they take, or promise to take in the future, political leaders will have a certain autonomy to act in ways counter to the public interest. Empirical work supports this idea, finding only a weak correlation between the views of the general public and policy outcomes, something we would not expect if elections made decision-makers highly responsive to the general population.[5] Instead, influence tends to go to those with the highest incomes or to special interests with structural advantages. In one particularly bleak study of the US, for example, Martin Gilens and Benjamin Page find that once you control for the preferences of economic elites and special interests, average Americans have only a 'minuscule' impact on public policy.[6] This suggests that the ability of inclusive elections to widen political leaders' circle of concern, and motivate them towards the common good, is much weaker than the conventional democratic solution would suppose.

The US may be an extreme case, of course, particularly following the Supreme Court's Citizens United decision which greatly expanded the ability of wealthy interests to influence politics. There are also many reforms which could help to reduce the influence of elites on public policy and promote the influence of elections. Some combination of campaign finance and lobbying regulations, the public funding of political parties, and increased restrictions on the 'revolving door' between the public and private sectors, would all help to limit the influence of wealthy individuals and special interests. The disproportionate influence of these groups can be seen in representative democracies more generally, however, and while these reforms certainly offer potential improvements, none of them change the basic epistemic position of voters in respect of political representatives. The best possible set of campaign finance laws can close down avenues for elite influence, and should

---

[5] Bartels (2016); Crouch (2004); Gilens (2012); Hacker and Pierson (2010); Jacobs and Shapiro (2000); Schlozman, Verba, and Brady (2012).

[6] Gilens and Page (2014).

186 INTELLIGENT DEMOCRACY

therefore be pursued, but they do not change the fact that voters face incentive and informational problems when trying to provide informed scrutiny and accountability. They will therefore likely continue in their struggle to incentivize electoral competition in the direction of the common good, and political leaders will retain a certain freedom to exercise their power self-servingly.

The limits of voter knowledge therefore undermine much of the promise of the conventional democratic solution to the motivational problem. While this is regrettable from the democratic perspective, such problems do not completely remove the force of this solution. While elections only moderately incentivize the adoption of the very best policies, there is a large amount of evidence suggesting that democracies are still better at avoiding many of the worst political decisions than their nondemocratic counterparts. Democracies are, for instance, found to be better than nondemocracies at securing basic goods such as nutrition and calories, low infant mortality, life expectancy and healthcare, and basic education, as well as safe water, public sanitation, and low air pollution.[7] Nondemocracies also suffer from more widespread corruption, provide less protection for human rights, and have worse safeguards against state repression than do democracies.[8] When it comes to avoiding many of the worst outcomes of political decisions, then, and some of the worst abuses and misuses of power, democracies tend to perform very well relative to alternative political systems.[9]

How are we to explain this good performance, however, given the limits of voter knowledge and its implications for the competence of elections? Some democratic sceptics, such as Jason Brennan, have argued that these outcomes have nothing to do with regular and inclusive elections, but rather the fact that these elections are so imperfect in practice.[10] The good performance of

---

[7] Blaydes and Kayser (2011); Franco, Álvarez-Dardet, and Ruiz (2004); Kudamatsu (2012); Besley and Kudamatsu (2006); Acemoglu, Naidu, Restrepo, and Robinson (2015); Gallego (2010); Harding and Stasavage (2014); Deacon (2009); Winslow (2005).

[8] Davenport (2007); Rock (2009). Some of this evidence suggests that the relationship between democracy and corruption is not linear but involves an inverted U-shape with corruption increasing with early democratization and falling later on.

[9] This claim does not require that I take a position of the procedure-independent standards used to judge political decisions, something ruled out by the framework I developed in Chapter 1. The cases I have listed are examples of some of the worst outcomes of political decisions—such as famine, widespread persecution, or violations of basic rights—all or most of which will be accepted as negative on any reasonable conception of justice or the common good. As Estlund (2009) argues, these outcomes represents certain 'primary bads' which all reasonable people will wish to avoid. Taken as a whole, these examples also help illustrate the relative lack of consideration for the public interest in many nondemocracies, even if readers wish to quibble about the value of certain specific examples.

[10] Brennan (2016a).

real world democracies is therefore attributed to the outsized influence of wealthy elites and special interests, and if they were more truly democratic in allowing the average citizen more political influence, then they would produce far worse decisions. If this is the case, however, then why do democracies outperform nondemocracies? While the latter also provide wealthy elites and special interests with outsized influence, they fail to achieve the same level of basic rights, needs provision, or protection against corruption and repression as that found in systems with regular and competitive elections. It is therefore more likely that the good performance of democracies has something to do with their democratic character and that elections are able to retain some motivational value despite the limits of voter knowledge.

The reason elections continue to have motivational value is that when it comes to many of the worst abuses and misuses of power, voters do not, in fact, require a significant amount of information to hold representatives accountable. The good performance of democracies is often related to the avoidance of the worst outcomes of political decisions or what David Estlund has referred to as 'primary bads'.[11] That is, they involve very costly and highly salient outcomes, such as wars, famines, state persecution, widespread corruption, and the deprivation of certain basic needs. While Estlund is interested in these outcomes because they are not subject to reasonable disagreement, I am interested in the epistemic burden they present to voters. When a political decision (or set of decisions) leads to disastrous or highly costly outcomes, or results in very significant abuses of political power, it often does not require a very large amount of knowledge on the part of voters to identify such failures and to punish political leaders accordingly. The reason why elections can disincentivize these primary bads, then, is that unlike the very best policies, they do not require much knowledge to identify.

Amartya Sen's empirically informed work linking famine to a lack of democratic accountability is perhaps the best-known example of this logic in practice.[12] He argued that the 1943 Bengal famine can be traced back to the unaccountability of British Rule which allowed political decision-makers to ignore the interests of the local population. Democracies with regular and competitive elections, however, are unable to ignore the wider population's interests in this way, and Sen argues that this explains why they are found not to experience famines at the same rate. Democracies are able to do this

[11] Estlund (2009, p. 163).
[12] Sen (1982, 1999).

188 INTELLIGENT DEMOCRACY

despite low levels of voter knowledge, however, because citizens do not require large amounts of information to recognize that significant portions of the population (possibly including themselves and their family) are starving. The same can be said for many of the worst uses and abuses of political power, whether it be large-scale corruption and persecution, or decisions which lead to significant scarcity of basic goods, such as public health, primary education, life expectancy, or infant mortality. These high-cost outcomes are obvious to most citizens, even if they lack much specific political knowledge.

There is therefore an asymmetry in the epistemic burden associated with identifying and avoiding the worst abuses and misuses of political power, and to identifying and motivating the very best decisions for the common good. Consider, for instance, decisions about healthcare policy. To determine which healthcare system best promotes the common good would require one to be very well informed about the intricacies of different systems and their effects on the wider population. It would require knowledge of the benefits of different public, private, and mixed insurance regimes, the consequences of different management styles, the benefits and costs of concentrating or dispersing hospitals and doctors' practices, and the trade-offs that come with funding alternative kinds of care. This is a very large epistemic burden which the average voter cannot be expected to overcome. If, alternatively, a healthcare system leaves almost the whole population without access to a doctor and life expectancy in its fifties, then one does not need the above information to determine that this is a bad system. These results are easily observable to individuals, and it does not require a great amount of additional knowledge on their part to determine that a systemic inaccessibility to doctors and low life expectancy are evidence of a bad policy.

Identifying a bad healthcare system and punishing the relevant political representatives is simply a less epistemically demanding task than identifying the very best healthcare system, and the same goes for many other areas of public policy. Determining which balance of local and centralized policing provides the very best protection against violent crime is, for instance, an information-intensive task for voters to engage in. However, judging that a police force that systematically abuses its powers and arrests the innocent is a bad police force requires one to know very little. In the latter case, these bad results are easily observable and even uninformed voters can recognize that there are significant failings with the policy being practised.

Given the different epistemic burdens associated with the different tasks facing voters, we can see that the conventional democratic solution to the motivational problem is half right. Elections can help motivate decision-makers away from many of the worst uses and abuses of political power but will likely struggle to motivate them to promote the best policies in terms of justice or the common good. While the latter involves information-intensive decisions which voters are unlikely to perform effectively, the former does not make significant epistemic demands in terms of voter knowledge. Elections can therefore be said to have *protective value* in the sense that they guard against the worst political decisions, but only limited *proactive value* in the sense that they only moderately incentivize the very best decisions for the public interest.[13] Although the motivational power of democratic elections is therefore weaker than the conventional solution suggests, it is important that we do not underappreciate their protective value. Political power can and has been exercised in many disastrous ways, either through intentional abuse or unintentional blunders, and this has resulted in enormous injustices to those affected. We should not therefore be too quick to overlook or dismiss the value of a mechanism which can help us to avoid political decisions which result in famines, persecution, low needs provision, or rampant corruption. That being said, elections are likely to provide only weak proactive value and will therefore struggle to incentivize the adoption of the very best policies. Given the strengths and weaknesses of democratic elections, then, the next question is whether the elitist alternatives of the new democratic sceptics can offer any improvement.

Political Meritocracy and Its Limits

Some new democratic sceptics, most prominently Daniel Bell, argue for the benefits of what they call political meritocracy.[14] The distinctive features of this system of government is that it selects political leaders not through regular and competitive elections, but rather through processes of examination and promotion which aim to identify those with the greatest 'political

[13] One critic of elections who may accept a version of this claim is Guerrero (2014, p. 149), who mentions in passing that elections may avoid large scale failures such as famines. Guerrero does not peruse this point further, however, and ends up rejecting elections in favour of a purely sortition based system. He therefore overlooks the significant value elections bring to a democratic system as guards against the worst uses and abuses of power, but also, as I argue in the following chapter, the vulnerability of a purely sortition based regime to these kinds of decisions.

[14] Bell (2009, 2016). Also see Bai (2019); Bell and Pei (2020). While these authors often draw on Confucianism to defend political meritocracy, others have argued for forms of Confucian democracy, including on epistemic grounds. See Ziliotti (2023).

190   INTELLIGENT DEMOCRACY

merit'. According to Bell, good political decision-making requires intellectual and academic abilities, effective social skills, and emotional intelligence,
as well as ethical virtues. Those who occupy positions of significant political
authority should therefore show evidence of academic qualifications, broad
reading in the social sciences and ethical philosophy, and good performance
at lower levels of government. Rigorous examinations should therefore be
used to test potential leaders in terms of their analytical abilities and knowledge, while systems of promotion within government should evaluate their
past performance as well as their social skills, emotional intelligence, and
communicative talent.

While democracies can and often do apply meritocratic procedures to professional bureaucrats and advisers, such as in the British Civil Service, political meritocracy is distinctive in applying these procedures to offices with
the power to make binding political decisions. They are applied to public
positions which are normally elected in a representative democracy. As inspiration for such a system, defenders of political meritocracy often look
to the examples of China or Singapore. As Bell describes them, 'Singapore
has institutionalized a rigorous system for the recruitment of political
talent that starts with the search for high academic achievers in the school
system, followed by a battery of examinations at key stages in the selection
and promotion process' and 'China has been learning from Singapore in
this respect', as well as drawing on its long history of political examination.[15]
Contemporary China and Singapore are, of course, only imperfect examples
of political meritocracies. Bell therefore argues that they require significant
reforms if they are to live up to their meritocratic potential. His version of
the 'China Model' would include stronger protections for the rule of law and
freedoms of speech, better Confucian education, more political experimentation, and even limited forms of democracy at the local level.

How well is this kind of political meritocracy likely to perform in
addressing the motivational problem when compared to a democratic
system based on inclusive elections? It is certainly the case that contemporary regimes which claim to be meritocratic suffer from significant failures
in this respect. Modern-day China, for instance, provides ample evidence of
abuses and misuses of power, with the mass detention and persecution of
its Uyghurs and other Muslim communities offering only the most recent

---

[15] Bell (2016, p. 80). Bell is less optimistic about the potential for political meritocracy in the democratic world, given people's strong commitments to democratic institutions.

example.[16] The country has long suffered from significant corruption at both higher and lower levels of government, from the suppression of political dissent and ethnic minorities, from violations of religious freedom and freedom of expression, and from weak protections for women's rights and disability rights.[17] Defenders of political meritocracy are not unaware of such problems. Bell, for instance, recognizes that decisions need to be taken in respect of the public interest if they are to be classed as good decisions, and he traces a version of the motivational problem through Chinese history as 'the problem of the bad emperor'. He then offers a range of solutions aimed at addressing the motivational failures of current political meritocracies.

Firstly, Bell argues that meritocratic selection procedures should be aimed not only at identifying those with the most knowledge and analytical skill, but also those intrinsically motivated towards the common good. They should look to empower those with ethical virtues by testing their knowledge of Confucian ethics and judging if they performed admirably at lower levels of political office. The problem with this solution, as many of Bell's critics have pointed out, is that when it comes to selecting for good motivations, meritocratic procedures can be easily gamed. While examinations may in principle be effective tools for identifying knowledge and analytical skills, potential candidates can correctly answer questions on ethical philosophy or moral dilemmas, without in fact possessing ethical virtues themselves. Similarly, candidates may act appropriately at lower levels of government knowing this will create a path to promotion, only to reap the rewards of corruption at higher levels on the political hierarchy. Selection based on examination and experience is therefore likely to provide a highly imperfect mechanism for promoting good motivations.

The more troubling problem for political meritocracies, however, is that even if they could reliably select for ethical virtue, they lack clear and effective accountability mechanisms for those who do slip through the net or perhaps have their motivations corrupted over time. By not including a role for regular and competitive elections, meritocratic regimes leave the general population with no effective mechanism for punishing leaders who do engage in significant abuses of power and remove them from office. If meritocratic leaders fail to meet the basic needs of large portions of their population, participate in blatant and widespread corruption, or persecute certain

---

[16] Van Schaack and Wang (2021).
[17] Amnesty International (2021); Human Rights Watch (2021); Wederman (2004).

192   INTELLIGENT DEMOCRACY

social groups, the population has little ability to punish these leaders or re-move them from office. Nonelected leaders may still fear the threat of revolution or regime change and will therefore likely seek some level of perceived legitimacy from the public. In China, for instance, such legitimacy has come through increasing economic growth and poverty reduction. However, the relative lack of accountability for those who do abuse and misuse their political power means that a political meritocracy is likely to have much less protective value than a representative democracy with regular and competitive elections.

Accepting that meritocratic procedures will be imperfect at selecting for good motivations, Bell proposes that they be combined with a second set of solutions to the problem of the bad emperor. These include increasing salaries for public officials to disincentivize corruption, allowing greater freedom of speech and freedom of the press, creating a positive culture among political officials which promotes good behaviour and shuns corruption, and establishing independent bodies aimed at monitoring and tackling corruption when it occurs. The aim of such reforms is therefore to provide mechanisms for accountability within a meritocratic system, which can increase its protective value without recourse to elections. Some of these policies may simply represent weak protections against abuses of power, however. While financial incentives provided by salaries may be effective at lower levels of government, for instance, they are unlikely to outweigh the spoils of political corruption at the top. Singapore currently leads the world in political salaries with the prime minister receiving $3.1 million, but this still pales in significance to the $2.7 billion former Chinese Prime Minister Wen Jiabao is estimated to have accumulated while in office.[18]

The more significant issue facing political meritocracy, however, is that many of the mechanisms Bell proposes are also utilized by democracies, and often made most effective by their inclusion within a broader system which also possesses regular and competitive elections. As the systemic approach teaches us, single institutions often achieve their value through their combination with others. Many democratic states therefore make use of independent bodies to check corruption and abuses of power (including an independent judiciary), cultivate positive political cultures, and allow for significant freedoms of speech and the press, but it is how they combine these measures with competitive elections which allows them to function

[18] Bell (2016, pp. 120–121).

most effectively. Freedom of speech and the press, for instance, pose a much greater constraint on those in power when they are backed up by the threat that declines in public opinion will lead to electoral losses, while a positive culture shunning abuses of power will be easier to maintain in a system with fewer opportunities for self-serving behaviour. Similarly, independent corruption bodies are important but often reliant on those with political power listening to their recommendations and abiding by their judgements. This compliance will again be more likely in a political system where leaders must fear the criticism of their political rivals and their possible removal at the ballot box if they are found to have engaged in corrupt practices, or not to have followed the regulations of independent watchdogs.

The kinds of policies Bell proposes are therefore likely to lack much of their protective value when they are not combined in a broader system with regular and competitive elections. None of this is to say that such elections are a perfect guard against abuses and misuses of political power. Democratic regimes also suffer from problems of corruption, persecution against minority groups, and can struggle to meet the basic needs of certain citizens. Elections can nevertheless provide significant protective value not found in a political meritocracy and they can also work to magnify the effectiveness of other mechanisms which check the exercise of political power. A political meritocracy which removes regular and competitive elections is therefore at a much greater risk of seeing the worst uses and abuses of political power than a representative democracy.

Could a political meritocracy still provide some benefits when it comes to proactive value, however? It is the ability of meritocratic procedures to select competent and knowledgeable leaders which attracts their supporters, so perhaps political meritocracies will perform better than their counterparts when it comes to the more epistemically burdensome task of selecting the very best policies. One may even accept some of the arguments just made but be willing to trade off a higher risk of abuse of power for a greater ability to select the best policies when government is working well. Let us assume, for the sake of argument, that we know which general skills and characteristics are important to good political leadership, and that systems of examination and promotion can in principle be designed to select for them. The problem is that political meritocracy's lack of protective value will likely also undermine its proposed proactive value, because its openness to abuses of political power is likely to include abuses of the meritocratic procedures used to select political leaders.

194 INTELLIGENT DEMOCRACY

As Samuel Bagg has argued, an important way political leaders try to entrench their power is by shaping the structural conditions which support it, and leaders in a political meritocracy have a much greater latitude to engage in this shaping due to the ambiguities of the concept of 'political merit'.[19] Even if we grant Bell's three categories of political merit—intellectual ability, social skills, and ethical virtue—each of these allows for significant differences in interpretation, and each could be tested in a myriad of different ways.[20] Those who sit atop a political meritocracy therefore have significant space to reinterpret and reform meritocratic procedures to favour their own interests, providing them with significant leeway to protect their position, favour their allies, and exclude their rivals. Bagg's interests in this respect are in the threats which come from the ability of political leaders to entrench their own power, and his concerns are mostly for what I have called protective value. If meritocratic leaders can entrench their political position, then political meritocracy will be even more open to the kinds of abuses just discussed. However, the manipulation of meritocratic procedures will also undermine such a regime's proactive value as they come to reflect the interests of those in power rather than any reasonable conception of political merit. Political leaders will therefore be increasingly selected on their willingness to support the ruling elite, rather than their knowledge, ability, and virtue, weakening any advantages such a system may have when it comes to the epistemically demanding task of promoting the very best policies.

The manipulation of meritocratic procedures can be seen in China today. As Bell himself repeatedly notes, the country has a history of political debate over the nature and form of meritocratic processes, and problems of imperfect examinations, cheating and fraud, tests for ideological purity, structural advantages for the wealthy, the direct purchasing of public offices, a lack of diversity in terms of the gender and background of those being selected, and the significant influence of connections and political loyalty to one's advancement up the political ladder.[21] While Singapore may be thought to offer a more promising example, research also suggests that meritocratic principles are eroding there as well, and it is likely that it always exhibited a significant level of cronyism.[22] Bell, for instance, speaks highly of Prime Minister

[19] Bagg (2018).
[20] The vagueness of Bell's description of these attributes has been a source of criticism. In her polemical critique, for instance, Fuller (2019) suggests that Bell offers little more than a list of attributes required for a job in middle-management.
[21] Bell (2016, pp. 67. 81–88, 125–126).
[22] Tan (2008).

Lee Hsien Loong's admittedly impressive academic credentials, but the fact that his father Lee Kuan Yew previously occupied the office of prime minister may have also had something to do with his rise to the top of Singaporean politics.[23]

Of course, democratic leaders can also shape democratic selection procedures, through practices such as voter suppression or gerrymandering. What is important to recognize, however, is that they are more constrained in their ability to do this due to their position within a broader democratic system. While any one mechanism is always open to abuses, it is its position within a wider system which can either limit or exacerbate this possibility. The threat of removal through elections constrains democratic leaders from engaging in flagrant abuses of electoral procedures, while the absence of electoral punishment provides meritocratic leaders more autonomy to manipulate meritocratic processes in self-serving ways. A democratic system also involves organized and official opposition groups, and democratic leaders must therefore fear that their rivals will themselves manipulate electoral procedures when they come to power. As a number of authors have argued, political competition can moderate abuses, since placing limits on self-serving behaviour can be in the long-term interest of all parties.[24] Electoral competition therefore enforces restraint between competitors who all risk being disadvantaged by the other side's future manipulations. A meritocratic system's lack of an official opposition therefore leaves it more vulnerable to procedural abuses.

Official and organized opposition groups can also create established sources of resistance and dissent within a democratic system. Rival groups can make legal and legislative challenges to abuses of electoral systems and can also work to undermine popular support given that they are public-facing. Rival groups or individuals within a political meritocracy, alternatively, will often operate within the same party apparatus and will likely be more constrained in their public statements due to fear of reprisals from those in power. The ability to corrode the perceived legitimacy of the current elite is therefore significantly reduced, and even if a public case can be made, opposition groups will have a harder time in convincing the public of wrongdoing, given the ambiguity of the concept of political merit. Such ambiguity provides ample space for leaders to offer self-serving justifications

---

[23] Bell (2016, p. 80).
[24] Bagg (2018); Przeworski (2005); Shapiro (2016).

196 INTELLIGENT DEMOCRACY

which present manipulations as well-meaning meritocratic reforms. While there is still ambiguity in a democratic system (e.g. are voter ID laws a form of voter suppression or a reasonable guard against fraud?), the principle of 'one person one vote' is less open to interpretation than the definition of political merit or the processes of examination and promotion which are meant to identify it.

For all the limitations of representative democracy, political meritocracy does not appear to offer much improvement. By removing inclusive elections it lacks protective value compared to a democracy and is therefore at greater risk of the worst uses and abuses of political power. While political meritocrats may attempt to make use of alternative accountability mechanisms to correct this problem, the effectiveness of these mechanisms is also often dependent on their inclusion in a broader system with competitive electoral procedures. This lack of protective value then leaves such regimes vulnerable to abuses of the very meritocratic procedures they rely on to select competent leaders. Political meritocracy's weak protective value therefore works to undermine any proactive value its supporters believe it to bring, as selection processes come to reflect the interests of the ruling elite, rather than any reasonable conception of political merit.

Epistocracy and Its Limits

While political meritocracy does not offer much improvement over democracy, perhaps a system of epistocracy can. Epistocracy refers to a political system based on 'rule by the knowers' and aims to make political power conditional on one's knowledge and competence. It is therefore similar in principle to a political meritocracy, although it can take a very different institutional form. I will focus here on restricted franchise approaches to epistocracy, given that they offer a clear alternative to Bell's China Model. Jason Brennan is the most prominent advocate for such an epistocracy, and defends this view based on the idea that we all possess a 'right to a competent government'.[25]

Given the significant consequences of political decisions, Brennan argues that the incompetent exercise of political power would impose an

---

[25] Brennan (2014, 2016a, 2018). Brennan does consider other approaches to epistocracy, alongside a restricted franchise.

ELECTIONS AND ELITE RULE 197

unreasonable and excessive level of risk on others. Just as no person can reasonably be expected to undergo an operation conducted by a surgeon without training or experience in medicine, no person should be reasonably expected to be ruled by people who are ignorant or irrational about politics. By granting all the right to vote, however, representative democracy allows even the most uninformed citizens to wield some political power over others. Brennan therefore suggests that voting rights should be conditional on one's educational qualifications or the ability to pass a political knowledge test. Just as we require surgeons to undergo examinations, and drivers to pass a driving test, we should want citizens to prove their political competence before they are allowed to vote. Such restrictions would not be aimed at selecting a small elite of wise and virtuous leaders, as in a political meritocracy, but rather at removing the most ignorant and incompetent citizens from the electorate.

Just how many citizens would be denied the right to vote in this form of epistocracy is somewhat unclear. Brennan sometimes suggests that epistocratic elections should aim to remove the bottom 5% of voters in terms of political knowledge.[26] However, his claims that the bottom 25% of voters know less than nothing about political affairs, and that nonvoters know even less than that, suggests that many more would fail any political knowledge test and should therefore be denied the vote.[27] Whatever the exact number disenfranchised, the important feature of this form of epistocracy is that it would continue to select political leaders through regular and competitive elections, but it would look to improve the epistemic quality of these elections by removing the least knowledgeable citizens. Educational requirements or political knowledge tests are therefore defended as mechanisms for producing a more competent electorate than that found in democracies with a universal franchise.

In considering the motivational problem, an epistocracy based on a restricted franchise would likely provide more protection against the worst uses and abuses of power than a political meritocracy. Unlike meritocratic leaders, epistocratic leaders must still fear electoral punishment if they engage in rampant corruption and persecution, or produce widespread policy failures. While an improvement on Bell's China model in respect of protective value, epistocratic elections still offer a less effective guard against misuses of power than inclusive democratic elections. While both democratic and

[26] Brennan (2016a, pp. 99, 182).
[27] Brennan (2016a, p. 188).

198   INTELLIGENT DEMOCRACY

epistocratic elections will likely guard against abuses which impact all or most of the population, the latter is still vulnerable to those which disproportionately impact the group of citizens excluded from the franchise, who also happen to be those most at risk of abuse.

As is now broadly acknowledged, epistocratic forms of politics confront what has become known as the 'demographic problem' or the 'demographic objection'.[28] This problem points to the fact that while epistocrats hope to restrict voting rights purely based on political knowledge or education, this is likely to disproportionately exclude certain already underprivileged groups. Empirical research shows that political knowledge varies with respect to resources and expectations, for instance, and this can produce significant demographic effects.[29] Background inequalities in the distribution of wealth and education will therefore lead an epistocracy to exclude those groups who already lack power and resources. Brennan himself has accepted this point, noting that his preferred system would disproportionately disenfranchise black women in the context of the US, given that they tend to score lower in terms of the kinds of political knowledge he sees as important.[30] While the demographic problem has been argued to introduce a range of issues for the prospects of epistocracy, what is important to our discussion is its impact on epistocracy's protective value.

Because educational requirements and knowledge tests are likely to disproportionately disenfranchise those who currently lack resources, opportunities, and social status, an epistocracy is likely to disproportionately disenfranchise those who are most at risk of suffering abuses and misuses of power. Those with resources and social standing can of course fall victim to political abuse, but it is those that lack such goods who tend to be most vulnerable. While elections therefore represent mechanisms for protecting against the worst uses of political power, making voting rights conditional on knowledge and education is likely to remove these mechanisms from the groups who are most in need of their protection. The demographic problem confronting epistocracy therefore weakens its protective value compared to democratic elections which are inclusive of the whole population. While the latter provides the most vulnerable with a mechanism to influence and punish those in power, epistocracy is likely to leave them with little

---

[28] Bhatia (2020); Estlund (2009); Ingham and Wiens (2021).
[29] Delli Carpini (2000); Verba, Burns, and Schlozman (1997); Verba, Schlozman, Brady, and Nie (1993); Wolak and McDevitt (2011).
[30] Brennan (2016a, pp. 226–227).

protection. A similar problem will inflict plural voting forms of epistocracy, most famously defended by John Stuart Mill.[31] Although not completely excluding the most vulnerable from voting, by distributing vote in proportion to political knowledge, such a system would similarly leave these groups with relatively less influence.

In attempting to defend his epistocratic proposal from this kind of challenge, Brennan has argued that excluded groups will lack the social scientific knowledge needed to protect their interests through voting, and that more competent voters will not act in ways which hurt the interest of the disenfranchised, given that they tend to vote altruistically.[32] Those disenfranchised should not therefore fear abuses of power, even when their voting rights are removed. Neither of these responses are convincing. Firstly, we have already seen that many of the worst uses and abuses of political power do not require significant amounts of information to identify. There is therefore no reason to think that disenfranchised groups cannot, just like everyone else, use their voting rights to protect themselves. Secondly, although there is empirical evidence to suggest that voters generally cast their votes based on what they think is best for the public interest, this does not stop their view of the public interest from being biased by their social positions.[33] As a number of critics of epistocracy have argued, one does not need to vote selfishly or maliciously to vote in ways which favour one's own interests over those of other groups.[34] Furthermore, given the incentive and information problems which confront voters when making decisions about the public good, it is also likely that they will simply be ignorant of many of the harms that public policies create for excluded groups. Even if well-intentioned, then, those included in epistocratic elections will likely lack knowledge about how their decisions impact the disenfranchised.

While Brennan's argument for a 'right to a competent government' is based on the idea that people should not be subjected to excessive and unreasonable risks, his preferred epistocracy does exactly this to those it is most likely to exclude. By making voting rights conditional on education or political knowledge, an epistocracy would disproportionately disenfranchise those groups who are already most at risk of the worst uses and abuses of political power. This is not to say that democratic elections are perfect or that

[31] Mill (2011).
[32] Brennan (2016a, pp. 227–228).
[33] Feddersen, Gailmard, and Sandroni (2009).
[34] Bhatia (2020); Estlund (2003).

democracies never subject vulnerable groups to harm, but it does suggest that elections with a restricted franchise offer less protective value than those with a universal franchise. Perhaps the weaknesses of epistocratic elections in terms of protective value can be offset, however, by improvements in proactive value. By restricting voting rights with respect to education or political knowledge, an epistocracy aims to create a more competent electorate who may be better at the information intensive task of identifying the best policies. So, although epistocracy may leave certain groups in a vulnerable position, it may in general still motivate better policies (at least for those who are included) than a democracy which extents voting rights to all.

We should generally be sceptical of the epistemic improvements which are reported to come from a restricted franchise, given that all (and not just a subset) of voters face the incentive and information problems highlighted in previous chapters. Removing the bottom 5% of voters in terms of political knowledge, as Brennan sometimes suggests, would have little influence on epistemic reliability, if much of the remaining 95% also face a large epistemic burden which they have little incentive to overcome. Epistocrats may, of course, increase the percentage excluded with the hope of producing a more competent electorate. However, the more that are excluded the greater the proportion of the population who cannot use voting rights to protect against abuses, and therefore the weaker epistocracy's protective value. There is therefore a conflict in epistocratic politics between restricting the franchise enough to make elections more likely to identify the best policies, and restricting it so much that it leaves the system even more vulnerable to the worst kinds of political decisions.

Even if we were to grant that a restricted franchise could in principle incentivize better policies than a universal franchise, epistocracy's weak protective value is also likely to undermine the procedures used to select competent voters. As Bagg and Ilya Somin point out, by introducing epistemic standards into the criteria for eligible voters, epistocracy creates significantly greater opportunities for political leaders to shape the voter base in favour of their interests.[35] While there are limits to the manipulation which can occur in a democracy through practices such as gerrymandering, the design of educational requirements and voter knowledge tests would allow leaders to drastically change the make-up of the electorate. Given that voting behaviour is correlated with levels of education, for instance, political parties

[35] Bagg (2018); Somin (2019).

could easily alter such requirements to disproportionately exclude opposition voters. They could also redesign political knowledge tests to favour their likely supporters, such as by only asking questions on their key issues. The scope for fundamentally reshaping the electorate in favour of the interests of those in power is therefore significantly increased when voting rights are made conditional on political knowledge or competence. This further reduces epistocracy's protective value, but also undermines its proactive value as voting requirements stop reflecting any reasonable conception of political competence.

An epistocracy with a restricted franchise would also provide less protection against procedural manipulations than a democracy. Firstly, as was the case with the idea of political merit, the concept of voter competence is similarly vague and open to interpretation and disagreement.[36] Although the principle of 'one person one vote' is often under attack, it is much easier to police than the principle that 'voting should be dependent on a sufficient level of political competence or knowledge'. This ambiguity in the latter principle increases the possibility that self-serving manipulations can be passed off as reasonable epistemic reforms. Secondly, the fact that even a 'manipulation free' epistocracy would disproportionately exclude the underprivileged, it will already exclude those most likely to be the target of voter disenfranchisement. Those most at risk from manipulations of selection procedures will therefore find it even more difficult to resist their further exclusion, given that a significant portion of their members are already left without voting rights. The demographic problem therefore also contributes to the undermining of epistocracy's proactive value.

Historical examples of competence requirements offer cautionary tales concerning just these kinds of problems. Literacy tests in Jim Crow America, for instance, were publicly advocated for as measures for improving the competency of the electorate, but had the poorly disguised aim of excluding nonwhite voters.[37] As Michelle Alexander explains, 'formally race-neutral devices were adopted to achieve the goal of an all-white electorate' in the

---

[36] Estlund (2003). Brennan's own conception of political competence has been disputed. Gunn (2019), for instance, takes particular objection to the position Brennan gives to neoclassical economics as a basis for good political knowledge. While economics is seen as an uncontroversial marker of knowledge by Brennan, as well as Caplan (2011), Gunn argues that the social sciences involves much greater pluralism and disagreement over the appropriateness of rational choice models.

[37] Literature tests were used in combination with poll taxes, grandfather clauses, and felon disenfranchisement laws to systematically exclude nonwhite voters. States would also directly violate legal voting rights knowing that the cost of litigation would stop them from being challenged.

202   INTELLIGENT DEMOCRACY

knowledge that black Americans would likely fail such tests due to their systematic denial of education.[38] Such discrimination was then reinforced by the unequal application of such requirements, where poll workers would simply choose not to administer such tests to white Americans. Similar abuses can be found in cases where literacy tests were applied to migration requirements both in the United States and under Australia's White Australia Policy.[39] In response to historical examples, Brennan argues that the 'fact that governments used to hide their racism beneath an epistocratic disguise does not show us that epistocratic exams are inherently objectionable' and that the question about such a system 'is just how badly it would be abused today'.[40] Given the kinds of abuses epistocratic procedures have suffered from in the past, and the kinds of voter suppression tactics used by contemporary politicians, it seems very likely that competence tests would be manipulated if enacted in the contemporary context.

Epistocracy therefore suffers from a similar problem to political meritocracy, although perhaps to a lesser extent. Both of these elitist regimes remove or reduce the protective value of elections and are therefore at greater risk of the worst uses and abuses of political power. This weakened protective value then works to undermine any proactive value these systems may be thought to bring, as abuses in power are likely to include manipulations of the very procedures used to select meritocratic leaders and competent voters. These procedures will therefore likely come to reflect the interests of the ruling elite rather than any reasonable conception of merit or competence, removing the proactive value their supporters hope they will bring by disempowering the ignorant.

Is Representative Democracy the Best We Can Do?

While previous chapters questioned the epistemic reliability of democratic elections, this chapter has defended their role in a democratic system. Regular, competitive, and inclusive elections can perform a vital function as guards against the worst uses and abuses of political power, and they can do this irrespective of low levels of voter knowledge. The epistemic limits of voters do not therefore stop elections from contributing to democracy's

---

[38] Alexander (2020, p. 187).
[39] Lake (2005).
[40] Brennan (2016a, p. 224).

intelligence. No matter how informed, political decisions cannot be intelligent if they only promote the interests of the privileged few, and inclusive elections provide a necessary check against such abuses. Democratic elections are still a highly imperfect solution to the motivational problem, however, given that they are unlikely to effectively perform the information intensive task of incentivizing political leaders towards the best policies. The new democratic sceptics have made much of these faults, but they overlook the benefits which can still come from democracy's protective value. Their preferred regimes of political meritocracy and epistocracy therefore end up weakening this value, with the result that they open themselves up to serious abuses and undermine their own ability to select more knowledgeable leaders and voters. This chapter has therefore charted a position between many epistemic democrats on the one hand, who often underestimate the problems voter knowledge present to the epistemic reliability of elections, and the elitist democratic sceptics on the other, who see voter ignorance as supporting the rejection of a universal franchise. Contrary to both, democratic elections are unlikely to motivate the very best decisions, but do offer effective guards against misuses and abuses of power.

Is representative democracy, with all its imperfections, therefore the best we can do? If it is, then this would seem to leave the intelligence of democracy in a rather weak position. If all we can hope for is democratic institutions which can avoid the worst uses of political power, and only moderately incentivize the adoption of the best policies, then they would not seem to make the best use of all the epistemic abilities highlighted in previous chapters. Democratic systems have been shown to possess the epistemic abilities of gathering and evaluating knowledge, engaging in experimentation and self-regulation, and utilizing cognitive diversity, but they would not seem to make the most of these abilities if they are only moderately motivated to exercise them to enhance the public interest. This appears to be the position that many contemporary democracies currently occupy, with political decisions disproportionately reflecting the preferences and interests of wealthy elites rather than those of the general population.

If we take a systemic perspective, however, democratic systems do not need to rely on elections alone to address the motivational problem. As noted repeatedly throughout this book, a systemic approach allows alternative mechanisms to be combined or connected, so that the weakness of one can be compensated for by others. Elections can therefore play an important role in a deliberative democratic system, helping it to avoid the worst uses and

204 INTELLIGENT DEMOCRACY

abuses of power, while other parts of the system may play a role in helping to motivate decision-makers towards the best policies. In the next chapter, I argue that this kind of division of labour can be achieved if we combine elections with institutions based on random sortition. I develop a proposal for a sortition branch of a deliberative system, which would institutionalize the use of random lotteries alongside regular elections as a new source of citizen scrutiny and accountability on elected officials. Through this proposal, I argue that the limitations of representative democracy do not require the greater exclusion of citizens, as claimed by the elitist democratic sceptics, but rather their greater inclusion in the processes of empowered political decision-making. By connecting elections and sortition in just the right way, we can produce a system more intelligent than either of these democratic institutions alone.

8

The Sortition Branch

The more elitist versions of the new democratic scepticism look to include only the best and brightest in politics, excluding those they see as most responsible for democracy's ills. We have already seen why their preferred alternatives fail to improve on even a very imperfect democracy. Yes, democratic elections possess weaknesses due to the limits of voter knowledge, but the removal of inclusive elections leaves more exclusionary systems vulnerable to the worst uses and abuses of power, and therefore to manipulations of the very procedures which are meant to select the best and brightest. Elite forms of rule are therefore likely to be less intelligent forms of rule, because they fail to motivate decisions towards the common good. This does not mean, however, that a representative democracy based on regular and competitive elections is the best we can do. A systemic perspective teaches us that the weaknesses of single institutions can be mitigated through their connection to others, and that an effective division of labour can make use of the strengths of alternative institutional forms. In this chapter, I argue that the weaknesses of elections can be overcome if they are appropriately combined with institutions based on random selection and develop a proposal for a sortition branch of a democratic system. While elections can play an effective role as guards against the worst uses and abuses of power, I argue that sortition can then better motivate elected leaders towards the common good.

Sortition refers to selection via random lotteries and has been considered a democratic mechanism since at least the ancient Greeks. By giving all an equal chance of being included, sortition expresses a form of political equality where all citizens are seen as having the capacity to participate in formal politics. For the Greeks, distributing political positions by lottery was seen as a guard against abuses of authority, with offices being randomly rotated to avoid concentrations of power among a few individuals. While contemporary epistemic democrats, such as Hélène Landemore, have focused on how random selection can promote greater diversity, I wish to return to sortition's

Intelligent Democracy. Jonathan Benson, Oxford University Press. © Oxford University Press 2024.
DOI: 10.1093/oso/9780197767283.003.0009

206   INTELLIGENT DEMOCRACY

motivational benefits.[1] By randomly selecting a small group of citizens to take part in an assembly, sortition provides the possibility for more informed public scrutiny of political decisions and accountability for elected officials. In other words, it may perform the kinds of epistemically demanding work individual voters struggle to do. The devil, however, is in the detail. While many democrats have recognized sortition's potential in overcoming the faults of our existing democracies, current proposals for combining random selection with elections leave much to be desired.

I consider two of the best-known and most popular sortition proposals: the greater use of 'deliberative mini-publics' and the establishment of a 'randomly selected legislator' as part of a bicameral system. To effectively improve the motivational value of a democratic system, sortition bodies must have *substantive power* so they can have influence on decisions, not be overly *burdensome* on their citizen members, and be able to resist forms of *elite capture* which aim to direct decisions towards specific interests. Drawing on previous debates over sortition, I argue that current approaches face significant problems in terms of these criteria. My main aim in this chapter, however, is to show that while these problems are serious, they are also dependent on institutional design and can therefore be overcome through the appropriate institutionalization of sortition.

I develop and defend a proposal for a sortition branch of a democratic system which would oversee the formation of many single-issue, short-term, and randomly selected assemblies with the power to veto legislation from an elected chamber or popular initiatives from the public sphere. I do not offer this proposal as a fixed blueprint, but rather as an illustration of how sortition can avoid the dilemmas of past approaches. I argue that through a division of labour and the rapid rotation of assemblies, sortition bodies can possess substantive powers to consider and vote on legislation while still not being overly burdensome on their members and avoiding pernicious forms of elite capture. I therefore aim to vindicate a specifically legislative role for sortition in a democratic system and in doing so show that the limits of elections are best overcome by democratic means. Contrary to the claims of the new democratic sceptics, I argue that the weaknesses of elections call for more, not less, direct involvement of citizens in political decision-making. A more intelligent democracy will therefore be a more inclusive and participatory democracy.

---

[1] For a full decision of Landemore's approach, see Chapter 6.

The Potential of Random Sortition

Distributing political positions through random lotteries has historically been viewed as a highly democratic procedure, often even more so than elections.[2] For Aristotle, sortition realized the democratic ideal of ruling and being ruled in turn by rotating citizens between positions of public office and everyday life as a member of the *polis*. Elections, on the other hand, were thought to reinforce a distinction between those chosen to rule and the rest of society, and as a result retained a certain similarity with oligarchy. Such concerns can still be seen in contemporary politics, with elections distinguishing a class of professional politicians from the rest of the public. Sortition has also often been thought of as democratic because it expresses a particularly strong form of political equality. Rather than 'one person one vote', random selection gives everyone an equal chance of being included in decision-making. It therefore not only expresses everyone's ability to pick their rulers, but their ability to directly engage in political decisions for themselves.

While perhaps most famously playing a role in the politics of ancient Athens, in the contemporary context sortition was for a long time confined to the judiciary, selecting juries for criminal trials, but not participants for political office. Random selection has, however, seen a revival of interest in both democratic theory and in the practice of contemporary democracies. Recent years have seen a proliferation of new forms of citizen participation, or 'democratic innovations', many of which make use of selection via lot.[3] Citizen juries and assemblies, consensus conferences, and deliberative polls all determine their members via means of random lottery, and represent a revival of this old democratic mechanism in modern politics. Support for sortition is often driven by the potential of random selection to address some of the limitations and shortcomings of electoral processes, and this potential can be seen in the analysis of this book.

The previous chapter argued that elections are able to guard against the worst uses and abuses of political power (they have protective value), but that they struggle to provide a strong incentive for political representatives to select the best policies (they lack proactive value). Although recognizing serious failures in political decision-making does not require

---

[2] Manin (1997).
[3] OECD (2020); Smith (2009).

208 INTELLIGENT DEMOCRACY

much information on the part of voters, determining the best policies for the common good confronts citizens with a significant epistemic burden. It requires large amounts of knowledge about alternative policies which individual voters cannot be expected to possess. This weakness results from the institutional structure of elections which leaves decisions to a large number of individual citizens spread throughout society. Sortition bodies, however, do not possess this same institutional structure. Random lotteries can be used to select a small group of citizens who are similar to the larger population, but who can be included in a collective assembly which can provide them with much more information and time to consider questions of public policy. While a sortition body will be unlikely to meet the standards of statistical representativeness, random selection can create an assembly with similar interests and values to the *demos* as a whole. It will look to reflect the feelings and beliefs of a population, even if it cannot act as a perfect 'simulation of what the population as a whole would decide if everyone were allowed to deliberate'.[4] Unlike the population as a whole, however, a sortition assembly is a more collective institution which can provide its members with the resources needed to make informed evaluations of public policy with respect to the common good.

As is the case with many democratic innovations, randomly selected assemblies can provide their members with the assessment of experts, the testimony of affected parties, and opportunities to deliberate with one another, allowing them to make more effective judgements about which decisions are more likely to promote the public interest. Consider, for instance, the British Columbia Citizens' Assembly (BCCA) which has become one of the most discussed modern examples of the political use of sortition.[5] Given the task of determining the preferred electoral system for the province, the assembly randomly selected 161 members from the general public to consider the issue. The members went through a learning phase which included expert testimony on social scientific knowledge, and a public consultation phase where participants heard the concerns of other citizens. It then provided members with significant time to discuss and deliberate with each other and come to a decision about the best electoral system. The BCCA allowed a group of citizens to become lay experts in electoral systems, and then come to a reasoned judgement about whether the current system should be replaced.

---

[4] Dryzek (2012).
[5] Herath (2007); Warren and Pearse (2008).

Unlike a whole electorate, the collective nature of a sortition body means that citizens can be provided with the information they need to evaluate public policy, while random selection can ensure a similarity between this more informed body and the broader public, in terms of their interests and values.

Sortition therefore has the potential to perform the epistemically demanding tasks which elections struggle to perform. It can allow for more informed and considered citizen scrutiny of political decisions which can better evaluate their implications for the common good or public interest, and therefore possibly improve the proactive value of a democratic system. If sortition has these benefits, however, then why not do away with elections completely and opt for a purely sortition based political system? Sometimes referred to as 'lottocracy', such a system would select all political leaders randomly and have political decisions taken by one or more sortition-based legislature.[6] The problem with lottocracy, however, is that by completely removing inclusive elections it is likely to lack protective value in a similar way to elite forms of politics. A lottocracy would allow decisions to be taken by more informed citizens, but without a system of elections it would leave them with significant autonomy to use their power in self-serving ways, just as a political meritocracy leaves its meritocratic leaders free to make decisions with little accountability or oversight. A purely sortition-based system is therefore likely to lack protective value and risk significant abuses and misuses of political power.[7]

A systemic approach, however, allows us to consider how sortition and elections may be combined, in order to overcome the limitations of both lottocracy and representative democracy. A deliberative system which made use of both mechanisms could reap the protective value of elections and proactive value of sortition. Elections could therefore play the role of guards against the worst uses and abuses of power, while sortition would better motivate decisions to promote the common good. Whether or not this prospect can be realized, however, will hinge on questions of institutional design. The wrong combination of these mechanisms can end up magnifying their vices, rather than combining their virtues. The question, then, is how can we best link or couple elections and sortition so that a democratic system can reap

---

[6] Guerrero (2014). Also see Landemore (2020).

[7] Lottocracy may still outperform political meritocracy in this respect. This is because meritocratic procedures are likely to attract those who most desire power, and therefore those who are perhaps most eager to advance their own position, while random selection is neutral on individuals' motivation for holding political office.

210 INTELLIGENT DEMOCRACY

the benefits of both? To date, there have been a host of academic and popular proposals for connecting random lotteries to the current institutions of representative democracy.[8] Drawing on the existing literature and focusing on two of the best known proposals—deliberative mini-publics and a randomly selected legislature—I will argue that existing approaches currently face significant problems, and struggle to realize the systemic benefits which could come from combining elections with sortition.

In evaluating these proposals, I will focus on three key criteria which are important to realizing the proactive value of sortition, and therefore improving the intelligence of a democratic system. Firstly, a sortition body must have *substantive powers* which allow it to influence political decisions. Without significant influence over decision-making, we cannot expect sortition bodies to improve policy in terms of the common good. Secondly, the sortition body must not be overly *burdensome* on its lay members. This criterion has two components: the body should not be overly burdensome in the sense that the task it performs is outside of the competence of lay members, and it should not demand too much time and energy from citizens who are not professional politicians and have other important commitments. Thirdly, the sortition body should also be able to limit *elite forms of capture*. If such a body is to better motivate democratic decisions towards the common good, then it needs to be able to resist influence from powerful subsections of the population. This includes *economic capture* by wealthy or special interests, *political capture* by elected representatives, and *technocratic capture* by experts or civil servants. While no system can eradicate the influence of these groups, an effective use of sortition must at least be able to limit or resist them if it is to motivate better political decision-making. The most popular proposals for linking sortition to a broader democratic system, however, fall short when judged by these criteria.

Deliberative Mini-Publics and Their Limits

Apart from the selection of criminal juries, the use of random sortition in modern democracies is rather limited. The exception is the growing use and experimentation with deliberative mini-publics. While the concept has

---

[8] Ackerman and Fishkin (2004); Barnett and Carty (1998); Callenbach, Phillips, and Sutherland (2008); Fishkin (2011); Gastil and Wright (2019); Hennig (2017); Landemore (2020); McCormick (2006); O'Leary (2006); Van Reybrouck (2016); Zakaras (2010).

received many definitions and refers to a range of institutions, mini-publics normally involve 'independent and facilitated group discussions among a (near) random sample of citizens who take evidence from experts and interested parties'.[9] They are typically one-off assemblies, formed to consider single policy issues, and include citizen assemblies and juries, consensus conferences, planning cells, G1000s, and deliberative polls. These initiatives are designed to be small enough to allow for genuine deliberation between randomly selected citizens, but also representative enough to be genuinely democratic.[10] They have therefore become very popular among deliberative democrats, even being described as 'the most advanced method to institutionalise deliberative democracy'.[11]

Varying types of mini-publics can be distinguished by their different design features, such as the number of citizens included. Citizen juries, for instance, often include fewer than twenty members, citizen assemblies between 100 and 150, and G1000s over one thousand. Some, like deliberative polls, rely on purely random selection to appoint members, while others often use stratified (or near random) sampling to ensure representation of key groups—the latter often being needed when the number of participants is small. Mini-publics can also have different aims or objectives, with some concluding with the formation of recommendations (as in citizen assemblies), post-deliberation surveys (as in deliberative polls), or in nonbinding votes on proposals (as in G1000s). All, however, tend to be one-off events commissioned to consider a single policy issue, with the aim of providing information or advice to elected politicians. There are some limited exceptions to this general rule. The Citizens' Assembly on Brexit in the UK, for instance, deliberated on both trade and immigration policy, while The Citizens' Assembly in Ireland considered a total of five issues.[12] The BCCA, alternatively, had its conclusions put to a popular referendum, and therefore had some agenda-setting powers as was the case for the Irish assembly's decisions on abortion. These cases remain exceptions, however, to the conventional use of mini-publics which involve single issues and recommendations.

---

[9] Setälä and Smith (2018, p. 301). For alternative definitions, see Fung (2003); Ryan and Smith (2014).

[10] Goodin and Dryzek (2006).

[11] Elstub and McLaverty (2014, p. 14). For critiques of mini-publics and/or sortition from a deliberative democratic perspective, see Chambers (2009); Lafont (2015); Böker (2017). Some of these critiques will be considered below.

[12] Farrell, Suiter, and Harris (2019); Renwick et al. (2018).

212 INTELLIGENT DEMOCRACY

Perhaps the greatest achievement of experiments with mini-publics has been to reply to the objection that a random group of lay citizens cannot intelligently and competently discuss issues of public policy. Many of those who are sceptical of sortition question whether the assessment of policy is a too cognitively burdensome task for the average citizen. They claim that citizen deliberation will at best be ill-informed and unsophisticated, and at worst an abusive shouting match. The evidence coming from mini-publics, however, rejects these concerns. There are now a wide range of experiments which show that citizen members are able to increase their level of information about the topic, deliberate in reasonable and respectful ways, and reflect on the issue under consideration. The BCCA is one such example. An analysis of the assembly tracked participants through a number of surveys conducted over their year-long deliberations, and found that they 'made choices that reflected a well-defined set of criteria appropriate to the choice of an electoral system'.[13] The criteria that members used to evaluate the alternative electoral systems remained stable throughout the assembly, but they changed their preferred electoral system as they gained new information and determined how the electoral systems fitted with their criteria. The researchers therefore concluded that 'the Assembly did indeed make a reasonable and intelligible choice'.[14]

Studies of deliberative polls, alternatively, have found that participants' policy attitudes and intentions are more predictable after deliberation, and their policy attitudes on collections of values become more correlated with empirical premises. Members have also been shown to change their mind not only in respect of receiving new information, but also through deliberation with others.[15] Other work has also shown that citizen members increase their understanding of opposing arguments during mini-publics and can form a 'meta-consensus' over the key dimensions of the dispute being considered.[16] As discussed in Chapter 6, there is also evidence that these forms of citizen deliberation can avoid common negative synergies or deliberative failures, such as group polarization. Combined with the fact that they only sit for relatively short periods, this evidence suggests that the demands mini-publics place on lay members are not overly burdensome.

[13] Blais et al. (2008, p. 138).
[14] Blais et al. (2008, p. 144).
[15] Fishkin (2011); Fishkin and Luskin (2005).
[16] Andersen and Hansen (2007); Hansen and Andersen (2004); Niemeyer and Dryzek (2007).

Despite these successes, the impact of mini-publics on political decision-making remains marginal. Apart from a few exceptions, these sortition bodies provide inputs into the political decision-making process, but final decisions are then taken by other actors such as elected representatives or civil servants. They are normally also commissioned by governments looking for informed public recommendation, and therefore represent a form of 'governance-driven democratization'.[17] Not only has this been the general practice, but also the role commonly advocated by supporters of mini-publics.[18] While this advisory role can be productive, it generally leaves mini-publics without substantive powers to influence political decision-making, and it is difficult to find examples where they have significantly impacted the policy process.[19] This advisory and one-off role also tends to leave mini-publics open to political and technocratic forms of capture. It is now well recognized that public authorities can be highly selective in both their adoption of the recommendations emerging from mini-publics and their initial establishment.[20] Elites can easily use them to their own advantage, commissioning them only when they support their ends and increase their perceived legitimacy. There have also been cases where such initiatives, such as NHS Citizens in the UK, simply found their funding drying up as their recommendations started contradicting the priorities of their commissioners.[21] While other mini-publics are commissioned by nongovernmental bodies, like the Australian Citizens' Parliament, this often leaves them disconnected from empowered institutions and actors.[22]

Mini-publics can avoid some forms of capture. The quality of their deliberation, for instance, suggests that they are not adversely influenced by expert witnesses or facilitators. There are also very few instances where mini-publics have been a target of significant economic capture by special interest groups or wealthy individuals. However, the lack of substantive powers possessed by mini-publics, combined with their one-off and temporary nature, leaves them open to capture by the politicians or technocrats who commission them. As a result, they risk being 'assimilated' into the broader political system and will struggle to provide an independent source of scrutiny which can motivate representatives towards the common good.[23] So while

---

[17] Warren (2009).
[18] Fishkin (1997, 2011); Lafont (2019); Parkinson (2006).
[19] Goodin and Dryzek (2006).
[20] Font, Smith, Galais, and Alarcon (2018); Hendriks (2016).
[21] Dean et al. (2020).
[22] Carson, Gastil, Hartz-Karp, and Lubensky (2013).
[23] Neblo (2015, p. 182).

214 INTELLIGENT DEMOCRACY

mini-publics have been 'internally' successful in terms of producing high-quality deliberation among their members, they have been less successful 'externally' in terms of their impact on the wider deliberative system and political decision-making in particular.[24]

Randomly Selected Legislators and Their Limits

Mini-publics have shown us that citizens can deliberate effectively and knowledgeably about issues of public policy, but their temporary nature and lack of influence means that they are unlikely to produce significant changes to the decision-making quality of democracy. The next step therefore seems to be to establish sortition as a permanent and more powerful component of a deliberative system. In this vein, proposals have been made to utilize sortition in a bi-cameral legislature where one chamber would be elected and the other would be selected by random lottery. Over twenty years ago Anthony Barnett and Peter Carty made such a proposal as a replacement for the UK's House of Lords (what they called the 'Athenian Option'), and more recently John Gastil and Erick Olin Wright have defended a coequal legislative assembly appointed by lot.[25] This section will focus on Gastil and Wright's more recent model, given that it offers a purer and more general proposal for the use of sortition, unlike Barnett and Carty's Athenian Option which involves only some members appointed by lot and is developed specifically within debates over UK parliamentary reform.

Gastil and Wright's proposal is for a bicameral legislative system where one chamber would be directly elected and the other would be selected by lottery. The latter, labelled the 'sortition assembly', would be filled by a random selection of the general public with the use of stratified sampling to ensure geographic and demographic representation, and with a limited set of rules for disqualification (e.g. those serving a current prison sentence). These lay members would sit for multiyear terms with only a portion being rotated at a time in order to retain experience. Gastil and Wright suggest either a two-year term with the possibility of serving another two or a five-year term where members can resign at any point but are expected to sit for at least two years. These members would not be party affiliated like those in the elected

---

[24] Curato and Böker (2016).
[25] Barnett and Carty (1998); Gastil and Wright (2019).

chamber, but could organize themselves into like-minded groups based on common values or priorities. An oversight committee would then review the selection of members, the assembly's procedural rules, and any complaints concerning misconduct. In terms of the sortition assembly's powers, it would be coequal with the fully elected chamber, with both chambers having the ability to initiate their own legislation as well as vote on legislation passed by the other. The sortition assembly would therefore not only have powers to scrutinize the laws and policies produced by elected representatives but would also have its own agenda-setting powers to form its own proposals, subject to approval from the elected assembly. In conducting these tasks, the randomly selected members would be given financial incentives to participate, extended training before taking up their position, and a staff to guide and advise them.

Compared to deliberative mini-publics, a randomly selected legislature along these lines would have significantly greater ability to influence policy decisions. Rather than a purely advisory assembly whose suggestions are enacted at the discretion of elected representatives, a legislative chamber would have the power to propose, form, scrutinize, and vote on laws, and any legislation coming from the elected chamber would need to gain the approval of the majority of randomly selected members. The sortition assembly would also be a fixed feature of the democratic system, so it could not be ignored or only consulted when it was politically expedient. The permanent nature of a legislative assembly therefore reduces the kinds of political and technocratic capture exhibited by mini-publics, while its increased powers make it much more consequential. However, the broader powers granted to a sortition assembly also make it a much greater target of capture by economic elites and special interests.

The effort that wealthy special interests make to influence an assembly will generally be proportional to the gains they can expect from capturing such a body. So although mini-publics have garnered little attention from such actors so far, this is likely due to their relative lack of influence, and we should expect this to increase with the power of the sortition body.[26] When it comes to Gastil and Wright's proposal, the gains from capture are considerable for two main reasons. Firstly, the sortition assembly has the power to both create and vote on pieces of legislation and therefore has significant influence over their content. Special interests would therefore have the expected benefit of

---

[26] Neblo (2015).

being able to shape legislation to fit their interests and veto legislation they object to. Secondly, the broad remit of the sortition assembly means that it possesses these substantial powers over all forms of legislation. Special interests could therefore expect influence not only over one or a limited range of policies, but over the whole policy agenda. Together, economic interests would have a very substantial incentive to try to capture such a body, and a legislative chamber appointed by lot is likely to experience many of the same forms of special interest influence which already inflict elected chambers.

While the absence of elections does remove campaign contributions as a mechanism of economic capture, a sortition legislature will still very likely see organized lobbying as well as 'revolving door' problems. The offer of lucrative employment options for themselves, or for family and friends, could easily lead to the capture of randomly selected members.[27] The absence of elections also means that members of the sortition chamber could not be removed from their position by the electorate if they do engage in such behaviour. Gastil and Wright's proposal does include an oversight committee which could have the power to review complaints and make recommendations to the full chamber who could vote on expulsion. However, although independent review bodies can certainly help to fight explicit corruption such as bribery, many forms of special interest influence are difficult to detect and can be designed to work around rules and regulations. While such oversight can and should be improved, the behaviours we see in current elected chambers suggest it may be inevitably limited.

The substantial power and broad remit of a legislative chamber therefore increases the risks that a sortition assembly would suffer from economic capture. The size of these responsibilities also increases the burden such an assembly would place on its lay members. Firstly, these members would be expected to take at least two years and possibly up to five away from their lives to participate in such an assembly. While financial incentives and salaries can be offered to compensate, these citizens would still be asked to put their life projects on hold for multiple years in order to become a full-time legislator. Whether this be raising children, running a small business, or completing a degree, such requirements create a sizeable burden on those citizens who are selected. Perhaps more troubling, however, is that the task which confronts those citizens who do take up positions is itself highly burdensome. As we have seen, there is ample evidence from mini-publics that lay citizens can

---

[27] Landa and Pevnick (2021).

become well informed on issues of public policy and deliberate on them in a competent and reasonable manner. Mini-publics, however, are for the most part conducted only on a single policy issue and at most a handful of such issues. They are also given the limited objective of scrutinizing a range of predetermined policy options, and perhaps offering small amendments.

A coequal legislative chamber, alternatively, would require its lay members to scrutinize, and therefore become informed about, all aspects of public policy. Rather than a clearly defined single issue, these nonprofessional legislatures would need to assess whole policy agendas over many years. They would also be expected to engage in the complex task of creating new policy proposals and new pieces of legislation from scratch. Members do not, of course, have to become experts on all issues. Elected politicians, for instance, often do not understand all the complexities of what they are voting on. However, elected politicians also operate within a more partisan environment and can rely on the apparatus of political parties to provide them with voting intentions and policy priorities. Randomly selected members, alternatively, are meant to play a less partisan game. In order to be an independent check on the elected chamber, they are given a more reflective role of considering the merits of the policy before them, rather than following the marching orders of political parties. Randomly selected members are therefore given a more demanding task than their elected counterparts.

Although mini-publics provide much support for the competence and abilities of lay citizens, they do not give us an example of citizens engaging in the wide range of responsibilities given to legislative chambers. In making a similar point, David Owen and Graham Smith argue that there are currently no examples of sortition bodies with such broad responsibilities, nor evidence that they can be effective when they move from single well-defined issues.[28] They also point out that even Ancient Athens did not grant a randomly selected assembly with the extensive powers found in a sortition legislature. The burdens which are placed on members create their own problems and are likely to reduce the effectiveness of such a chamber. They also reintroduce issues of political and technocratic capture, although in a different form to those seen in mini-publics. Confronted with the daunting task of scrutinizing all legislation and formulating original policy, lay members are much more likely to defer judgement to elected representatives, civil servants, and experts. Unable to become informed on every issue put before

---

[28] Owen and Smith (2019).

218   INTELLIGENT DEMOCRACY

them, members are likely to become overly reliant on their advisers and staff, or may simply take their lead from political parties in the elected house. Having some affinity with a political party before being appointed as a legislator, members may use party positions as a shortcut or heuristic to deal with their broad responsibilities, with the result that the sortition assembly ends up simply reflecting the partisan dynamics of the elected chamber rather than offering independent scrutiny. So, while a permanent legislative assembly cannot simply be ignored by elected politicians and civil servants like a mini-public, these actors will likely retain a significant influence given the demands placed on lay members.

A randomly selected legislative assembly certainly has greater substantive powers than any conventional mini-public. However, these wide-ranging responsibilities create a significant burden on its lay members and open it up to economic capture, as well as alternative forms of political and technocratic capture. Neither of the best-known proposals for connecting sortition to democratic elections therefore appears to be able to realize the potential systemic benefits which could come from combining these two mechanisms. Both proposals struggle to simultaneously achieve substantive powers and low burdensomeness, and both are vulnerable to elite forms of capture, although in different forms (see Table 8.1). Although many of the problems just discussed will be familiar to those interested in the political use of sortition, the important question is whether there is some institutional design which can avoid them. In other words, is it possible to arrange sortition within a deliberative system in such a way that it can have substantive powers, while not becoming overly burdensome on its members and continuing to guard against elite forms of capture? In the following sections, I will attempt to offer just such an institutional design in the form of a sortition branch of a deliberative democratic system, and I will argue that it can vindicate a legislative role

Table 8.1 Strengths and Weaknesses of Popular Sortition Proposals

	Substantive Power	Burden on Members	Political Capture	Technocratic Capture	Economic Capture
Deliberative Mini-Publics	X	✓	X	X	✓
Randomly Selected Legislators	✓	X	X	X	X

for sortition. While I build on the work of previous advocates of random selection, I argue that the sortition branch can overcome the significant limitations of existing proposals, and that sortition is therefore a viable mechanism for improving the intelligence of democracy.

The Sortition Branch of a Deliberative System

The proposal I will outline and defend in the rest of this chapter is for the creation of what I will call the sortition branch of a deliberative democratic system. Importantly, I do not offer this proposal as a fixed blueprint to be enacted exactly as described. Instead, I wish to use it as an illustration of how sortition can be effectively incorporated into a democratic system in a way which can improve its motivational value and therefore the quality of its political decisions. My focus will be on showing how a model along these lines can avoid the problems and dilemmas which have inflicted past proposals for combining elections with random lotteries. I therefore offer the sortition branch more as a possibility proof, rather than a fixed roadmap, and I hope it will offer grounds for greater experimentation with more influential and permanent uses of sortition. Given this aim, I will leave certain aspects of the model flexible or underspecified in order that it can be modified to fit specific contexts or simply the personal tastes of the reader, instead focusing on how the proposal can overcome existing problems and vindicate a legislative role for sortition.

The sortition branch would institutionalize random lotteries as an indefinite feature of a deliberative system. This branch or sphere of the system would involve a set of permanent institutions which would have the task of creating many short-term deliberative assemblies for particular purposes. Membership of these assemblies would be determined via random selection, with the aid of stratified sampling to ensure representation among key demographic groups.[29] This will likely include gender, ethnicity, race, social economic status, age, and geography, but possibly further characteristics

---

[29] One may question the practicality of having many sortition assemblies and therefore the need to frequently select citizen members. It is worth pointing out, however, that many countries already frequently engage in such selection in their judicial systems, filling the juries of the many criminal trials which occur each year. It is not therefore farfetched to imagine this kind of selection forming a normal part of political life as well.

220 INTELLIGENT DEMOCRACY

important to a particular polity (such as indigenous or linguistic representation). Members will also be provided with financial compensation for their participation. The formation of one of these short-term assemblies can be triggered in one of two ways, each of which represent a different function of the sortition branch. The first function is to scrutinize a piece of legislation coming from an elected legislative chamber. These assemblies would scrutinize this legislation and would have the right to an up or down vote. If a majority approves then it would become law (subject to judicial review) but if the majority rejects then the legislation would return to the elected chamber with an accompanying justification.[30] At this point the elected chamber would have the opportunity, if they so choose, to revise the legislation and try again. The sortition branch therefore requires that legislation originating in an elected chamber must be approved by a randomly selected assembly of citizens, although a different assembly each time. The result is that the elected chamber faces public security and accountability not only via elections, but also via a specially formed sortition body.

The second function of the sortition branch would be to review popular initiatives which attract significant public support. The formation of an assembly is not therefore triggered by the passing of a piece of legislation from the elected chamber, as in the first function, but rather by a popular proposal which attracts a sufficient number of signatures. In this case the assembly would again have the right to vote on the proposal so that it would become law if approved by a majority (subject to judicial review), and any decision would be accompanied with a written and publicly available justification. The sortition branch is, therefore, connected to two parts of the deliberative system. It can review proposals coming from empowered space, specifically from a more traditional elected chamber, and proposals coming directly from the public sphere. Both types of sortition assembly are formed by a new group of randomly selected citizens each time and are only given this one specified task. To help in the performance of this task, members will be provided with initial training, expert testimony, the testimony of affected parties, and the testimony of representatives of political parties within the elected chamber. They will also engage with each other in both general and small group deliberation in a similar manner to a conventional mini-public. Each assembly will then review a specified single piece of legislation for a limited

---

[30] Depending on the political system, legislation may have to pass through the executive branch and be approved by a president or governor. I will leave this option open so that the proposal could apply to parliamentary or presidential systems. All laws would, however, be subject to judicial review.

period before being disbanded. Given the experience of mini-publics, the period could be as little as a week or as long as a month depending on the issue under consideration.[31]

How does such a model shape up against past proposals in terms of our three criteria? When it comes to substantive powers, the individual short-term sortition assemblies have significantly greater powers than conventional mini-publics but fall short of a full legislative chamber. Rather than a purely advisory role, the assemblies in the sortition branch would have the ability to approve or veto legislation. An elected chamber would therefore have a very significant incentive to account for the concerns of the general public, knowing that any legislation they pass must also be approved by a random selection of citizens before it can become law. Not only would they need to pass policies which can help them to be re-elected—a weak motivation towards the common good—but policies which can be agreed to by a well-informed group of citizens who have the time and resources to scrutinize them in depth and hold elected officials to account. As well as the power to vote down legislation, the written justification provided with any rejection would also provide these sortition assemblies with some additional influence over content. By providing areas where the legislation would need to be improved to become law, they would be able to exercise some control over the form that policies take. Each assembly would therefore have significant powers, but these would be less broad than those of a full randomly selected legislature as they only consider one piece of legislation rather than the whole policy agenda. When we take the sortition branch as a whole, however, all legislation does have to pass via the informed scrutiny of a group of randomly selected citizens possessing veto powers. All legislation is therefore reviewed

---

[31] Given the two functions of the sortition branch, the proposal represents an amalgamation of existing proposals for the use of random lotteries. The first function of reviewing a single piece of legislation is similar to some uses of traditional mini-publics but with the power to reject laws, while similar powers can be seen in proposals for full legislative chambers but for all legislation rather than single pieces. Zakaras (2010), for instance, advocates for a single sortition-based legislative chamber with the authority to vote up or down on all legislation. The use of many randomly selected assemblies rather than just one, can also be seen in other proposals. Guerrero (2014), for instance, suggests the use of many assemblies specialized in particular policy areas but in a purely sortition-based system, Bouricius (2019) suggests the use of single-issue assemblies as a method of transitioning to a pure sortition system, while Owen and Smith (2019) discuss the use of single-issue assemblies to review legislation in a similar way to the first function of the sortition branch. Leib (2010), alternatively, has proposed the use of sortition to review popular initiatives in the US context, in a similar way to the second function (although requiring a two-thirds majority). The proposal of this chapter therefore owes much to earlier work. My argument, however, is that the sortition branch combines the different features of earlier proposals in such a way as to avoid the current problems facing the use of random sortition.

222 INTELLIGENT DEMOCRACY

by a sortition body in this proposal, as was the case with a randomly selected legislative chamber, but with a division of labour between many short-term single-issue assemblies.

Where the sortition branch's powers certainly do fall short of those of a full legislative chamber is in terms of agenda setting. Control of the agenda is a critical area where elites can exert a disproportionate influence, determining which issues receive attention and how these issues are framed. I am therefore sympathetic to Gastil and Wright's aim of breaking the elective chamber's monopoly over such powers within empowered spaces. As the previous section argued, however, it is difficult to see how a chamber of randomly selected citizens can deal with the intimidating task of forming priorities and creating original legislation. When it comes to the first function of the sortition branch, then, agenda setting powers remain in the hands of elected representatives. Their monopoly over agenda setting is instead broken by the second function. The ability to review popular initiatives emanating from the broader public sphere creates new sources of agenda setting power outside of the formal institutions of an elected chamber. So while sortition assemblies are reserved for reviewing predetermined proposals, these proposals do not have to come solely from elected representatives. Together, then, the first and second function of the sortition branch provide very significant powers which could substantively influence the formation of policy.

While the powers of the sortition branch are much greater than a conventional mini-public, the burden placed on lay members is not significantly increased. Firstly, citizens are only asked to sit in short-term assemblies and their participation can be expected to last up to a month. Even if this period needs to be extended in special circumstances, the time lay members sit would still be significantly lower than the two or more years involved in Gastil and Wright's legislative assembly. More importantly, the task given to these lay members in the sortition branch is also much closer to that of mini-publics. Each short-term assembly is tasked with scrutinizing and voting on a single piece of predetermined legislation on a well-defined issue, and the experience of mini-publics provides good evidence that citizens can perform this task effectively. The sortition branch can therefore perform many of the core functions of a full legislative chamber, but without the unreasonable burdens such a chamber would create on lay citizens. Rather than overburdening a single assembly with reviewing a whole legislative agenda, there is a division of labour which spreads this task among a number of sortition bodies. This is also likely to increase the quality of scrutiny, given that lay members have only one well-defined task to perform.

Unlike conventional mini-publics or a full legislative chamber, the sortition branch is able to combine substantive powers with low burdensomeness. What, however, about elite capture? Starting with economic capture, a full legislative chamber posed significant problems as its substantial powers and broader remit made it a large target for special interests. The spreading of responsibilities among many short-term assemblies in the sortition branch, on the other hand, reduces the risk of economic capture in three core ways. Firstly, the benefits to be gained by capturing any one assembly are reduced. Rather than being able to influence a whole policy agenda, capturing one short-term assembly only provides influence over one piece of legislation. Such assemblies also do not have agenda setting powers, limiting the autonomy that members have to form policy in line with economic interests. The potential benefits and incentive to engage in economic capture are therefore reduced through the structure of the sortition branch. Secondly, the sortition branch spreads the risks of economic capture for the same reason. If one assembly does happen to come under the influence of economic interests then this will only come at the expense of one piece of legislation, rather than all legislation and agenda-setting powers. While a full legislative assembly therefore puts all its eggs in one basket, the sortition branch spreads these risks across many sortition bodies.

Thirdly, while the sortition branch reduces the benefits and risks of economic capture, it also increases its difficulty. By having legislation reviewed by multiple short-term assemblies, special interests would need to repeatedly capture multiple sortition assemblies over time to gain a significant influence over the policy agenda. Having a permanent assembly where long-term members check all legislation, as in a randomly selected second chamber, makes it easy to identify the targets of capture. Special interests know exactly who will have influence over the legislation they care about, and they will likely have pre-existing relationships with sympathetic members. Having a new set of citizens randomly selected to review legislation, alternatively, makes it more difficult to identify targets of capture, while limiting the length of members' participation reduces the scope that economic interests have to form relationships over time and bring members under their influence. The opportunities for economic capture are therefore reduced by the structure of the sortition branch, particularly its rotation of citizens between pieces of legislation. As Owen and Smith have argued, the Ancient Athenians

224 INTELLIGENT DEMOCRACY

combined their use of sortition with the rapid rotation of citizens in order to resist capture or concentrations of power.[32] Sortition alone leaves too many opportunities for wealthy interests to influence members and must therefore be combined with rotation if it is to improve decision-making in terms of the public good. The sortition branch's use of many short-term assemblies is, therefore, an example of this combination of random selection with rapid rotation.

Like Gastil and Wright's proposal, the sortition branch can make use of oversight committees and procedures for the removal of members to further guard against corrupt behaviour. It can also utilize other general safeguards such as secret ballots, the protection of members' personal details, and using a large number of members to reduce the influence of any one bad actor. What is important about the sortition branch, however, is that it combines these general measures with a broader institutional design which works to reduce the risks of economic capture. This is not to say that such a system would be free of special interest influence. No political system could reasonably be expected to eradicate such influence, as long as there are significant inequalities of wealth in the broader society. However, the sortition branch involves an institutional design which can guard against and limit such influence, despite its substantive powers.

An alternative entry point for economic capture, however, is through the second function of the sortition branch. A well-known problem with popular initiatives is that they can favour wealthy and organized interest groups, who have the resources to put forward proposals and campaign to achieve the respective number of signatures.[33] This problem has been long observed in the US, for instance, where popular initiatives are used in a number of states.[34] Rather than capturing one of the sortition branch's short-term assemblies, special interests could instead aim to influence the support for popular initiatives in the broader public sphere in order to gain some control over agenda setting. Economic influence along these lines is unlikely to be eliminated. It is important to recognize, however, that popular initiatives also allow other actors who are often excluded from agenda setting to put proposals on the table. Organized groups of citizens can and do use

---

[32] Owen and Smith (2019).

[33] Some procedures will be required to check against fraud in the collection of signatures. Leib (2010, p. 14), for instance, suggests the adoption of Colorado's method of verifying a random sample of the signatures collected to determine if significant fraud has taken place.

[34] Magleby (1995).

THE SORTITION BRANCH   225

popular initiatives to force issues of public concern onto the political agenda. Through grass roots campaigns or social movements popular initiatives can provide the wider public space with an avenue to propose new policy. Furthermore, the sortition branch's use of popular proposals has significant advantages over current uses because it combines them with randomly selected assemblies. Rather than having popular initiatives put back to voters in a referendum or to elected politicians in the legislature, any initiative must instead pass the scrutiny of a group of well-informed citizens who can weed out proposals which are only to the benefit of wealthy special interests.[35] The second function of the sortition branch therefore involves a check on the influence that economic interests can currently have on popular initiatives.

At this point, the sortition branch seems to avoid some of the problems inflicting previous proposals for combining elections with sortition. It possesses substantive powers which can influence political decision-making, while not becoming overly burdensome, and still protecting against economic capture. It may also be thought to avoid the kinds of political and technocratic capture seen in mini-publics or a legislative chamber. Unlike mini-publics, the randomly selected assemblies in the sortition branch are permanent features of the democratic system with substantive powers, and cannot therefore be simply ignored by politicians or civil servants. Unlike a legislative chamber, alternatively, these sortition assemblies also do not overburden their members and will not therefore make them overly reliant on civil servants or elected politicians in completing their duties. Despite this, the short-term nature of these assemblies does introduce another potential source of political and technocratic capture.

As Dimitri Landa and Ryan Pevnick argue, short participation times can produce inexperienced lay members who may be more easily manipulated by bureaucratic and political actors who wish to influence legislation.[36] The less time lay members sit, the less they will be open to economic capture and the influence of special interests, but the more vulnerable they will be to the influence of expert witnesses, civil servants, and elected politicians due to their relative lack of experience. While members may be provided with basic training before taking part, this would not be equivalent to years of experience dealing with professional actors. There therefore seems to be a trade-off between limiting economic capture in a sortition body through rapid

---

[35] Also see Leib (2010).
[36] Landa and Pevnick (2021)

226 INTELLIGENT DEMOCRACY

rotation of members and limiting certain forms of technocratic and political capture.

The evidence from mini-publics is optimistic about lay citizens' abilities to critically engage with experts and policymakers, and come to their views about the issue under consideration. However, the reason for this may again be that the limited power of mini-publics deters efforts to influence on the part of experts, civil servants, and politicians. Of course, how concerning we find such threats will in part depend on how able we believe citizens to be at forming their own judgements in the face of attempts to lead them astray. The experience of mini-publics provides an optimistic picture, but it is certainly no guarantee. One method of reducing these threats, however, is to structure the short-term assemblies so that members are subjected to a diverse range of perspectives and interests, reducing the influence of any one group or individual. All political parties with representation in the elected parliament could be given allotted time to provide testimony to the assembly, a broad range of expert testimony can be determined by an independent and bi-partisan commission (following the practices of mini-publics), and avenues for public engagement could be created through spoken and written testimony by affected parties or even larger public engagement in cases of significant pieces of legislation. Members themselves could also be provided with the right to call their own witnesses, in order to give them more control over the perspectives on offer. Combining all this with the diverse views of the randomly selected members themselves, can help to guard against the undue influence of any one group on lay members' judgements.

Of course, elected politicians or technocrats may look to manipulate the procedures which aim to ensure a diversity of perspectives are heard in order to favour their side of the debate. To guard against this, changes to procedures could be set within the purview of an oversight commission and require the agreement of a specially convened sortition assembly, with perhaps more members and needing a two-thirds majority. Such designs would limit the influence of other political actors by taking the power to alter procedures out of their hands. Furthermore, while attempts at manipulation may still take place, these will also be moderated by party competition. As discussed in the previous chapter, political competition can regulate abuses of power and self-serving manipulations of procedures, as political actors risk their opponents engaging in similar practices when they come to power. This is why safeguards protecting procedures from manipulation are more stable in a democracy than in something like a political meritocracy. The sortition

THE SORTITION BRANCH 227

branches position within a broader deliberative system therefore provides it with the means to guard against political and technocratic capture, despite its use of rapid rotation alongside random selection.

As a whole, then, the sortition branch is able to institutionalize the random selection of citizens in a way which is better able to avoid the problems and balance the tensions which limited previous proposals for combining elections with lotteries. Its use of many short-term and single-issue sortition bodies allows it to possess substantive powers, while not becoming overly burdensome on its citizen members, and still protecting against many of the most pernicious forms of elite capture. Of course, the sortition branch is itself imperfect and tensions will exist between its different design features. Such tensions are, however, a fact of life for the design of any legislative institution, including elected or elite chambers.[37] What the sortition branch shows is that these tensions can be effectively (although imperfectly) balanced through an appropriate institutional design, and that random selection is therefore a viable mechanism for improving the intelligence of a democratic system. Having the decisions of elected leaders checked by a well-informed group of citizens has the potential to increase the motivational value of democracy, forcing politicians to better account for the common good.

At the very least, it is unlikely that policies designed to favour only special interests or elite minorities will pass the scrutiny of a representative selection of citizens with the knowledge and time to understand its implications. Many laws and policies passed in contemporary democracies are transparently designed to favour particular interests and would be unlikely to gain the assent of the public if they were informed of their content. The sortition branch's motivational value goes beyond cases of explicit capture or corruption, however. The decisions of elected representatives can become biased towards certain interests in many more implicit ways, particularly given the limited incentives, accountability, and feedback provided by elections. Even in the absence of more overt capture or corruption, having decisions reviewed by a representative group of citizens can inject a greater concern for the general interest and public good into political decision-making. The sortition branch's remit is therefore more extensive than Samuel Bagg's proposal

---

[37] There is, for example, an ongoing tension over the length of time between election cycles or whether to have term limits. Long terms with no limits may allow representatives to gain experience and take longer-term decision, but also provide them with more autonomy to use their power self-servingly, to be captured by special interests, or to restrict the emergence of new political leaders. Short electoral cycles with term limits, alternatively, have the opposite set of trade-offs.

228   INTELLIGENT DEMOCRACY

for Citizen Oversight Juries which would be tasked with reviewing specific allegations of corruption.[38] The sortition branch is not limited to anti-corruption but plays a more direct legislative role in reviewing all legislation in terms of whether it is likely to promote justice and the common good, and randomly selected members should use their veto powers and accompanying justifications to motivate elected representatives to give the greatest regard to the public interest. While others reject a legislative role for sortition due to concerns for elite manipulation, the sortition branch's use of rapid rotation and a division of labour between randomly selected assemblies has been argued to reduce the risk of elite influence from economic, political, and technocratic interests. It is therefore the specific institutional design of the sortition branch which allows it to perform many of the legislative functions of a second chamber, while still avoiding problems of over burdensomeness and elite capture.

The Sortition Branch as a Democratic Proposal

I have defended a sortition branch of a democratic system as a viable proposal for improving the intelligence of democracy. While elections may be an effective guard against the worst uses and abuses of power, the sortition branch can allow for more informed citizen scrutiny and accountability which can better motivate elected representatives towards the common good. Unlike the new democratic sceptics who claim that the limits of elections encourage us to restrict the role of citizens in politics, I have argued that they require us to increase it. The sortition branch therefore represents a democratic proposal for improving the intelligence of democracy. That said, some democrats may have concerns about this proposal, either because it cannot fully realize the epistemic virtues of democracy or because they question the democratic credentials of random selection. Although I have already rejected the alternatives of the new sceptics in previous chapters, it is important that my own proposal does not itself threaten democratic values.

---

[38] Bagg (2024). I think Bagg underestimates the potential of random selection because he sees reducing the power and remit of sortition bodies as the main way of avoiding problems of capture and manipulation. I, alternatively, have argued that a division of labour and rapid rotation of assemblies is just as important. These measures allow for sortition bodies with more significant legislative powers while still avoiding the problems of previous proposals.

THE SORTITION BRANCH   229

In defending her experimental model of epistemic democracy, for instance, Elizabeth Anderson places much emphasis on the role of dissent and the ability of minorities to be heard in decision-making.[39] A more structured political process such as the sortition branch, however, may be thought less able to provide avenues for such voices than more open processes of electoral campaigns and civil society. It is important to remember, however, that the sortition branch only represents one part of a larger democratic system. Such a system will still involve elections and an active public sphere which can include protests, petitions, and other forms of dissent both before and after policy decisions. Many of the avenues of dissent and minority voice that Anderson sees as important are therefore alive and well in this systemic model. Furthermore, the sortition branch adds to these avenues by providing more opportunities for minority groups to be heard in the decision-making process. While such groups tend to suffer from lower levels of representation within formal political institutions, sortition assemblies provide a descriptive representation of the population and therefore offer such groups greater voice within formal bodies. It also provides them with further opportunities to engage in dissent. On the proposal defended here, the policy decisions of the majority party or coalition must pass the scrutiny of a random selection of the public, which will include those on the losing side in the last election. The sortition branch therefore provides a second chance for dissenters to voice their concerns about the policies favoured by the majority.

The idea that the sortition branch only represents one part of a democratic system also helps respond to an alternative set of democratic concerns. Although historically associated with democracy, sortition has also found critics among contemporary democratic theorists who see it as falling short on key democratic values. While providing everyone an equal chance of being included, these critics argue that random selection will inevitably leave most citizens outside of any sortition assembly, and therefore limits the extent to which they can participate in politics. Simone Chambers, for instance, questions whether deliberative democrats have abandoned mass democracy through their interest in small scale mini-publics.[40] However, it is important to again recognize that the sortition branch only represents one part of a broader system which involves many other opportunities for participation. This includes voting in elections as well as engagement in the broader public

[39] Anderson (2006).
[40] Chambers (2009). Also see Pateman (2012).

230   INTELLIGENT DEMOCRACY

sphere, through protests, social movements, and campaigns. The sortition branch would not therefore involve 'giving up on mass democracy' but would instead increase participation within empowered spaces which are normally inaccessible to average citizens. It is also important to remember that my systemic model involves greater political decentralization, which allows for the use of sortition on more local levels, where more individuals can be involved.

Developing a similar theme to Chambers, Cristina Lafont directly objects to the empowerment of sortition in legislative decision-making, arguing that it involves forms of 'blind deference' contrary to the ideal of democratic self-government.[41] Just as citizens must blindly defer to meritocrats in a political meritocracy, they must defer to randomly selected citizens in any sortition body. Sortition is therefore argued to 'shortcut' mass justification by requiring those not included to follow the decisions of a small group of more informed citizens. While citizens must also defer to elected representatives, this is not 'blind deference' as voters can in principle monitor representatives and remove them through elections. Such a critique does allow sortition bodies a role in contributing to wider public debate and opinion formation, what Simon Niemeyer calls 'deliberation making', but they should not be empowered to take political decisions themselves.[42] The sortition branch does not necessarily require blind deference to randomly selected assemblies, however. While they vote on legislation the sortition bodies in this proposal are also connected to an elected chamber and to the wider public sphere, as all legislation originates with either elected representatives or popular initiatives. The sortition branch does not, therefore, clearly involve blind deference in the way that a purely lottery-based system would. In fact, it may be seen to lessen deference to elected officials, given that it introduces a new mechanism of citizen accountability. It is also possible to reduce deference to sortition bodies further, if one would want to, by for instance allowing the elected chamber to overrule sortition assemblies with a two-thirds majority.

Furthermore, I sympathize with Mark Warren in claiming that democracy in complex societies cannot function without 'shortcuts' where citizens allow others to make decisions on their behalf. Warren argues that 'in complex mass democracies, no person can participate in but a few of those forces that affect their lives, however ideal they might be'.[43] This point coheres with the analysis of this book which has highlighted the epistemic limits of individuals

---

[41] Lafont (2015, 2019).
[42] Niemeyer (2014, p. 179).
[43] Warren (2020, p. 85).

in large societies, and the need for democratic systems to rely on many divisions of labour. Citizens in existing democracies must constantly defer to the decisions of parliaments, government agencies and bureaucracies, judges and courts, independent commissions, central banks, and public service providers, if only to be able to focus on what is most important to them. There are, of course, undemocratic ways this could happen, such as giving over the task of politics to a dictator or philosopher king. However, we can also defer to others because we have good reason to think that they are aligned with the interests and values of the wider citizenry. The sortition branch is one version of this. Because random selection produces a descriptively representative group of fellow citizens, sortition assemblies normally fit well with the interests and values of the public. Rather than restricting participation or the judgements of citizens, then, the sortition branch is one way of making participatory democracy possible in a large and complex society.

Finally, even if the sortition branch has the benefits I have attributed to it, some may wonder how such a proposal could ever be enacted. While I consider promising developments in the conclusion, some may outright object that elected politicians will never agree to a proposal which would reduce their own power. If this objection came from the new democratic sceptics then it would be unconvincing, given that their preferred alternatives require the very same thing. Even elitist alternatives, which grant more power to political leaders, assume that they will empower different leaders to those elected in democracies, and would therefore require current officials give up their power. It is also simply not true that elected leaders never give up power. The move towards independent central banks across contemporary democracies involved elected leaders giving up much control over monetary policy, while privatization policies can and have decreased their influence over key industries. As Gastil and Wright point out, many experiments with citizens' engagement are also initiated by political parties who ran campaigns on such initiatives.[44] The BCCA was advocated by an existing political party, participatory budgeting in Brazil emerged from a political party's empowerment platform, while recent attempts to institutionalize random selection in Belgium received cross-party support.[45] The fact that sortition branches would introduce new limits to the power of elected officials does not therefore

---

[44] Gastil and Wright (2019, p. 37).
[45] See the conclusion for more details on these initiatives.

232 INTELLIGENT DEMOCRACY

necessarily rule out its implementation. In fact, elected members can come to power on the back of campaigns to enhance citizen participation.

Intelligent Democracy as a More Participatory Democracy

While the previous chapter argued that the elitist alternatives offered by the new democratic sceptics fail to provide improvements over representative democracy, this chapter has argued that the intelligence of democracy can be enhanced through a greater legislative role for sortition. While elections offer only limited motivation for representatives to take those decisions which best promote the common good, the sortition branch provides space for more informed citizen accountability which can scrutinize policy choices and force elected leaders to more substantively consider the public interest. If legislation and policy needed to pass the judgement of a group of citizens who represented a cross section of society, and who were given the time and information needed to understand and evaluate it, then this would likely change the kinds of political decisions taken. Not only will policies explicitly aimed at promoting the interests of wealthy or special interests be unlikely to gain support among this group of citizens, but they will also be able to give greater consideration to whether its content is likely to promote justice or the common good. While elections certainly have their limits, it is by combining them with mechanisms of random selection within a wider deliberative system that the full motivational value of democracy can be achieved. By making use of elections and sortition, a democratic system can not only help us to avoid the worst uses and abuses of political power but can also help motivate elected leaders to take those decisions which are best for the common good.

Over the last two chapters, I have argued that improving the intelligence of democracy does not require the exclusion of citizens, as claimed by the new democratic sceptics, but rather their greater involvement in processes of political decision-making. I therefore agree with Jane Addams's often quoted phrase that 'the cure for the ills of democracy is more democracy'.[46] What is important to recognize, however, is that the sortition branch offers a different form of democracy to the one we currently find in representative

---

[46] Addams (2013).

democracies. An intelligent democratic system cannot confine the role of citizens to simply voting in elections but must also include them more directly in empowered institutions. While citizens may struggle to acquire the information they need in elections, sortition provides an environment for a more informed and more deliberative form of citizen participation. The limitations of voters should not therefore lead us to the conclusion that citizens cannot competently engage in politics or that they need to be excluded from political life. Instead, it should lead us to look for new forms of inclusion and participation, which allow citizens to do things which elections cannot. The sortition branch is, of course, an ideal model and I do not offer it as a fixed blueprint. What it helps us to see, however, is the potential of random selection and citizen engagement, and how they provide more hope for increasing the epistemic value of our politics than the elite alternatives favoured by the new sceptics. It helps us to see that greater democracy of an inclusive and participatory kind can be a pathway towards a more intelligent politics.

Conclusion

A More Intelligent Democracy

In recent years a number of philosophers, economists, and political scientists have been taking an increasingly critical line with respect to democracy. They have argued that modern social science has confirmed that citizens know little of politics, that their biases and prejudices make them irrational in public debate, or that centralized democratic governments are ignorant and ineffective. These authors are also unconvinced that these epistemic failings can be fixed through some kind of democratic reform, as they are said to come 'built into democracy'.[1] The ills of our contemporary democracies are not therefore accidental, but rather the logical result of the structure of democratic institutions. These authors therefore see democracy as inevitably flawed and advocate for its restriction or even removal in favour of some more desirable and competent alternative. While some wish to get away from politics, shrink the state, and place more power in the hands of free markets or polycentric governance, others want to move politics in a more elitist direction, restricting voting rights to the knowledgeable, or appointing political leaders through examinations. What unites this new democratic scepticism, however, is the belief that if we want a more intelligent form of governance, then we must start to look beyond democracy.

While many democrats may simply dismiss these new sceptics, we should be wary of taking their objections too lightly. While a democratic self-confidence may have been reasonable following the end of the Second World War and then the fall of the Berlin Wall, today we live in a moment of democratic discontent. Democratic countries around the world are experiencing the rise of political parties and leaders who place little value in democratic norms, and public dissatisfaction with democracy is at a record high. The concerns that many citizens have for the outcomes of democratic institutions are also far from unreasonable. Yes, these institutions respect our equality in

---

[1] Brennan (2016b).

Intelligent Democracy. Jonathan Benson, Oxford University Press. © Oxford University Press 2024.
DOI: 10.1093/oso/9780197767283.003.0010

CONCLUSION 235

ways other regimes cannot, but they also have considerable influence over our lives and over the justness of our societies. Democrats cannot and should not therefore simply wave aside the objections of the new sceptics with appeals to procedural fairness. If democracy really is as hopelessly ignorant and irrational as the critics claim, then the prospects of convincing our fellow citizens that it really is the best form of rule will be greatly diminished. While some fear that a consideration of epistemic values only opens the door to the possibility of nondemocratic forms of rule, I believe the greater threat is to leave these values to the critics and let their claims about democratic incompetence go unaddressed. It is for this reason that I have aimed to meet head-on the challenges of the new democratic scepticism by defending what I see as the unique intelligence of democracy.

Democracy's intelligence comes from the fact that it possesses a range of epistemic abilities which allow it to make good decisions with respect to any reasonable conception of justice or the common good. When we consider which form of government is best, our task is like that faced by a handyman selecting a toolbox. A handyman does not know in advance the exact task they will be set. They may need to plug a leak, put up a shelf, rehinge a door, or fix an electrical socket. Given this range of ends, they will require a toolbox containing a range of tools which will help them achieve any of these various goals. In politics we similarly cannot say in advance what ends we will aim at. People reasonably differ in their preferred conceptions of justice and the common good, and these conceptions produce a range of potential goals for our political institutions. We may want them to pursue more material equality, greater individual freedom, broader opportunity, or perhaps increased security. Like the handyman's toolbox, then, we will want political institutions to possess a range of epistemic tools which can help them to achieve these various goals. What I have argued in this book is that democracy is intelligent because it possesses a larger and better set of these tools than any of its alternatives. Whatever end we may wish our political institutions to pursue, it is democracy which has the best chance of achieving it.

This view does not deny that value can be found in the fairness, equality, or freedom of democratic procedures. When determining how to take decisions about the path our societies should follow, we should pay attention to the intrinsic value of political equality. Finding institutions which can pick the preferred path in a fair manner is only part of the problem, however, as we also want institutions which can effectively guide us down the path we end up choosing. In other words, our political procedures do not only affect the way

236 INTELLIGENT DEMOCRACY

in which we select the ends our societies should pursue, but also our ability to achieve or approximate these ends. It is therefore important that democracy can possess epistemic as well as procedural values. It is this epistemic value of democracy which the new democratic sceptics so vehemently reject, and which I have set out to defend in this book. I have argued that democracy should be valued not only as a fair procedure for deciding which path our societies should follow, but also as a set of institutions which can most effectively guide us down our chosen path. It is democracy which gives us the best chance of reaching whichever destination we end up preferring.

Key to understanding the intelligence of democracy has been a systemic account of its epistemic value. Unlike previous epistemic democrats, I have argued that no one institution or mechanism can possibly demonstrate democracy's superiority over all its various alternatives. No election or deliberative assembly can on its own acquire all the information needed to address social problems, experiment with all promising solutions, or motivate decisions towards the common good. I have therefore argued that we need to understand democracy not as a single institution, but rather as a network of different bodies and spaces which connect and interact in ways which make up a larger system. We can then identify democracy's epistemic abilities by looking at how the different components of this system interact to produce divisions of labour, distributed functions, and emergent properties. The weaknesses and faults of any one institution can therefore be compensated for by others, and a democratic system can achieve epistemic values not found in any one of its parts.

We have seen, for instance, that democracy's ability to gather and evaluate information cannot be performed through a single electoral mechanism or deliberative forum taken in isolation but requires a division of labour between formal and informal spaces. On the one hand, any centralized democratic body would be cut off from the sea of knowledge which surrounds it, and therefore would require the many institutions of the democratic public sphere which have the autonomy to search out and collect knowledge distributed across society. On the other hand, this more open public sphere is susceptible to distortion by bias and inequality, and therefore relies on the more structured and formal institutions of empowered space to evaluate information and correct its errors. A democratic system can therefore both gather and evaluate information because its different spaces offer alternative strengths and can offset each other's weaknesses.

CONCLUSION   237

The same is true of democracy's ability for experimentation and self-regulation. A systemic approach allows for a polycentric form of democracy where many actors test out new ways of gathering information, representing interests, and solving social problems. A democratic system therefore allows for forms of learning and self-correction not possible in any one institution, and points to greater forms of political decentralization as ways of better realizing these benefits. Finally, we have also seen that elections can be effective guards against the worst uses and abuses of political power, but struggle to motivate the adoption of the very best policies due to the limits of voter knowledge. Such limits are not fatal to democracy's motivational value, however, if we combine elections with sortition in a broader system. A randomly selected group of citizens not only possesses valuable cognitive diversity but can also provide the kind of informed and considered scrutiny of public policy which elections inevitably lack.

Although this book therefore owes much to previous work on epistemic democracy, it claims that democracy's intelligence cannot be properly understood without taking a systemic approach. In other words, we cannot advance an epistemic justification of democracy if we do not take a systemic perspective. Once such a perspective is adopted, we can better identify democracy's ability to gather and evaluate information, engage in experimentation and self-regulation, benefit from cognitive diversity, and motivate decision-makers towards justice and the common good. Of course, even with this list of epistemic abilities democracy will be far from perfect. I have argued for the relative epistemic value of democracy, not that it is omnipotent or omniscient. Given that social problems are complex and uncertain, and that people are limited in their knowledge and virtues, we cannot expect any institution to always promote the common good. My claim that democracy is intelligent therefore leaves much room for democratic blunders and mishaps, as well as intentional wrongdoing on behalf of elected leaders and citizens. Bad decisions are simply a fact of life, and this is as true for democracies as it is for any other form of governance. It is through comparing imperfect alternatives, however, that we can see the unique intelligence of democracy.

Today's democratic sceptics have moved beyond calls for autocracy or monarchy, but they still fail to offer a convincing alternative to democratic politics. While supporters of political meritocracy and epistocracy produce new arguments for leaving politics to the best and brightest, they still fall victim to many of the old problems confronting elite forms of rule. By removing inclusive elections, these elitist regimes struggle to motivate

238 INTELLIGENT DEMOCRACY

decisions towards the public interest and leave the system vulnerable to the worst misuses of political power. Free-market and polycentric sceptics may then offer more original alternatives to democratic politics but at the cost of producing another set of problems. Wishing to shrink the scope of politics, these sceptics end up prioritizing the exit mechanism, and overburdening individuals with the complex and epistemically demanding decisions which are best taken by collective institutions. While democracy involves individual decision-making in the form of voting, its intelligence comes from its recognition of its limits and its ability to incorporate individual action within a broader system which also makes room for more collective forms of political participation.

While their alternatives therefore leave much to be desired, the work of the new democratic sceptics has certainly helped inform a better understanding of democracy's epistemic value. Many chapters of this book rejected a certain brand of the new scepticism but then used this as a platform for better understanding the benefits of democracy. Exploring the limits of markets, for instance, helped develop an understanding of the problems faced by voters in elections, and foregrounded the necessary role of collective democratic institutions. Similarly, it was Hayek's division of knowledge which pointed to the necessary epistemic role of the public sphere; the sceptics' focus on political bias which motivated a concern for trust and error correction; and the critics' adoption of the Ostroms which opened the door to a polycentric understanding of democracy. While my defence of democracy's intelligence builds significantly on recent work in epistemic and deliberative democracy, it therefore also owes much to Hayekian political economy, Ostrom's institutional economics, and a broad range of work coming from political science and social psychology. The result is a more robust and interdisciplinary argument than would have been produced by considering the work of democratic theorists alone.

The benefits which come from directly engaging with democracy's sceptics should not be surprising. It is often those who are most critical of democracy who more clearly describe its problems and limitations, and it is by considering nondemocratic alternatives that we can best understand the relative benefits of democratic politics. When examined on their own, democracy's failures and weaknesses can easily lead us to be pessimistic about the possibility of a competent democratic politics, and such pessimism is alive and well today. Whether it be the rise of misinformation, the election of far-right politicians, or the failures of public deliberation, many have soured on the

CONCLUSION   239

idea that democracy offers a competent form of government. While in isolation such problems can appear damning, it is by viewing them in relation to the faults and failings of democracy's alternatives that we can more easily see the reasons why we should place value in this form of rule. Democracy has epistemic value not because it is omnipotent or omniscient, but because it has more and better epistemic abilities than the alternatives offered up by those who wish to restrict or replace it.

Of course, the form of democracy I have argued to be intelligent does look markedly different from those we see today. As I mentioned in the introduction, my aim from the start has not been to defend our current democratic status quo against the growth of the new democratic scepticism, but to engage with the critics to produce a positive case for transforming democracy. While current democracies have advantages over nondemocratic systems, realizing their full epistemic potential requires significant changes to the way we do democratic politics. One key failing in the intelligence of contemporary democracies is the extent to which decisions are taken for the benefit of particular interests, rather than the public good. The limited knowledge of voters combined with the influence of wealthy individuals reduces elected leaders' circle of concern to a group far smaller than the whole population, and in the US this problem is so stark that public policy now has almost no relationship to the views of average Americans.[2] While reforms to electoral and campaign finance rules, as well as tighter controls on lobbying and regulatory capture, offer improvements, representative democracy is likely to retain a motivational problem as long as citizens lack the information needed to evaluate the decisions of representatives.

I have therefore argued for a more radical change and for making random sortition a permanent and much more powerful part of our democratic systems. By bringing together representative groups of citizens who can evaluate public policy in a more informed and deliberate manner, random selection has the potential to provide a more effective check on elected leaders. To do this, however, lotteries need to become more than a marginal actor in our democratic systems. Rather than the sporadic use of deliberative minipublics and the relegation of citizen deliberation to the role of advice and recommendation, we need to give groups of citizens powers which can capture the attention of elected representatives. In other words, they need the power to force representatives to broaden their circle of concern, and account for

---

[2] Gilens and Page (2014).

240 INTELLIGENT DEMOCRACY

the interests of the whole population. Determining how best to do this raises interesting issues of institutional design and I have made my own proposal for a sortition branch which would require all legislation to pass the informed scrutiny of a representative group of citizens.

The sortition branch is, of course, an idealized model which is not likely to come about overnight. One role of political and democratic theory, however, is to offer appealing solutions to social problems, even if they are likely to be long-term projects. The problems facing our democracies are large and we may require significant and radical reforms. Political theorists can take the first steps in making such proposals politically possible by showing their potential value, and starting a conversation about how they can be realized in practice. The sortition branch is also not a fixed blueprint to be implemented exactly as described, but a demonstration that an effective use of random selection and direct citizen participation is possible. In this respect, the sortition branch is only one possibility and is unlikely to represent the best possible use of random selection. This proposal was greatly informed by the experience of existing mini-publics and citizen assemblies, and our understanding of sortition will likely grow as new initiatives are tried out and tested. The sortition branch should not therefore be seen as a fixed destination but rather as an example of the possibilities for sortition, and as a call for more experimentation with new ways of doing democracy.

The hope is that future experimentation will involve granting sortition-based bodies greater influence over policy decisions and more permanence in our political systems. Conventional mini-publics can tell us a lot but their mostly advisory role makes them an imperfect guide to situations where the political stakes are much higher. Experimentation with more permanent and influential uses of random selection is therefore needed, and we can find signs of such innovation taking place. The British Columbia Citizens' Assembly on Electoral Reform, for instance, involved a precommitment to put its decision to a referendum, while Ireland's Citizen Assembly's recommendations on the legalization of abortion formed the basis of a national vote. Although they did not take the final decision, these examples show an increased willingness to allow sortition bodies more political influence. There is also a new willingness to give sortition an established role in our political systems. The city of Gdansk in Poland, for instance, has established legal rules which would allow a citizen assembly to be formed on any issue if it garners enough public support, and a similar policy can be found in Vorarlberg, Austria. In the Polish case, the collection of one thousand signatures is required for an assembly to be considered, while five thousand forces the mayor to establish an assembly.

Perhaps the most ambitious experiment comes from Belgium, where in 2019 the Ostbelgien parliament (the German-speaking community of Belgium) decided to establish a permanent sortition-based council as a complement to their elected chamber. This 'Citizens' Council' is made up of 24 citizens rotated every eight months and plays an agenda-setting role. It does not itself make recommendations, but rather determines which issues should be debated by a set of more temporary 'Citizen Assemblies'. These latter assemblies are made up of 50 randomly selected members, consider the single issues set by the Citizen Council, and provide recommendations. Although the decisions of these Citizen Assemblies will not be legally binding, the parliament is required by law to debate and respond to their recommendations, and the permanent Citizen Council plays a role in overseeing parliamentary debates and monitoring the implementation of any agreed actions. The Ostbelgien model falls short of the more extensive powers average citizens would be granted in my sortition branch proposal, but it represents a significant progression in the contemporary use of lotteries and an important step towards a more permanent and powerful use of random selection.

More generally, recent years have seen a 'deliberative wave' with a surge of interest and experiments with citizen-based participation and deliberation, very often based on principles of random selection.[3] This includes the use of sortition at the local and city level, as well as national and even transnational levels within the European Union. While many of these initiatives fall into the more conventional uses of mini-publics criticized in the previous chapter, the speed at which they are gaining popularity, combined with new models for making lotteries more permanent and influential, provide much promise for the development of sortition. Vigilance, as well as enthusiasm, should accompany this deliberative wave. There will always be an incentive for elected leaders and special interest groups to weaken sortition initiatives or to design them in ways which reduce their influence. Many experiments with citizen participation come from the platforms of political parties—the Ostbelgien model, for instance, received cross-party support—and this will likely continue to be an important source of innovation into the future. However, it is important to guard against their capture by political actors. If the use of random selection is always subordinated to the interests of elected

[3] OECD (2020).

242   INTELLIGENT DEMOCRACY

leaders, then it will struggle to develop into an independent check on their power and improve the quality of democratic decisions.

There is also a threat that the use of sortition and citizen assemblies become synonymous with deliberative democracy, and we come to ignore the importance of other parts of the democratic system. There are signs that this may be becoming a trend with the increasing use of mini-publics often being referred to as a 'rise in deliberative democracy'. Throughout this book, however, we have seen how elections and an active public sphere are also vital parts of any functional democratic system, and why a deliberative democracy cannot be reduced to sortition and lotteries alone. Random selection has an important role in a democracy, a role it is currently not being allowed to play, but we also require an open and energetic civil society. Another important ingredient is political decentralization. Reducing decision-making to more local levels can help to bring democratic bodies closer to citizens, as well as increase the opportunity for experimentation with new ways of addressing social problems. Cities, for instance, are often seen as key sites for innovation around climate policy, and test beds for lower emission strategies. While national governments are often risk averse, and have to juggle many policy priorities, more local levels of decision-making have greater latitude to try something new.

While allowing for the emergence of new public policy, decentralization can also lead to more experimentation with democratic institutions. Many of the most ambitious sortition projects have been conducted away from national politics where the stakes are lower and the ability to innovate is larger. It is therefore likely that the local level will continue to be a site for innovation with citizen participation, and this will only increase with a greater decentralization of power. We may also be more likely to find initial support for sortition at the smaller scale, where the population from which people are selected is lower, and the chance of being included (or having someone you know included) is greater. Success at the local level may then provide a springboard for change higher up the political ladder. This is not to say that local democracy should be seen as merely a means to inspire reform at higher levels. While it can have this effect, we should not lose sight of the fact that more local forms of democracy have many advantages of their own, and local innovation in citizen participation should therefore also be valued for its direct contribution to democracy's epistemic value.

Achieving a more intelligent democracy will, of course, be neither simple nor guaranteed. Over the course of this book, however, I hope that I have shown why it represents a better route towards a more competent politics than efforts to either restrict or reject democracy. We are unlikely to improve our current political systems by simply reserving the political sphere for elites, nor will we produce better decisions by giving up on politics altogether and placing more power in the hands of the market. Democracy already possesses many epistemic virtues, and we can increase these further, if only we are willing to place trust in the capacity of citizens to competently contribute to politics. While the new democratic sceptics see democracy's epistemic problems as a reason to limit equal inclusion, we should instead be looking at how new forms of citizen participation can correct or compensate for these ills. It is true that our current representative democracies face many challenges, but they also do not represent the full range of democratic possibilities. The contribution average citizens can make to politics is not determined by their natural abilities alone, but by the institutions which structure their participation. The road to a more intelligent politics will therefore involve experimenting with new ways of doing democracy, which do not relegate citizens to voting in periodic elections, but instead allow them to contribute in a more direct, deliberative, and informed manner. Discovering these new forms of democratic participation is no easy task, but it is far preferable to any of the paths laid out for us by the new democratic scepticism.

References

Acemoglu, D., Naidu, S., Restrepo, P., & Robinson, J. A. (2015). Democracy, redistribution, and inequality. In A. B. Atkinson & F. Bourguignon (Eds.), *Handbook of income distribution* (Vol. 2, pp. 1885–1966). Elsevier.

Achen, C. H., & Bartels, L. M. (2017). *Democracy for realists: Why elections do not produce responsive government*. Princeton University Press.

Ackerman, B. A., & Fishkin, J. S. (2004). *Deliberation day*. Yale University Press.

Addams, J. (2013). *Democracy and social ethics*. Harvard University Press.

Akerlof, G. A. (1978). The market for 'lemons': Quality uncertainty and the market mechanism. In P. Diamond & M. Rothschild (Eds.), *Uncertainty in economics* (pp. 235–251). Elsevier.

Alexander, M. (2020). *The New Jim Crow: Mass incarceration in the age of colorblindness*. The New Press.

Aligica, P. D. (2014). *Institutional diversity and political economy: The Ostroms and beyond*. Oxford University Press.

Aligica, P. D. (2018). *Public entrepreneurship, citizenship, and self-governance*. Cambridge University Press.

Aligica, P. D., & Boettke, P. J. (2009). *Challenging institutional analysis and development: The Bloomington school*. Routledge.

Aligica, P. D., Boettke, P. J., & Tarko, V. (2019). *Public governance and the classical-liberal perspective: Political economy foundations*. Oxford University Press.

Aligica, P. D., & Tarko, V. (2012). Polycentricity: from Polanyi to Ostrom, and beyond. *Governance, 25*(2), 237–262.

Allcott, H., & Gentzkow, M. (2017). Social media and fake news in the 2016 election. *Journal of Economic Perspectives, 31*(2), 211–236.

Amnesty International. (2021). Amnesty International Report 2020/21: The state of the world's human rights. Retrieved from https://www.amnesty.org/en/countries/asia-and-the-pacific/china/report-china/

Ancell, A. (2017). Democracy isn't that smart (but we can make it smarter): On Landemore's democratic reason. *Episteme, 14*(2), 161–175.

Andersen, V. N., & Hansen, K. M. (2007). How deliberation makes better citizens: The Danish Deliberative Poll on the euro. *European Journal of Political Research, 46*(4), 531–556.

Anderson, E. (1995). *Value in ethics and economics*. Harvard University Press.

Anderson, E. (2006). The epistemology of democracy. *Episteme, 3*(1–2), 8–22.

Anderson, E. (2011). Democracy, public policy, and lay assessments of scientific testimony. *Episteme, 8*(2), 144–164.

Arechar, A. A., Nancy, J., Allen, L., Berinsky, A., Cole, R., Epstein, Z., . . . Rand, D. (2022). Understanding and combating online misinformation across 16 countries on six continents. *PsyArXiv*. doi:10.31234/osf.io/a9frz

Aristotle. (1991). *Rhetoric* (H. Lawson-Tancred, Trans.). Penguin Classics.

246 REFERENCES

Arlen, G., & Rossi, E. (2018). Is this what democracy looks like? (Never mind epistocracy). *Inquiry, 65*(1), 1–14.

Arneson, R. (2018). Democracy is not intrinsically just. In M. Cahan & R. B. Talisse (Eds.), *Political philosophy in the twenty-first century* (pp. 181–198). Routledge.

Bächtiger, A., Niemeyer, S., Neblo, M., Steenbergen, M. R., & Steiner, J. (2010). Disentangling diversity in deliberative democracy: Competing theories, their blind spots and complementarities. *Journal of political philosophy, 18*(1), 32–63.

Bagg, S. (2018). The power of the multitude: Answering epistemic challenges to democracy. *American Political Science Review, 112*(4), 891–904.

Bagg, S. (2024). Sortition as anti-corruption: Popular oversight against elite capture. *American Journal of Political Science, 68*(1), 93–105.

Bago, B., Rand, D. G., & Pennycook, G. (2020). Fake news, fast and slow: Deliberation reduces belief in false (but not true) news headlines. *Journal of experimental psychology: general, 149*(8), 1608–1613.

Bai, T. (2019). *Against political equality: The Confucian case.* Princeton University Press.

Barber, M., & Pope, J. C. (2019). Does party trump ideology? Disentangling party and ideology in America. *American Political Science Review, 113*(1), 38–54.

Barnett, A., & Carty, P. (1998). *The Athenian option: Radical reform for the House of Lords.* Demos.

Bartels, L. M. (1996). Uninformed votes: Information effects in presidential elections. *American Journal of Political Science, 40*(1), 194–230.

Bartels, L. M. (2016). *Unequal democracy.* Princeton University Press.

Bednar, J. (2009). *The robust federation.* Cambridge University Press.

Bell, D. A. (2009). *Beyond liberal democracy: Political thinking for an East Asian context.* Princeton University Press.

Bell, D. A. (2016). *The China model: Political meritocracy and the limits of democracy.* Princeton University Press.

Bell, D. A., & Pei, W. (2020). *Just hierarchy: Why social hierarchies matter in China and the rest of the world.* Princeton University Press.

Benson, J. (2018). Environmental law & the limits of markets. *Cambridge Journal of Economics, 42*(1), 215–230.

Benson, J. (2019a). Deliberative democracy and the problem of tacit knowledge. *Politics, Philosophy & Economics, 18*(1), 76–97.

Benson, J. (2019b). Knowledge and communication in democratic politics: markets, forums and systems. *Political Studies, 67*(2), 422–439.

Benson, J. (2020). Exit, Voice and Technocracy. *Critical Review, 32*(1–3), 32–61.

Benson, J. (2021). The epistemic value of deliberative democracy: How far can diversity take us? *Synthese, 199*, 8257–8279.

Berinsky, A. J. (2017). Rumors and health care reform: Experiments in political misinformation. *British Journal of Political Science, 47*(2), 241–262.

Besley, T., & Kudamatsu, M. (2006). Health and democracy. *American Economic Review, 96*(2), 313–318.

Bhatia, U. (2020). Rethinking the epistemic case against epistocracy. *Critical Review of International Social and Political Philosophy, 23*(6), 706–731.

Bhatia, U. (2022). Indirect elections as a constitutional device of epistocracy. *International Journal of Constitutional Law, 20*(1), 82–111.

REFERENCES 247

Blais, A., Carty, R. K., & Fournier, P. (2008). Do citizens' assemblies make reasoned choices? In M. Warren & H. Pearse (Eds.), *Designing deliberative democracy: The British Columbia citizens' assembly* (pp. 127–144). Cambridge University Press.

Blaydes, L., & Kayser, M. A. (2011). Counting calories: democracy and distribution in the developing world. *International Studies Quarterly, 55*(4), 887–908.

Boettke, P. J. (2018). *FA Hayek: Economics, political economy and social philosophy.* Palgrave Macmillan.

Boettke, P. J., & Coyne, C. J. (2009). An entrepreneurial theory of social and cultural change. In V. Pérez-Díaz (Ed.), *Markets and civil society: The European experience in comparative perspective* (pp. 77–103). Berghahn Books.

Böker, M. (2017). Justification, critique and deliberative legitimacy: The limits of mini-publics. *Contemporary Political Theory, 16*(1), 19–40.

Boulstridge, E., & Carrigan, M. (2000). Do consumers really care about corporate responsibility? Highlighting the attitude-behaviour gap. *Journal of Communication Management, 4*(4), 355–368.

Bouricius, T. (2019). Why hybrid bicameralism is not right for sortition. In J. Gastil & E. O. Wright (Eds.), *Legislature by lot* (pp. 313–332). Verso.

Bray, J., Johns, N., & Kilburn, D. (2011). An exploratory study into the factors impeding ethical consumption. *Journal of Business Ethics, 98*(4), 597–608.

Brennan, J. (2014). Epistocracy within public reason. In A. E. Cudd & S. J. Scholz (Eds.), *Philosophical perspectives on democracy in the 21st century* (pp. 191–204). Springer.

Brennan, J. (2016a). *Against Democracy.* Princeton University Press.

Brennan, J. (2016b, November 10). The problem with our government is democracy. *Washington Post.* Retrieved from https://www.washingtonpost.com/news/in-theory/wp/2016/11/10/the-problem-with-our-government-is-democracy/.

Brennan, J. (2018). Does the demographic objection to epistocracy succeed? *Res Publica, 24*(1), 53–71.

Brennan, J., & Jaworski, P. (2015). *Markets without limits: Moral virtues and commercial interests.* Routledge.

Bronstein, M. V., Pennycook, G., Bear, A., Rand, D. G., & Cannon, T. D. (2019). Belief in fake news is associated with delusionality, dogmatism, religious fundamentalism, and reduced analytic thinking. *Journal of Applied Research in Memory and Cognition, 8*(1), 108–117.

Broockman, D. E., & Butler, D. M. (2017). The causal effects of elite position-taking on voter attitudes: Field experiments with elite communication. *American Journal of Political Science, 61*(1), 208–221.

Callenbach, E., Phillips, M., & Sutherland, K. (2008). *A people's parliament/A citizen legislature.* Imprint Academic.

Campbell, A., Converse, P. E., Miller, W. E., & Stokes, D. E. (1980). *The American voter.* University of Chicago Press.

Caplan, B. (2011). *The myth of the rational voter: Why democracies choose bad policies. New edition.* Princeton University Press.

Carrigan, M., & Attalla, A. (2001). The myth of the ethical consumer: Do ethics matter in purchase behaviour? *Journal of consumer marketing, 18*(7), 560–578.

Carrington, M. J., Neville, B. A., & Whitwell, G. J. (2010). Why ethical consumers don't walk their talk: Towards a framework for understanding the gap between the ethical purchase intentions and actual buying behaviour of ethically minded consumers. *Journal of Business Ethics, 97*(1), 139–158.

248 REFERENCES

Carson, L., Gastil, J., Hartz-Karp, J., & Lubensky, R. (2013). *The Australian Citizens' Parliament and the future of deliberative democracy*. Penn State University Press.

Chambers, S. (1996). *Reasonable democracy: Jürgen Habermas and the politics of discourse*. Cornell University Press.

Chambers, S. (2009). Rhetoric and the public sphere: Has deliberative democracy abandoned mass democracy? *Political Theory, 37*(3), 323–350.

Chambers, S. (2018). Human life is group life: Deliberative democracy for realists. *Critical Review, 30*(1–2), 36–48.

Chambers, S. (2021). Truth, deliberative democracy, and the virtues of accuracy: Is fake news destroying the public sphere? *Political Studies, 69*(1), 147–163.

Chappell, Z. (2011). Justifying deliberative democracy: Are two heads always wiser than one? *Contemporary Political Theory, 10*(1), 78–101.

Christiano, T. (2008). *The constitution of equality: Democratic authority and its limits*. Oxford University Press.

Christiano, T. (2009). Debate: Estlund on democratic authority. *Journal of Political Philosophy, 17*(2), 228–240.

Christiano, T. (2012). Rational deliberation among experts and citizens. In J. Parkinson & J. Mansbridge (Eds.), *Deliberative systems: Deliberative democracy at the large scale* (pp. 27–51). Cambridge University Press.

Christiano, T. (2018). *The rule of the many: Fundamental issues in democratic theory*. Routledge.

Citrin, J., & Stoker, L. (2018). Political trust in a cynical age. *Annual Review of Political Science, 21*, 49–70.

Coady, C. A. J. (1994). *Testimony: A philosophical study*. Oxford University Press.

Cohen, J. (1986). An epistemic conception of democracy. *Ethics, 97*(1), 26–38.

Cohen, J. (2005). Deliberation and democratic legitimacy. In D. Matravers & J. Pike (Eds.), *Debates in contemporary political philosophy* (pp. 352–370). Routledge.

Collins, H., & Evans, R. (2008). *Rethinking expertise*. University of Chicago Press.

Conover, P. J., & Feldman, S. (1989). Candidate perception in an ambiguous world: Campaigns, cues, and inference processes. *American Journal of Political Science, 33*(4), 912–940.

Crouch, C. (2004). *Post-democracy*. Polity.

Curato, N., & Böker, M. (2016). Linking mini-publics to the deliberative system: A research agenda. *Policy Sciences, 49*(2), 173–190.

Curato, N., Hammond, M., & Min, J. B. (2019). *Power in deliberative democracy*. Palgrave Macmillan.

Davenport, C. (2007). *State repression and the domestic democratic peace*. Cambridge University Press.

De Pelsmacker, P., Driesen, L., & Rayp, G. (2005). Do consumers care about ethics? Willingness to pay for fair-trade coffee. *Journal of Consumer Affairs, 39*(2), 363–385.

De Pelsmacker, P., & Janssens, W. (2007). A model for fair trade buying behaviour: The role of perceived quantity and quality of information and of product-specific attitudes. *Journal of Business Ethics, 75*(4), 361–380.

Deacon, R. T. (2009). Public good provision under dictatorship and democracy. *Public Choice, 139*(1–2), 241–262.

Dean, R., Boswell, J., & Smith, G. (2020). Designing democratic innovations as deliberative systems: the ambitious case of NHS citizen. *Political Studies, 68*(3), 689–709.

REFERENCES 249

DeCanio, S. (2014). Democracy, the market, and the logic of social choice. *American Journal of Political Science, 58*(3), 637–652.

Delli Carpini, M. X. (2000). In search of the informed citizen: What Americans know about politics and why it matters. *The Communication Review, 4*(1), 129–164.

Dewey, J. (1923). *Democracy and education: An introduction to the philosophy of education.* Aakar Books.

Dewey, J. (1927). *The public and its problems.* Henry Holt and Company.

Dewey, J. (1969–1991). *The collected works of John Dewey: The early works, the middle works, the latter works.* (J. A. Boydston Ed. 37 vols). Southern Illinois University Press.

Dietrich, F. (2008). The premises of Condorcet's jury theorem are not simultaneously justified. *Episteme, 5*(1), 56–73.

diZerega, G. (1989). Democracy as a spontaneous order. *Critical Review, 3*(2), 206–240.

diZerega, G. (2011). Spontaneous order and liberalism's complex relation to democracy. *The Independent Review, 16*(2), 173–197.

Downs, A. (1957a). *An economic theory of democracy.* Harper and Row.

Downs, A. (1957b). An economic theory of political action in a democracy. *Journal of Political Economy, 65*(2), 135–150.

Druckman, J. N., & McGrath, M. C. (2019). The evidence for motivated reasoning in climate change preference formation. *Nature Climate Change, 9*(2), 111–119.

Dryzek, J. S. (1987). Complexity and rationality in public life. *Political Studies, 35*(3), 424–442.

Dryzek, J. S. (2009). Democratization as deliberative capacity building. *Comparative Political Studies, 42*(11), 1379–1402.

Dryzek, J. S. (2010). Rhetoric in democracy: A systemic appreciation. *Political Theory, 38*(3), 319–339.

Dryzek, J. S. (2012). *Foundations and frontiers of deliberative governance.* Oxford University Press.

Dryzek, J. S. (2017). The forum, the system, and the polity: three varieties of democratic theory. *Political Theory, 45*(5), 610–636.

Dryzek, J. S., Ercan, S. A., Hendriks, C. M., Niemeyer, S., Manin, B., Landemore, H., . . . Lafont, C. (2017). The prospects & limits of deliberative democracy. *Journal of the American Academy of Arts & Sciences, 146*(3), 6–166.

Elstub, S., & McLaverty, P. (2014). *Deliberative democracy: Issues and cases.* Endinburgh University Press.

Erikson, R. S., MacKuen, M. B., & Stimson, J. A. (2002). *The macro polity.* Cambridge University Press.

Estlund, D. (1994). Opinion leaders, independence, and Condorcet's jury theorem. *Theory and Decision, 36*(2), 131–162.

Estlund, D. (1997). Beyond fairness and deliberation: The epistemic dimension of democratic authority. In J. Bohman & W. Rehg (Eds.), *Deliberative democracy: Essays on reason and politics* (pp. 173–204). The MIT Press.

Estlund, D. (2003). Why not epistocracy. In N. Reshotko (Ed.), *Desire, identity and existence: Essays in honor of TM Penner* (pp. 53–69). Academic Printing and Publishing.

Estlund, D. (2009). *Democratic authority: A philosophical framework.* Princeton University Press.

Estlund, D., & Landemore, H. (2018). The epistemic value of democratic deliberation. In A. Bächtiger, J. S. Dryzek, J. Mansbridge, & M. E. Warren (Eds.), *The Oxford handbook of deliberative democracy* (pp. 113–131). Oxford University Press.

250 REFERENCES

Estlund, D., Waldron, J., Grofman, B., & Feld, S. L. (1989). Democratic theory and the public interest: Condorcet and Rousseau revisited. *American Political Science Review*, 83(4), 1317–1340.

Evans, A. J., & Friedman, J. (2011). 'Search' vs. 'browse': A theory of error grounded in radical (not rational) ignorance. *Critical Review*, 23(1–2), 73–104.

Farrell, D. M., Suiter, J., & Harris, C. (2019). 'Systematizing' constitutional deliberation: The 2016–18 citizens' assembly in Ireland. *Irish Political Studies*, 34(1), 113–123.

Fazey, I., Fazey, J. A., & Fazey, D. M. (2005). *Ecology and Society*, 10(2).

Fazey, I., Fazey, J. A., Salisbury, J. G., Lindenmayer, D. B., & Dovers, S. (2006). The nature and role of experiential knowledge for environmental conservation. *Environmental conservation*, 33(1), 1–10.

Fazey, I., Proust, K., Newell, B., Johnson, B., & Fazey, J. A. (2006). Eliciting the implicit knowledge and perceptions of on-ground conservation managers of the Macquarie Marshes. *Ecology and Society*, 11(1).

Feddersen, T., Gailmard, S., & Sandroni, A. (2009). Moral bias in large elections: Theory and experimental evidence. *American Political Science Review*, 103(2), 175–192.

Ferguson, A. (1996). *An essay on the history of civil society*. Cambridge University Press.

Festenstein, M. (2019). Does Dewey have an 'epistemic argument' for democracy? *Contemporary Pragmatism*, 16(2–3), 217–241.

Fishkin, J., Kousser, T., Luskin, R. C., & Siu, A. (2015). Deliberative agenda setting: Piloting reform of direct democracy in California. *Perspectives on Politics*, 13(4), 1030–1042.

Fishkin, J. S. (1997). *The voice of the people: Public opinion and democracy*. Yale University Press.

Fishkin, J. S. (2011). *When the people speak: Deliberative democracy and public consultation*. Oxford University Press.

Fishkin, J. S. (2018). *Democracy when the people are thinking: Revitalizing our politics through public deliberation*. Oxford University Press.

Fishkin, J. S., He, B., Luskin, R. C., & Siu, A. (2010). Deliberative democracy in an unlikely place: Deliberative polling in China. *British Journal of Political Science*, 40(2), 435–448.

Fishkin, J. S., & Luskin, R. C. (2005). Experimenting with a democratic ideal: Deliberative polling and public opinion. *Acta Politica*, 40(3), 284–298.

Fleuß, D. (2021). *Radical proceduralism: Democracy from philosophical principles to political institutions*. Emerald Group Publishing.

Foa, R. S., Claystone, A., Slade, M., Rand, A., & Williams, R. (2020). *The global satisfaction with democracy report 2020*. Bennett Institute for Public Policy, University of Cambridge.

Font, J., Smith, G., Galais, C., & Alarcon, P. (2018). Cherry-picking participation: Explaining the fate of proposals from participatory processes. *European Journal of Political Research*, 57(3), 615–636.

Forestal, J. (2021). Constructing digital democracies: Facebook, Arendt, and the politics of design. *Political Studies*, 69(1), 26–44.

Franco, Á., Álvarez-Dardet, C., & Ruiz, M. T. (2004). Effect of democracy on health: ecological study. *British Medical Journal*, 329(7480), 1421–1423.

Fricker, M. (2007). *Epistemic injustice: Power and the ethics of knowing*. Oxford University Press.

Friedman, J. (1998). Public ignorance and democratic theory. *Critical Review*, 12(4), 397–411.

REFERENCES 251

Friedman, J. (2019). *Power without knowledge: A critique of technocracy*. Oxford University Press.

Friedman, J. (2020). Political epistemology, technocracy, and political anthropology: Reply to a symposium on power without knowledge. *Critical Review, 32*(1–3), 242–367.

Fuerstein, M. (2008). Epistemic democracy and the social character of knowledge. *Episteme, 5*(1), 74–93.

Fuller, R. (2019). *In defence of democracy*. Polity Press.

Fung, A. (2003). Survey article: Recipes for public spheres: Eight institutional design choices and their consequences. *Journal of Political Philosophy, 11*(3), 338–367.

Futerra, S. (2005). *The rules of the game: The principals of climate change communication*. Department for Environment, Food and Rural Affairs, London.

Gallego, F. A. (2010). Historical origins of schooling: The role of democracy and political decentralization. *Review of Economics and Statistics, 92*(2), 228–243.

Gastil, J., & Wright, E. O. (2019). *Legislature by lot: Transformative designs for deliberative governance*. Verso Books.

Gaus, G. (1997a). Does democracy reveal the voice of the people? Four takes on Rousseau. *Australasian Journal of Philosophy, 75*(2), 141–162.

Gaus, G. (1997b). Reason, justification, and consensus: Why democracy can't have it all. In J. Bohman & W. Rehg (Eds.), *Deliberative democracy: Essays on reason and politics* (pp. 205–242). The MIT Press.

Gaus, G. (2011). On seeking the truth (whatever that is) through democracy: Estlund's case for the qualified epistemic claim. *Ethics, 121*(2), 270–300.

Gaus, G. (2019). What might democratic self-governance in a complex social world look like. *San Diego Law Review, 56*, 967.

Gaus, G. (2021). *The open society and its complexities*. Oxford University Press.

Gerber, A., & Green, D. (1999). Misperceptions about perceptual bias. *Annual Review of Political Science, 2*(1), 189–210.

Gilens, M. (2012). *Affluence and influence: Economic inequality and political power in America*. Princeton University Press.

Gilens, M., & Page, B. I. (2014). Testing theories of American politics: Elites, interest groups, and average citizens. *Perspectives on Politics, 12*(3), 564–581.

Goldman, A. I. (2001). Experts: Which ones should you trust? *Philosophy and Phenomenological Research, 63*(1), 85–110.

Goodin, R. E. (2005). Sequencing deliberative moments. *Acta Politica, 40*(2), 182–196.

Goodin, R. E., & Dryzek, J. S. (2006). Deliberative impacts: The macro-political uptake of mini-publics. *Politics & Society, 34*(2), 219–244.

Goodin, R. E., & Niemeyer, S. J. (2003). When does deliberation begin? Internal reflection versus public discussion in deliberative democracy. *Political Studies, 51*(4), 627–649.

Goodin, R. E., & Spiekermann, K. (2018). *An epistemic theory of democracy*. Oxford University Press.

Greenwood, D. (2007). The halfway house: Democracy, complexity, and the limits to markets in green political economy. *Environmental Politics, 16*(1), 73–91.

Gribben, C., & Gitsham, M. (2007). *Food labelling: Understanding consumer attitudes and behaviour*. Ashridge.

Grinberg, N., Joseph, K., Friedland, L., Swire-Thompson, B., & Lazer, D. (2019). Fake news on Twitter during the 2016 US presidential election. *Science, 363*(6425), 374–378.

252 REFERENCES

Grönlund, K., Herne, K., & Setälä, M. (2015). Does enclave deliberation polarize opinions? *Political Behavior*, *37*(4), 995–1020.

Guerrero, A. A. (2014). Against elections: The lottocratic alternative. *Philosophy & Public Affairs*, *42*(2), 135–178.

Guerrero, A. A. (2016). Living with ignorance in a world of experts. In R. Peels (Ed.), *Perspectives on ignorance from moral and social philosophy* (pp. 168–197). Routledge.

Guess, A., & Coppock, A. (2020). Does counter-attitudinal information cause backlash? Results from three large survey experiments. *British Journal of Political Science*, *50*(4), 1497–1515.

Guess, A., Nagler, J., & Tucker, J. (2019). Less than you think: Prevalence and predictors of fake news dissemination on Facebook. *Science Advances*, *5*(1), 1197–1201.

Gunn, P. (2014). Democracy and epistocracy. *Critical Review*, *26*(1–2), 59–79.

Gunn, P. (2019). Against epistocracy. *Critical Review*, *31*(1), 26–82.

Gutmann, A., & Thompson, D. F. (2009). *Why deliberative democracy?* Princeton University Press.

Habermas, J. (1975). *Legitimation Crisis* (T. McCarthy, Trans.). Polity Press.

Habermas, J. (1984). *The theory of communicative action, Vol. 1*. Beacon.

Habermas, J. (1990). *Moral consciousness and communicative action*. The MIT Press.

Habermas, J. (1994). *Justification and Application: Remarks on discourse ethics* (C. Cronin, Trans.). The MIT Press.

Habermas, J. (2006a). Political communication in media society: Does democracy still enjoy an epistemic dimension? The impact of normative theory on empirical research. *Communication Theory*, *16*(4), 411–426.

Habermas, J. (2006b). Religion in the public sphere. *European Journal of Philosophy*, *14*(1), 1–25.

Habermas, J. (2015). *Between facts and norms: Contributions to a discourse theory of law and democracy*. Polity Press.

Hacker, J. S., & Pierson, P. (2010). *Winner-take-all politics: How Washington made the rich richer--and turned its back on the middle class*. Simon & Schuster.

Hansen, K. M., & Andersen, V. N. (2004). Deliberative democracy and the deliberative poll on the Euro. *Scandinavian Political Studies*, *27*(3), 261–286.

Harding, R., & Stasavage, D. (2014). What democracy does (and doesn't do) for basic services: School fees, school inputs, and African elections. *Journal of Politics*, *76*(1), 229–245.

Hayek, F. A. (1937). Economics and knowledge. *Economica*, *4*(13), 33–54.

Hayek, F. A. (1945). The use of knowledge in society. *The American Economic Review*, *35*(4), 519–530.

Hayek, F. A. (1978). *New studies in philosophy, politics, economics, and the history of ideas*. Routledge.

Hayek, F. A. (2002). Competition as a discovery procedure. *Quarterly Journal of Austrian Economics*, *5*(3), 9–23.

Hayek, F. A. (2011). *The constitution of liberty: The definitive edition*. University of Chicago Press.

Hayek, F. A. (2013). *Law, legislation and liberty: A new statement of the liberal principles of justice and political economy*. Routledge.

He, B., & Warren, M. E. (2011). Authoritarian deliberation: The deliberative turn in Chinese political development. *Perspectives on Politics*, *9*(2), 269–289.

REFERENCES 253

Hendriks, C. M. (2016). Coupling citizens and elites in deliberative systems: The role of institutional design. *European Journal of Political Research*, *55*(1), 43–60.

Hennig, B. (2017). *The end of politicians*. Unbound Publishing.

Herath, R. (2007). *Real power to the people: A novel approach to electoral reform in British Columbia*. University Press of America.

Herzog, L. (2020). The epistemic division of labour in markets: Knowledge, global trade and the preconditions of morally responsible agency. *Economics & Philosophy*, *36*(2), 266–286.

Hong, L., & Page, S. E. (2004). Groups of diverse problem solvers can outperform groups of high-ability problem solvers. *Proceedings of the National Academy of Sciences*, *101*(46), 16385–16389.

Horwitz, S. (2004). Monetary calculation and the unintended extended order: The Misesian microfoundations of the Hayekian great society. *Review of Austrian Economics*, *17*(4), 307–321.

Human Rights Watch. (2021). *World Report 2021*. Retrieved from https://www.hrw.org/world-report/2021/country-chapters/china-and-tibet#49dda6

Hume, D. (2007). *An enquiry concerning human understanding*. Oxford University Press.

Ingham, S. (2013). Disagreement and epistemic arguments for democracy. *Politics, Philosophy & Economics*, *12*(2), 136–155.

Ingham, S., & Wiens, D. (2021). Demographic objections to epistocracy: A generalization. *Philosophy & Public Affairs*, *49*(4), 323–349.

Jacobs, L. R., & Shapiro, R. Y. (2000). *Politicians don't pander: Political manipulation and the loss of democratic responsiveness*. University of Chicago Press.

Jeffrey, A. (2018). Limited epistocracy and political inclusion. *Episteme*, *15*(4), 412–432.

Johnston, D. (1997). Hayek's attack on social justice. *Critical Review*, *11*(1), 81–100.

Jörke, D. (2010). The epistemic turn of critical theory: Implications for deliberative politics and policy-making. *Critical Policy Studies*, *3*(3–4), 440–446.

Kahan, D. M. (2012). Ideology, motivated reasoning, and cognitive reflection: An experimental study. *Judgment and Decision Making*, *8*(4), 407–424.

Kahan, D. M. (2017). Misconceptions, misinformation, and the logic of identity-protective cognition. Cultural Cognition Project Working Paper Series No. 164, Available at SSRN: doi:https://dx.doi.org/10.2139/ssrn.2973067

Kahan, D. M., Peters, E., Dawson, E. C., & Slovic, P. (2017). Motivated numeracy and enlightened self-government. *Behavioural Public Policy*, *1*(1), 54–86.

Kahan, D. M., Peters, E., Wittlin, M., Slovic, P., Ouellette, L. L., Braman, D., & Mandel, G. (2012). The polarizing impact of science literacy and numeracy on perceived climate change risks. *Nature Climate Change*, *2*(10), 732–735.

Kahneman, D. (2011). *Thinking, fast and slow*. Macmillan.

Kelly, J. T. (2014). Democracy as the rule of a small many. *Critical Review*, *26*(1–2), 80–91.

Kirzner, I. M. (1985). *Discovery and the capitalist process*. University of Chicago Press.

Kirzner, I. M. (2015). *Competition and entrepreneurship*. University of Chicago Press.

Knight, J., & Johnson, J. (2007). The priority of democracy: A pragmatist approach to political-economic institutions and the burden of justification. *American Political Science Review*, *101*(1), 47–61.

Knight, J., & Johnson, J. (2011). *The priority of democracy: Political consequences of pragmatism*. Princeton University Press.

Kolodny, N. (2014a). Rule over none I: What justifies democracy? *Philosophy & Public Affairs*, *42*(3), 195–229.

254 REFERENCES

Kolodny, N. (2014b). Rule over none II: Social equality and the justification of democracy. *Philosophy & Public Affairs, 42*(4), 287–336.

Kudamatsu, M. (2012). Has democratization reduced infant mortality in sub-Saharan Africa? Evidence from micro data. *Journal of the European Economic Association, 10*(6), 1294–1317.

Kuehn, D. (2017). Diversity, ability, and democracy: A note on Thompson's challenge to Hong and Page. *Critical Review, 29*(1), 72–87.

Ladha, K. K. (1992). The Condorcet jury theorem, free speech, and correlated votes. *American Journal of Political Science, 36*(3), 617–634.

Lafont, C. (2015). Deliberation, participation, and democratic legitimacy: Should deliberative mini-publics shape public policy? *Journal of Political Philosophy, 23*(1), 40–63.

Lafont, C. (2019). *Democracy without shortcuts: A participatory conception of deliberative democracy*. Oxford University Press.

Lake, M. (2005). From Mississippi to Melbourne via Natal: The invention of the literacy test as a technology of racial exclusion. In A. Curthoys & M. Lake (Eds.), *Connected Worlds: History in Transnational Perspective* (pp. 209–230). Australian National University Press.

Landa, D., & Pevnick, R. (2021). Is random selection a cure for the ills of electoral representation? *Journal of Political Philosophy, 29*(1), 46–72.

Landemore, H. (2013a). Deliberation, cognitive diversity, and democratic inclusiveness: an epistemic argument for the random selection of representatives. *Synthese, 190*(7), 1209–1231.

Landemore, H. (2013b). *Democratic reason: Politics, collective intelligence, and the rule of the many*. Princeton University Press.

Landemore, H. (2014). Yes, we can (make it up on volume): Answers to critics. *Critical Review, 26*(1–2), 184–237.

Landemore, H. (2017). Beyond the fact of disagreement? The epistemic turn in deliberative democracy. *Social Epistemology, 31*(3), 277–295.

Landemore, H. (2020). *Open democracy*. Princeton University Press.

Landemore, H., & Mercier, H. (2010). 'Talking it out': Deliberation with others versus deliberation within. Available at SSRN: http://dx.doi.org/10.2139/ssrn.1660695.

Landémore, H., & Mercier, H. (2012). Talking it out with others vs. deliberation within and the law of group polarization: Some implications of the argumentative theory of reasoning for deliberative democracy. *Análise Social, 47*(205), 910.

Landemore, H., & Page, S. E. (2015). Deliberation and disagreement: Problem solving, prediction, and positive dissensus. *Politics, Philosophy & Economics, 14*(3), 229–254.

Las Heras, J., & Ribera-Almandoz, O. (2017). When corporatism fails: trade union strategies and grassroots resistance to the Spanish economic crisis. *Journal of Labor and Society, 20*(4), 449–466.

Lazer, D. M., Baum, M. A., Benkler, Y., Berinsky, A. J., Greenhill, K. M., Menczer, F., . . . Rothschild, D. (2018). The science of fake news. *Science, 359*(6380), 1094–1096.

Leib, E., & He, B. (2006). *The search for deliberative democracy in China*. Palgrave Macmillan.

Leib, E. J. (2010). *Deliberative democracy in America: A proposal for a popular branch of government*. Penn State University Press.

Lenz, G. S. (2013). *Follow the leader? How voters respond to politicians' policies and performance*. University of Chicago Press.

REFERENCES 255

Lepoutre, M. (2020). Democratic group cognition. *Philosophy & Public Affairs*, 48(1), 40–78.

Levinson, S. (2014). A Welcome defense of democracy. *Critical Review*, 26(1–2), 92–100.

Lippert-Rasmussen, K. (2012). Estlund on epistocracy: A critique. *Res Publica*, 18(3), 241–258.

List, C., & Goodin, R. E. (2001). Epistemic democracy: Generalizing the Condorcet jury theorem. *Journal of Political Philosophy*, 9(3), 277–306.

Lister, A. (2013). The 'mirage' of social justice: Hayek against (and for) Rawls. *Critical Review*, 25(3–4), 409–444.

López-Guerra, C. (2011). The enfranchisement lottery. *Politics, Philosophy & Economics*, 10(2), 211–233.

Lukes, S. (1997). Social justice: The Hayekian challenge. *Critical Review*, 11(1), 65–80.

Lupia, A. (1992). Busy voters, agenda control, and the power of information. *American Political Science Review*, 86(2), 390–403.

Lupia, A. (2006). How elitism undermines the study of voter competence. *Critical Review*, 18(1–3), 217–232.

Luskin, R. C., Fishkin, J. S., & Jowell, R. (2002). Considered opinions: Deliberative polling in Britain. *British Journal of Political Science*, 32(3), 455–487.

Luskin, R. C., Sood, G., Fishkin, J. S., & Hahn, K. S. (2022). Deliberative distortions? Homogenization, polarization, and domination in small group deliberations. *British Journal of Political Science* 53, 1205–1225.

Mackie, G. (2006). Does democratic deliberation change minds? *Politics, Philosophy & Economics*, 5(3), 279–303.

Mackie, G. (2012). Rational ignorance and beyond. In H. Landemore & J. Elster (Eds.), *Collective wisdom: Principles and mechanisms* (pp. 290–318). Cambridge University Press.

Magleby, D. B. (1995). Governing by Initiative: Let the voters decide? An assessement of the initiative and referendum process. *University of Colorado Law Review*, 66, 42.

Manin, B. (1997). *The principles of representative government*. Cambridge University Press.

Mansbridge, J. (1986). *Why we lost the ERA*. University of Chicago Press.

Mansbridge, J. (1999a). Everyday talk in the deliberative system. In S. Macedo (Ed.), *Deliberative politics* (pp. 211–242.). Oxford University Press.

Mansbridge, J. (1999b). Should blacks represent blacks and women represent women? A contingent 'yes'. *Journal of Politics*, 61(3), 628–657.

Mansbridge, J., Bohman, J., Chambers, S., Christiano, T., Fung, A., Parkinson, J., . . . Warren, M. E. (2012). A systemic approach to deliberative democracy. In J. Parkinson & J. Mansbridge (Eds.), *Deliberative systems: Deliberative democracy at the large scale* (pp. 1–26). Cambridge University Press.

Mansbridge, J., Bohman, J., Chambers, S., Estlund, D., Føllesdal, A., Fung, A., . . . Martí, J. L. (2010). The place of self-interest and the role of power in deliberative democracy. *Journal of Political Philosophy*, 18(1), 64–100.

Manson, N. C., & O'Neill, O. (2007). *Rethinking informed consent in bioethics*. Cambridge University Press.

Martí, J. L. (2006). The epistemic conception of deliberative democracy defended: Reasons, rightness and equal political. In J. L. Martí & S. Besson (Eds.), *Deliberative democracy and its discontents* (pp. 27–56). Routledge.

May, K. O. (1952). A set of independent necessary and sufficient conditions for simple majority decision. *Econometrica: Journal of the Econometric Society*, 20(4), 680–684.

256 REFERENCES

McCormick, J. P. (2006). Contain the wealthy and patrol the magistrates: Restoring elite accountability to popular government. *American Political Science Review*, *100*(2), 147–163.

McKay, S., & Tenove, C. (2020). Disinformation as a threat to deliberative democracy. *Political Research Quarterly*, *74*(3), 703–717.

Mercier, H., & Sperber, D. (2011). Why do humans reason? Arguments for an argumentative theory. *Behavioral and Brain Sciences*, *43*(2), 57–74.

Mercier, H., & Sperber, D. (2017). *The enigma of reason*. Harvard University Press.

Mill, J. S. (2008). *On liberty and other essays*. Oxford Paperbacks.

Mill, J. S. (2011). *Considerations on representative government*. Cambridge University Press.

Min, J. B., & Wong, J. K. (2018). Epistemic approaches to deliberative democracy. *Philosophy Compass*, *13*(6), e12497.

Misak, C. (2013). *The American pragmatists*. Oxford University Press.

Moore, A. (2017). *Critical elitism: Deliberation, democracy, and the problem of expertise*. Cambridge University Press.

Moraro, P. (2018). Against epistocracy. *Social Theory and Practice*, *44*(2), 199–216.

Morrell, M. E. (2014). Participant bias and success in deliberative mini-publics. In K. Grönlund, A. Bächtiger, & M. Setälä (Eds.), *Deliberative mini-publics: Involving citizens in the democratic process* (pp. 157–176). Rowman & Littlefield.

Mosleh, M., Pennycook, G., Arechar, A. A., & Rand, D. G. (2021). Cognitive reflection correlates with behavior on Twitter. *Nature communications*, *12*(1), 1–10.

Muirhead, R. (2014). The politics of getting it right. *Critical Review*, *26*(1–2), 115–128.

Müller, J. F. (2019). *Political pluralism, disagreement and justice: The case for polycentric democracy*. Routledge.

Neblo, M. A. (2015). *Deliberative democracy between theory and practice*. Cambridge University Press.

Nicholls, A., & Lee, N. (2006). Purchase decision-making in fair trade and the ethical purchase 'gap': 'Is there a fair trade twix?' *Journal of Strategic Marketing*, *14*(4), 369–386.

Niemeyer, S. (2014). Scaling up deliberation to mass publics: Harnessing mini-publics in a deliberative system. In K. Grönlund, A. Bächtiger, & M. Setälä (Eds.), *Deliberative mini-publics: Involving citizens in the democratic process* (pp. 177–201). Rowman & Littlefield.

Niemeyer, S., & Dryzek, J. S. (2007). The ends of deliberation: meta-consensus and intersubjective rationality as ideal outcomes. *Swiss Political Science Review*, *13*(4), 497–526.

Nyhan, B., & Reifler, J. (2010). When corrections fail: The persistence of political misperceptions. *Political Behavior*, *32*(2), 303–330.

Nyhan, B., Reifler, J., & Ubel, P. A. (2013). The hazards of correcting myths about health care reform. *Medical Care*, *51*(2), 127–132.

O'Leary, K. (2006). *Saving democracy: A plan for real representation in America*. Stanford University Press.

O'Neill, J. (2002). The rhetoric of deliberation: Some problems in Kantian theories of deliberative democracy. *Res Publica*, *8*(3), 249–268.

O'Neill, J. (2012). Austrian economics and the limits of markets. *Cambridge Journal of Economics*, *36*(5), 1073–1090.

Oakeshott, M. (1991). *Rationalism in politics and other essays*. Liberty Fund.

OECD. (2020). *Innovative citizen participation and new democratic institutions*. OECD Publishing. Available at https://doi.org/10.1787/339306da-en

REFERENCES   257

Oreskes, N., & Conway, E. M. (2011). *Merchants of doubt: How a handful of scientists obscured the truth on issues from tobacco smoke to global warming.* Bloomsbury Publishing.

Osmundsen, M., Bor, A., Vahlstrup, P. B., Bechmann, A., & Petersen, M. B. (2021). Partisan polarization is the primary psychological motivation behind 'fake news' sharing on Twitter. *American Political Science Review, 115*(3), 999–1015.

Ostrom, E. (1972). Metropolitan reform: Propositions derived from two traditions. *Social Science Quarterly, 53*(3), 474–493.

Ostrom, E. (1998). The comparative study of public economies. Presented upon acceptance of the Frank E. Seidman Distinguished Award in Political Economy. PK Seidman Foundation.

Ostrom, E. (2009). *Understanding institutional diversity.* Princeton University Press.

Ostrom, E. (2010). Beyond markets and states: Polycentric governance of complex economic systems. *American Economic Review, 100*(3), 641–672.

Ostrom, V., & Ostrom, E. (1965). A behavioral approach to the study of intergovernmental relations. *The AnnALs of the American Academy of Political and Social Science, 359*(1), 137–146.

Ostrom, V., Tiebout, C. M., & Warren, R. (1961). The organization of government in metropolitan areas: a theoretical inquiry. *American Political Science Review, 55*(4), 831–842.

Owen, D., & Smith, G. (2015). Survey article: Deliberation, democracy, and the systemic turn. *Journal of Political Philosophy, 23*(2), 213–234.

Owen, D., & Smith, G. (2019). Sortition, rotation, and mandate: Conditions for political equality and deliberative reasoning. In J. Gastil & E. O. Wright (Eds.), *Legislature by lot* (pp. 279–299). Verso.

Page, S. E. (2008). *The difference: How the power of diversity creates better groups, firms, schools, and societies. New edition.* Princeton University Press.

Page, S. E. (2010). *Diversity and complexity.* Princeton University Press.

Parkinson, J. (2006). *Deliberating in the real world: Problems of legitimacy in deliberative democracy.* Oxford University Press.

Parkinson, J. (2012). Democratizing deliberative systems. In J. Parkinson & J. Mansbridge (Eds.), *Deliberative systems: Deliberative democracy at the large scale* (pp. 151–172). Cambridge University Press.

Parkinson, J., & Mansbridge, J. (2012). *Deliberative systems: Deliberative democracy at the large scale.* Cambridge University Press.

Pateman, C. (2012). Participatory democracy revisited. *Perspectives on politics, 10*(1), 7–19.

Pehlivanoglu, D., Lin, T., Deceus, F., Heemskerk, A., Ebner, N. C., & Cahill, B. S. (2021). The role of analytical reasoning and source credibility on the evaluation of real and fake full-length news articles. *Cognitive Research: Principles and Implications, 6*(1), 1–12.

Pennington, M. (2001). Environmental markets vs. environmental deliberation: a Hayekian critique of green political economy. *New Political Economy, 6*(2), 171–190.

Pennington, M. (2003). Hayekian political economy and the limits of deliberative democracy. *Political Studies, 51*(4), 722–739.

Pennington, M. (2005). Liberty, markets, and environmental values: A Hayekian defense of free-market environmentalism. *The Independent Review, 10*(1), 39–57.

Pennington, M. (2010). Democracy and the deliberative conceit. *Critical Review, 22*(2–3), 159–184.

258 REFERENCES

Pennington, M. (2011). *Robust political economy: Classical liberalism and the future of public policy*. Edward Elgar.

Pennington, M. (2017). Robust political economy and the priority of markets. *Social Philosophy and Policy*, *34*(1), 1–24.

Pennycook, G., Epstein, Z., Mosleh, M., Arechar, A. A., Eckles, D., & Rand, D. G. (2021). Shifting attention to accuracy can reduce misinformation online. *Nature*, *592*, 590–595.

Pennycook, G., McPhetres, J., Zhang, Y., Lu, J. G., & Rand, D. G. (2020). Fighting COVID-19 misinformation on social media: Experimental evidence for a scalable accuracy-nudge intervention. *Psychological Science*, *31*(7), 770–780.

Pennycook, G., & Rand, D. G. (2019). Lazy, not biased: Susceptibility to partisan fake news is better explained by lack of reasoning than by motivated reasoning. *Cognition*, *188*, 39–50.

Pennycook, G., & Rand, D. G. (2020). Who falls for fake news? The roles of bullshit receptivity, overclaiming, familiarity, and analytic thinking. *Journal of Personality*, *88*(2), 185–200.

Pennycook, G., & Rand, D. G. (2021). The psychology of fake news. *Trends in Cognitive Sciences*, *25*(5), 388–402.

Pereira, A., Van Bavel, J. J., & Harris, E. A. (2023). Identity concerns drive belief: The impact of partisan identity on the belief and dissemination of true and false news. *Group Processes & Intergroup Relations*, *26*(1), 24–47.

Persily, N. (2017). The 2016 US election: Can democracy survive the internet? *Journal of Democracy*, *28*(2), 63–76.

Peter, F. (2007). Democratic legitimacy and proceduralist social epistemology. *Politics, Philosophy & Economics*, *6*(3), 329–353.

Peter, F. (2008). Pure epistemic proceduralism. *Episteme*, *5*(1), 33–55.

Pincione, G., & Tesón, F. R. (2006). *Rational choice and democratic deliberation: A theory of discourse failure*. Cambridge University Press.

Polanyi, M. (1997). The tacit dimension. In L. Prusak (Ed.), *Knowledge in Organistions* (pp. 135–146). Butterworth-Heinemann.

Polanyi, M. (2013). *The logic of liberty: Reflections and rejoinders*. Routledge.

Polanyi, M. (2015). *Personal Knowledge: Towards a post-critical philosophy*. University of Chicago Press.

Polanyi, M. (1962). The republic of science: its political and economic theory. *Minerva*, *1*(1), 54–73.

Przeworski, A. (2005). Democracy as an equilibrium. *Public choice*, *123*(3), 253–273.

Quirk, P. J. (2014). Making it up on volume: Are larger groups really smarter? *Critical Review*, *26*(1–2), 129–150.

Rawls, J. (1971). *A theory of justice*. Harvard University Press.

Raymond, C. M., Fazey, I., Reed, M. S., Stringer, L. C., Robinson, G. M., & Evely, A. C. (2010). Integrating local and scientific knowledge for environmental management. *Journal of Environmental Management*, *91*(8), 1766–1777.

Remer, G. (2008). Genres of political speech: Oratory and conversation, today and in antiquity. *Language & Communication*, *28*(2), 182–196.

Renwick, A., Allan, S., Jennings, W., Mckee, R., Russell, M., & Smith, G. (2018). What kind of Brexit do voters want? Lessons from the Citizens' Assembly on Brexit. *The Political Quarterly*, *89*(4), 649–658.

Rini, R. (2017). Fake news and partisan epistemology. *Kennedy Institute of Ethics Journal*, *27*(2), E–43–E–64.

REFERENCES 259

Rock, M. T. (2009). Corruption and democracy. *Journal of Development Studies*, *45*(1), 55–75.

Roemer, J. (1994). *A future for socialism*. Harvard University Press.

Ross, R. M., Rand, D. G., & Pennycook, G. (2021). Beyond 'fake news': Analytic thinking and the detection of false and hyperpartisan news headlines. *Judgment & Decision Making, 16*(2), 484–504.

Ryan, A. (1995). *John Dewey and the high tide of American liberalism*. Norton.

Ryan, M., & Smith, G. (2014). Defining mini-publics. In K. Grönlund, A. Bächtiger, & M. Setälä (Eds.), *Deliberative mini-publics: Involving citizens in the democratic process* (pp. 9–26). Rowman & Littlefield.

Ryan, S. (2017). Fake news, epistemic coverage and trust. *The Political Quarterly, 92*(4), 606–612.

Ryle, G. (1945). Knowing how and knowing that: The presidential address. *Proceedings of the Aristotelian Society, 46*(1945–1946), 1–16.

Sagoff, M. (2007). *The Economy of the Earth: Philosophy, law, and the environment*. Cambridge University Press.

Sanders, L. M. (1997). Against deliberation. *Political Theory, 25*(3), 347–376.

Satz, D. (2010). *Why some things should not be for sale: The moral limits of markets*. Oxford University Press.

Schlozman, K. L., Verba, S., & Brady, H. E. (2012). *The unheavenly chorus*. Princeton University Press.

Schumpeter, J. A. (1996). *Capitalism, socialism and democracy*. Routledge.

Schwartzberg, M. (2015). Epistemic democracy and its challenges. *Annual Review of Political Science, 18*, 187–203.

Scott, E., Kallis, G., & Zografos, C. (2019). Why environmentalists eat meat. *PloS One, 14*(7), e0219607.

Scott, J. C. (1998). *Seeing like a state: How certain schemes to improve the human condition have failed*. Yale University Press.

Sen, A. (1982). *Poverty and famines: an essay on entitlement and deprivation*. Oxford University Press.

Sen, A. (1999). *Development as freedom*. Oxford University Press.

Setälä, M., & Smith, G. (2018). Mini-publics and deliberative democracy. In A. Bächtiger, J. Dryzek, J. Mansbridge, & M. Warren (Eds.), *The Oxford handbook of deliberative democracy* (pp. 300–314). Oxford University Press.

Shapiro, I. (2016). *Politics against domination*. Harvard University Press.

Simon, W. H. (2012). The institutional configuration of Deweyan democracy. *Contemporary Pragmatism, 9*(2), 5–34.

Siu, A. (2009). *Look who's talking: Examining social influence, opinion change, and argument quality in deliberation*. Stanford University Press.

Sloman, S. F., Philip. (2017). *The knowledge illusion: The myth of individual thought and the power of collective wisdom*. Penguin Random House.

Slovic, P. (1987). Perception of risk. *Science, 236*(4799), 280–285.

Slovic, P. (2000). *The perception of risk*: Earthscan.

Smith, A. (2010). *The wealth of nations: An inquiry into the nature and causes of the wealth of nations*. Harriman House Limited.

Smith, G. (2009). *Democratic innovations: Designing institutions for citizen participation*. Cambridge University Press.

260 REFERENCES

Somin, I. (2010). Deliberative democracy and political ignorance. *Critical Review*, *22*(2–3), 253–279.

Somin, I. (2016). *Democracy and political ignorance: Why smaller government is smarter.* Stanford University Press.

Somin, I. (2019). The promise and peril of epistocracy. *Inquiry*, *65*(1), 1–8.

Sperber, D., Clément, F., Heintz, C., Mascaro, O., Mercier, H., Origgi, G., & Wilson, D. (2010). Epistemic vigilance. *Mind & Language*, *25*(4), 359–393.

Stevenson, H., & Dryzek, J. S. (2014). *Democratizing global climate governance.* Cambridge University Press.

Stich, S. G. (2014). When democracy meets pluralism: Landemore's epistemic argument for democracy and the problem of value diversity. *Critical Review*, *26*(1–2), 170–183.

Stiglitz, J. E. (1996). *Whither socialism?* The MIT Press.

Strickland, A. A., Taber, C. S., & Lodge, M. (2011). Motivated reasoning and public opinion. *Journal of health politics, policy and law*, *36*(6), 935–944.

Sunstein, C. R. (2002). The law of group polarization. *Journal of Political Philosophy*, *10*(2), 175–195.

Sunstein, C. R. (2000). Deliberative trouble? Why groups go to extremes. *Yale Law Journal*, *110*(1), 71–119.

Sunstein, C. R. (2009). *Going to extremes: How like minds unite and divide.* Oxford University Press.

Talisse, R. B. (2011). A farewell to Deweyan democracy. *Political Studies*, *59*(3), 509–526.

Tan, K. P. (2008). Meritocracy and elitism in a global city: Ideological shifts in Singapore. *International Political Science Review*, *29*(1), 7–27.

Tappin, B. M., Pennycook, G., & Rand, D. G. (2020). Bayesian or biased? Analytic thinking and political belief updating. *Cognition*, *204*, 104375.

Taub, A. (2017). The real story about fake news is partisanship. *New York Times*. Retrieved from https://www.nytimes.com/2017/01/11/upshot/the-real-story-about-fake-news-is-partisanship.html

Tebble, A. J. (2009). Hayek and social justice: a critique. *Critical Review of International Social and Political Philosophy*, *12*(4), 581–604.

Tebble, A. J. (2016). *Epistemic liberalism: a defence.* Routledge.

The Economist. (2018). The partisan brain: Why psychology experiments tell you why people deny facts. *The Economist*. Retrieved from https://www.economist.com/united-states/2018/12/08/what-psychology-experiments-tell-you-about-why-people-deny-facts

Thompson, A. (2014). Does diversity trump ability? *Notices of the American Mathematical Society*, *61*(9), 1024–1030.

Thompson, D. F. (2004). *Just elections: Creating a fair electoral process in the United States.* University of Chicago Press.

Urbinati, N. (2014). *Democracy disfigured.* Harvard University Press.

Van Bavel, J. J., & Pereira, A. (2018). The partisan brain: An identity-based model of political belief. *Trends in cognitive sciences*, *22*(3), 213–224.

Van Reybrouck, D. (2016). *Against elections: The case for democracy.* Random House.

Van Schaack, B., & Wang, M. (2021). 'Break their lineage, break their roots': China's crimes against humanity targeting Uyghurs and other Turkic Muslims. Human Rights Watch & Mills Legal Clinic of Stanford Law School.

Vegetti, F., & Mancosu, M. (2020). The impact of political sophistication and motivated reasoning on misinformation. *Political Communication*, *37*(5), 678–695.

Verba, S., Burns, N., & Schlozman, K. L. (1997). Knowing and caring about politics: Gender and political engagement. *Journal of Politics, 59*(4), 1051–1072.

Verba, S., Schlozman, K. L., Brady, H., & Nie, N. H. (1993). Race, ethnicity and political resources: Participation in the United States. *British Journal of Political Science, 23*(4), 453–497.

Von Mises, L. (2002). *Epistemological problems of economics*. Ludwig von Mises Institute.

Von Mises, L. (2012). *Human action: A treatise on economics*. Martino Publishing

Wagner, R. E. (2005). Self-governance, polycentrism, and federalism: recurring themes in Vincent Ostrom's scholarly oeuvre. *Journal of Economic Behavior & Organization, 57*(2), 173–188.

Waldron, J. (1995). The wisdom of the multitude: some reflections on book 3, chapter 11 of Aristotle's politics. *Political Theory, 23*(4), 563–584.

Waldron, J. (1999). *Law and disagreement*. Oxford University Press.

Wall, D. (2018). *Elinor Ostrom's rules for radicals*. Pluto Press.

Wall, S. (2007). Democracy and equality. *Philosophical Quarterly, 57*(228), 416–438.

Warren, M. E. (2009). Governance-driven democratization. *Critical Policy Studies, 3*(1), 3–13.

Warren, M. E. (2017). A problem-based approach to democratic theory. *American Political Science Review, 111*(1), 39–53.

Warren, M. E. (2020). Participatory deliberative democracy in complex mass societies. *Journal of Deliberative Democracy, 16*(2), 81–88.

Warren, M. E., & Gastil, J. (2015). Can deliberative minipublics address the cognitive challenges of democratic citizenship? *Journal of Politics, 77*(2), 562–574.

Warren, M. E., & Pearse, H. (2008). *Designing deliberative democracy: The British Columbia citizens' assembly*. Cambridge University Press.

Wederman, A. (2004). The intensification of corruption in China. *China Quarterly, 180*, 895–921.

Weisberg, M. (2012). *Simulation and similarity: Using models to understand the world*. Oxford University Press.

Westbrook, R. B. (2015a). *Democratic hope*: Cornell University Press.

Westbrook, R. B. (2015b). *John Dewey and American democracy*. Cornell University Press.

Winslow, M. (2005). Is democracy good for the environment? *Journal of Environmental Planning and Management, 48*(5), 771–783.

Wolak, J., & McDevitt, M. (2011). The roots of the gender gap in political knowledge in adolescence. *Political Behavior, 33*(3), 505–533.

Wood, T., & Porter, E. (2019). The elusive backfire effect: Mass attitudes' steadfast factual adherence. *Political Behavior, 41*(1), 135–163.

Yack, B. (2006). Rhetoric and public reasoning: An Aristotelian understanding of political deliberation. *Political Theory, 34*(4), 417–438.

Young, I. M. (2011). *Justice and the politics of difference*. Princeton University Press.

Zakaras, A. (2010). Lot and democratic representation: A modest proposal. *Constellations, 17*(3), 455–471.

Zaller, J. R. (1992). *The nature and origins of mass opinion*. Cambridge University Press.

Ziliotti, E. (2023). An epistemic case for confucian democracy. *Critical Review of International Social and Political Philosophy, 26*(7), 1005–1027.

Index

For the benefit of digital users, indexed terms that span two pages (e.g., 52–53) may, on occasion, appear on only one of those pages.

accountability
  in democracy via elections, 75, 181–86, 187–88, 193, 195–96
  in democracy via lotteries, 205–6, 209–10, 219–20, 221–22, 227–28, 230
  in dictatorship, 181–82
  in epistocracy, 197–99, 200–2
  in lottocracy, 209
  in political meritocracy, 191–95, 196
Achen, Christopher, 20n.1, 96n.1, 184–85
advertising, 56–57, 86–88, 91–92
agenda setting, 74–75, 145–46, 211, 214–15, 222, 223, 224–25, 241
agent-based modules, 7–8, 156–59
aggregation, 59, 61–62, 72, 118
Aligica, Paul Dragos, 4–5, 127–33, 135–36
ancient Greeks, 205–6. *See also* Athenian democracy
Anderson, Elizabeth, 9, 32–33, 36, 42–44, 105n.26, 106n.30, 110–11, 149–50, 151–52, 229
argument, 163–64, 170–71
argumentative theory of reasoning, 117–18
aristocracy, 1, 32, 154, 158–59
Aristotle, 21n.6, 106n.29, 109, 207
Athenian democracy, 207, 217–18, 223–24
Austrian economics, 11–12, 38–39, 42–44, 46, 59–61. *See also* Hayek, Friedrich von
authority, 107, 119, 128
autonomy
  and deliberation, 99–100, 107n.32
  and exit, 148–49
  and markets, 43–44
  and political leaders, 185, 195, 209, 223, 227n.37
  and public sphere, 82–84, 123, 236

backfire effect, 112–13, 114–15
bad emperor problem, 190–93
Bagg, Samuel, 194, 200–1, 227–28
Bartels, Larry, 20n.1, 49n.22, 96n.1, 184–85
basic needs, 26–27, 150–51, 186–89, 191–92, 193
Bell, Daniel, 4, 82n.26, 189–96, 197–98
Berlin wall, 3, 234
bicameralism, 206, 214–19
black lives matter, 78–79
Bloomington school. *See* Ostrom, Elinor
Boettke, Peter, 36, 129–31, 135–36
bounded rationality, 42
Brennan, Jason, 4, 24n.13, 49n.24, 96, 111–12, 175, 186–87, 196–202, 234
brexit, 2, 96, 113

campaign finance, 182–83, 185–86, 239
centralization, 3–4, 38–39, 63–65, 66–67, 68–69, 88–94, 129, 130–31, 141–42, 150–52. *See also* decentralization
Chambers, Simone, 99–100, 113, 118, 163, 184n.4, 229–30
China, 2, 4, 34, 190–92, 194–95
Christiano, Thomas, 20, 102
Churchill, Winston, 35–36
citizen assemblies, 72–73, 118, 158–59, 165, 210–11, 240–42
  in Austria, 240–41
  in Belgium, 231–32, 241–42
  on brexit, 211
  in British Columbia, 208–9, 211–12, 231–32, 240–41
  in Ireland, 211, 240–41
  in Poland, 240–41
citizen juries, 92, 122, 207, 211

264 INDEX

Citizens United US Supreme Court decision, 185–86
classical reasoning, 116–17
Clinton, Hillary, 115
cognitive bias, 3–4, 112–13, 114–15, 116, 117–18, 119, 121–23. *See also* motivated reasoning
cold war, 6
collective intelligence, 154–55, 156–57
common good, 5–7, 21–22, 24–29, 31–32, 44–47, 69–70, 133–35, 179, 227, 235–36. *See also* justice
community associations, 7, 79
competition
  in democracy, 150, 181–84, 192–93, 195–96, 226–27
  interterritorial *vs.* intraterritorial, 135–36
  in markets, 34, 39, 40–41, 134–35
  in polycentricity, 126, 128–33, 134–36, 150
complexity, 35–36, 91, 92, 160–61, 163, 170–71, 177–78
Condorcet jury theorem, 7–8, 25–26, 61–62, 72
conference of parties (COP), 78, 80–81
Confucianism, 4, 189n.14, 190, 191˙
consensus conference, 207, 210–11
consumer knowledge, 42–44, 47–61, 88–94, 133–40
Conway, Erick M, 61–62
coordination, 33–35, 59–61, 69–70, 71–72, 129, 151
corruption, 131–32, 186–89, 190–93, 197–98, 216, 227–28. *See also* elite capture
criminal juries, 21–22, 120, 158–59, 176, 207, 219n.29

DeCanio, Samuel, 38n.1, 136–37
decentralization, 10–11, 63–64, 68–69, 77–78, 148–51, 152–53, 229–30, 242. *See also* centralization
deference, 230–31
deliberation day, 94–95n.34
deliberative democracy, 71–72, 99–100, 106–9, 118, 163, 210–11, 229–31, 242
  the systems approach, 9–10, 72–76, 124, 143–44

deliberative polls, 118, 120, 175–77, 207, 210–11, 212. *See also* citizens assemblies
deliberative structure, 82, 85–86, 97–99, 118–24, 145–46, 175–77, 207–8, 223–24, 226, 229
deliberative wave, 241–42
democratic innovations, 207, 208–9. *See also* citizens assemblies
democratic scepticism, 3–6, 11–12, 18, 20, 29, 38–39, 66, 96–97, 111–12, 126–27, 154, 180, 234–35, 237–39
demographic objection, 198–99, 201
Dewy, John, 8–9, 41, 42–44, 53
dictatorship, 181–83
diminishing returns, 165–71
disagreement, 49, 160–62, 201. *See also* reasonable disagreement
dissent, 142, 195–96, 229
diversity
  of cognitive skills, 156–59, 165–71
  of institutions, 11–12, 32–55, 79–80, 84–85, 129–30
  of opinions, 118–19, 120, 121
  of perspectives, 84–85, 226–27
diversity trumps ability theorem, 156–62, 170–71
division of labour, 7–9, 76–87, 90–91, 92–93, 122–24, 144, 205, 221–23, 227–28, 230–31, 236
Downs, Anthony, 41–42
Dryzek, John, 9–10, 74–76, 144, 207–8
dual-process theory, 113–14, 116

elite capture, 210, 227–28
  economic capture, 213, 215–16, 223–25
  political capture, 213–14, 215, 217–19, 225–27
  technocratic capture, 213–14, 217–19, 225–27
  See also corruption
emergence, 76, 103, 128–29, 145–46
empathy, 119
empowered space, 7, 74, 76–78, 81–83, 87–94, 122–24, 144–46, 147–48, 152–53
emulation, 150–52
energy policy, 45, 48, 51–52, 53, 54–55

INDEX 265

environmental problems, 26–27, 45, 48, 50, 51–52, 54–55, 60–61, 87–88, 103, 104, 160

epistemic burden, 7–8, 52–59, 62, 71, 76–77, 79–80, 92–93, 133–40, 141–42, 144–45, 148–49, 187–89, 193, 200

epistemic democracy, 7–10, 11–12, 21–23, 24–29, 32–33, 36, 236–37

epistemic filter, 122–23

epistemic injustice, 119

epistemic responsibility, 110–11

epistocracy, 4, 154, 156, 172–73, 196–202, 237–38

equality. *See* political equality

Erdoğan, Recep Tayyip, 2

error correction, 29–30, 121–24, 131–32, 148, 236, 238. *See also* self-regulation

Estlund, David, 22–23, 186n.9, 187, 198

ethical consumerism, 49–51

ethos, 106–11

everyday talk, 74–75

examinations. *See* political examinations

exit, 14–15, 131–40, 148–49, 237–38. *See also* foot voting

experimentation, 33–35

  in democracy, 10–11, 43–44, 53–59, 142–43, 146, 147–52, 229

  in markets, 43–44, 53–59, 133–40

  in polycentricity, 132–40

expertise, 68, 71, 77–78, 79–80, 89, 98, 101–2, 107–10. *See also* scientific knowledge

fake news, 2, 96, 113–14, 115–17

famine, 187–88, 189n.13

far-right, 2, 238–39

federalism, 147–49

Ferguson, Adam, 128–29

Fishkin, James, 94–95n.34, 120. *See also* deliberative polls

foot voting, 4–5, 132–33. *See also* exit

free cities, 148–49

freedom of association, 83–84, 121, 144–46

freedom of speech, 83–84, 121, 144–46, 190–91, 192–93

freedom of the press, 82, 192–93. *See also* news media

Fricker, Miranda, 119. *See also* epistemic injustice

full information, 43–44

Gastil, John, 214–19, 222–23, 224, 231–32

Gaus, Gerald, 25, 28–29

general knowledge. *See* scientific knowledge

gerrymandering, 195–96, 200–1. *See also* voter suppression

group polarization, 175–77, 212

Guerrero, Alexandar, 189n.13, 209, 221n.31

Habermas, Jürgen, 73n.15, 80n.25, 85, 99–100, 124, 163

hate speech, 83–84n.27

Hayek, Friedrich von, 4–5, 32–33, 36, 38–39, 46

  on experimentation, 43–44, 142–43

  on general and local knowledge, 42–43, 68–71, 86, 89, 90–91

  on price signals, 59–61, 69–70

  on social justice, 31–32

health care, 42–43, 186, 188

Herzog, Lisa, 54n.34, 141–42

heuristics, 57–58

Hong, Lu, 157–58

Hume, David, 104–5

ideal speech situation, 163–64

identity, 112, 113, 115, 184–85

identity-protective cognition, 112

illiberal democracy, 2

imperfect procedural justice, 21–22, 23

impersonal reason, 98–106

inclusion, 42–43, 84–85, 109–10, 154–55, 156, 181–83, 186–87, 196, 198–99, 232–33

institutional economics, 11–12, 238. *See also* Ostrom, Elinor

institutionalism, 35–37

institutional models, 7–8, 36–37, 72

institutional priority, 32–35, 39, 44–46, 61–62, 71, 129–31, 134–35, 146

intelligence, 5–7, 29–32, 235

interdisciplinarity, 11–12, 238

intergovernmental panel on climate change (IPCC), 78, 80–81, 85, 98–99

266 INDEX

invisible hand arguments, 59
  and elections, 61–62
  and markets, 59–61, 69–70
  and polycentricity, 134–35

Jim crow, 201–2
Johnson, Boris, 2, 3–4
Johnson, James, 33–35, 129–30, 132
judiciary, 144, 192–93, 207, 219–21.
    See also criminal juries
justice, 5–7, 21–23, 24–29, 44–47,
    69–70, 133–35, 179, 227–28, 235.
    See also reasonable disagreement

Kahan, Dan, 112–14
Knight, Jack, 33–35, 129–30, 132
knowledge tests. *See* political knowledge tests

Lafont, Cristina, 230–31
Landemore, Hélène, 7–8, 32–33, 36n.37,
    72, 118, 154–55, 156–62, 163, 169,
    171, 172–73, 177, 205–6
Lee Hsien Loong, 194–95
Lee Kuan Yew, 194–95
limits of reason, 163–64
literacy tests, 201–2. *See also* political
    knowledge tests
lobbying, 75, 80–81, 122, 185–86, 216, 239
local Knowledge, 42–43, 52–59, 68–71, 77–
    79, 84, 90–91, 105n.26, 134–40, 148
lottocracy, 209–10

Manin, Bernard, 207
Mansbridge, Jane, 9–10, 72–73, 74–75,
    120n.73, 143–47
markets
  and deliberation, 86–88, 91–92
  and democratic scepticism, 4–5, 11–12,
    32–33, 38–39, 66–67, 237–38
  and experimentation, 43–44, 52–59,
    135–40
  and general knowledge, 89
  and local knowledge, 42–43, 52–59, 69–
    70, 90–91, 135–40
  a priority of, 38–39, 44–46, 63–64
  and rational ignorance, 42, 47–52
  See also invisible hand arguments and
    price system

Mill, John Stuart, 36, 41–42, 83–84n.27,
    198–99
mini-publics, 71–73, 118–19, 175–76,
    210–14. *See also* citizen's assemblies
minorities, 229
miracle of aggregation, 62, 72
mirage of social justice, 31–32. *See also*
    justice
Mises, Ludwig von, 36
motivated reasoning, 111–15, 117–18

neoclassical economics, 33n.31, 49n.24,
    201n.36
news media, 74–75, 87–88, 91. *See also*
    freedom of the press
non-governmental organisations (NGOs),
    74–75, 79, 146, 147

Oakeshott, Michael, 103n.19, 103n.21
oligarchy, 11–12, 32, 156, 207
O'Neill, John, 70–71, 106–7
opposition groups, 182, 195–96, 200–1
oracle assumption, 159–62, 163–64,
    170–71
Orbán, Viktor, 2
Oreskes, Naomi, 56–57
Ostrom, Elinor, 11–12, 126, 127–28, 129,
    131–32, 238
Ostrom, Vincent, 126, 127–28, 129, 238

Page, Scott, 157–58, 161–62,
    164n.26, 166–67
parliamentary committees, 75, 80–81,
    92–93
parliaments, 7, 64, 68–69, 71–72, 75, 144,
    214, 241
participatory budgeting, 231–32
participatory democracy, 11, 230–31,
    232–33
partisanship, 96–97, 110, 112–13, 114–17,
    118–19
Pennington, Mark, 4–5, 46, 66, 68–69,
    71–72, 86–87
Pennycook, Gordon, 116–17
persecution, 181, 187–88, 190–91,
    193, 197–98
platform for people affected by mortgages
    (PAH), 78–79, 81

Plato, 1, 4
plural voting, 41n.4, 198–99
Polanyi, Michael, 36, 102–3, 104, 127–28
policing, 78–79, 188
political competence, 196–97, 200–2. *See also* political merit
political culture, 192–93
political equality, 5–6, 11, 20, 21, 23, 28–29, 207, 235–36
political examination, 4, 189–90, 191, 193–96. *See also* political knowledge tests
political knowledge tests, 4, 196–97, 198–99, 200–2. *See also* political examination
political merit, 189–90, 194, 195–96. *See also* political competence
political meritocracy, 4, 11–12, 32–33, 95, 154, 189–96
political parties, 40–41, 62, 184–85, 195–96, 214–15, 217–18, 220–21, 226–27, 231–32
popular initiatives, 220–21, 222, 224–25, 230
populism, 2
prejudice, 119
price system, 38–39, 46, 59–61, 69–70, 86–87, 90, 141–42. *See also* markets
primary bads, 186n.9, 187
priority of democracy, 32–35, 129–31, 146. *See also* institutional priority
proceduralism, 20–23
procedural justice, 21–22, 23
procedure independent standards, 21–23, 24–29, 44–46
product labelling, 56–57, 91–92
protest, 43–44, 74–75, 80–81, 92–93, 229
public satisfaction with democracy, 2–3, 20–21, 234–35
public sphere/public space, 10–11, 74–75, 76–88, 94–95, 98–99, 121–24, 144–47, 220–21, 224–25, 229–30, 236

rational choice theory, 42, 201n.36
rational ignorance
in collective institutions, 64, 148–49, 207–8
in elections, 41–42, 47–52, 183–84, 185–86

in epistocracy, 199, 200
in markets, 42, 47–52, 91–92, 133–35, 139
in polycentricity, 133–35, 139, 148–49
Rawls, John, 21–22, 117–18
reasonable disagreement, 6–7, 23, 24–29, 34–35, 44–46, 49, 61, 62, 134–35, 187, 235. *See also* disagreement
representation, 78–79, 146–47, 158–59, 184–85, 211, 214–15, 219–20, 229
restricted franchise. *See* epistocracy
rhetoric, 9–10, 72–73, 99–100, 113n.42, 185
right to competent government, 196–97, 199–200
rotation, 223–24, 225–28
rule of law, 144–45, 190
rules, 39, 82, 119, 121, 128–29, 130–31, 144–46, 175–76

Schumpeter, Joesph, 3, 4
scientific knowledge, 68, 70–71, 78, 80, 89. *See also* specialized knowledge
Scott, James C, 102n.17, 103n.19
self-interest, 29–31, 44–47, 61, 63–64, 69–70, 90–91, 106, 135–40, 181–83
self-regulation, 8–9, 11, 131–32, 134–35, 146–48. *See also* error correction
Sen, Amartya, 187–88
Singapore, 4, 190, 192, 194–95
situated knowledge, 104–6, 107–9
Smith, Adam, 30–31
Smith, Graham, 217–18, 221n.31, 223–24
social bias, 119–20, 176–77, 199
social domination, 176–77
socialist calculations debate, 38n.1
social movements, 74–75, 79–80, 81, 82, 83, 87–88, 121, 144, 146–47, 224–25, 229–30
Somin, Ilya, 41–42, 96, 111–12, 148–49, 200–1
specialized knowledge, 92, 101–2, 107–9
spontaneous orders
and democracy, 82, 145–46
and markets, 38–39, 59–61
and polycentricity, 128–29, 131–32
storytelling, 119

tacit knowledge, 102–4, 107–9
testimony, 106–11

268 INDEX

transmissions, 75, 76–78, 80–82, 89–92, 114, 122–24
Trump, Donald, 2, 3–4, 115

uncertainty, 92, 111, 137, 160, 169
unions, 7, 74–75, 79–80, 83, 98, 110–11, 147
United States of America, 2–3, 126, 185–86, 201–2
utilitarianism, 24, 44–45, 61, 134–35

value pluralism, 160–61.
   See also reasonable disagreement
voter knowledge, 10, 41–44, 49, 51–59, 62, 72, 183–89, 197, 199, 200, 202–3, 207–8, 237

voter knowledge tests. See political knowledge tests
voter suppression, 195–96, 201–2.
   See also gerrymandering

Waldron, Jeremy, 21n.6
war, 187
Warren, Mark, 76–77, 213, 230–31
Wen Jiabao, 192
wisdom of the multitude, 21n.6
witness testimony, 104–6
world war two, 3, 234
Wright, Erick Olin, 214–19, 222–23, 224, 231–32